Palgrave's Critical Policing Studies

Laura Huey
Dept Socio, Social Sci Ctr, Rm 5401
University of British Columbia
London, ON, Canada

Bethan Loftus
Bangor University
Bangor, UK

Ali Malik
Northumbria University
Newcastle upon Tyne, UK

Monique Marks
Durban University of Technology
Durban, South Africa

Angus Nurse
Hendon campus
Middlesex University
London, UK

Louise Porter
Griffith University
South East Queensland, Australia

Pamela Ugwudike
Southampton University
Southampton, UK

James J Willis
George Mason University
Heidelberg, Germany

Andrew Wooff
Edinburgh Napier University
Edinburgh, UK

K. Jaishankar
International Institute of Justice
and Police Sciences
Karnataka, India

In a period where police and academics benefit from coproduction in research and education, the need for a critical perspective on key challenges is pressing. Palgrave's Critical Policing Studies is a series of high quality, research-based books which examine a range of cutting-edge challenges and developments to policing and their social and political contexts. They seek to provide evidence-based case studies and high quality research, combined with critique and theory, to address fundamental challenging questions about future directions in policing.

Through a range of formats including monographs, edited collections and short form Pivots, this series provides research at a variety of lengths to suit both academics and practitioners. The series brings together new topics at the forefront of policing scholarship but is also organised around who the contemporary police are, what they do, how they go about it, and the ever-changing external environments which bear upon their work.

The series will cover topics such as: the purpose of policing and public expectations, public health approaches to policing, policing of cybercrime, environmental policing, digital policing, social media, Artificial Intelligence and big data, accountability of complex networks of actors involved in policing, austerity, public scrutiny, technological and social changes, over-policing and marginalised groups, under-policing and corporate crime, institutional abuses, policing of climate change, ethics, workforce, education, evidence-based policing, and the pluralisation of policing.

Michelle N. Eliasson

Who Gets Believed?

Police, Victims, and the Credibility Dilemma in Domestic and Non-Domestic Batteries

palgrave
macmillan

Michelle N. Eliasson
School of Criminology and Criminal Justice
Florida Atlantic University
Boca Raton, FL, USA

ISSN 2730-535X ISSN 2730-5368 (electronic)
Palgrave's Critical Policing Studies
ISBN 978-3-032-22252-7 ISBN 978-3-032-22253-4 (eBook)
https://doi.org/10.1007/978-3-032-22253-4

Cover illustration: CoverZoo

This Palgrave Macmillan imprint is published by the registered company Springer Nature Switzerland AG
The registered company address is: Gewerbestrasse 11, 6330 Cham, Switzerland

Acknowledgments

This book has been a part of my life for several years, and it stands as one of the greatest accomplishments of my junior career. When I began this project, one of my dreams was to one day hold my own book in my hands, and now that dream has become true. I am deeply grateful for the opportunity to publish this book and for all the people who believed in me. Thank you to everyone who contributed to making this book possible.

Specifically, I would like to thank Dr. Barbara Zsembik, Dr. Jodi Lane, Dr. Lonn Lanza-Kaduce, and Dr. Mary Watt at the University of Florida for serving on my dissertation committee, for asking the hard questions, and for offering professional guidance and support. Your insight was monumental to the work I have done. Additionally, thank you to all my friends and colleagues, with special mentions to Dr. Pilar Morales Giner, Dr. Elizabeth Hartsell, Dr. David Cañarte, Dr. Gissel Perez, Lizanne H, and Lisa T, for your unwavering support from day one of this research through to today. Thank you to PEO for the immense support, especially chapters in Gainesville, FL and Sanford, FL.

Furthermore, I want to thank all the officers and staff at Gainesville Police Department for believing in me and helping me with this research. I could not have done any of this without you. The many hours I spent in police cars were filled with meaningful conversations that inspired me in ways words cannot fully express. Those experiences paved the way for my career and motivated me to continue on my path in academia. I also extend my gratitude to the staff at the Gainesville Police Department Records Unit and the Alachua County Records Unit for assisting me with my many, many, many requests for documents.

I must also thank a very special little fluff ball, my cat Alma, who is one of the most important beings in my life. I know you cannot read this, Alma, but thank you for saving me, for waiting for me after every ride-along, and for lying next to me through all the hours I spent writing this book. Finally, thank you to my family and friends back home in Sweden. Your love and support have meant everything to me. Tack mamma och Oscar för att ni alltid är vid min sida. Tack Mikael, Cecilia, Benjamin, Jonathan, Filippa och Josefine. Tack till alla andra som varit med längst vägen och hejat på, ni gav mig elden och motivationen att fortsätta framåt. Tack till änglarna som tittat ner och gett mig styrka, tack mormor, morfar och pappa.

Ethics Approval This study was approved IRB202103033 at the University of Florida. Informed consent to participate in the study was obtained from participants. All information shared in this book is information that can be obtained through a public records request.

Competing Interests The author has no competing interests to declare that are relevant to the content of this manuscript.

Contents

Abbreviations

A	Asian
Adv	Advise
B	Black
BA	Baker Acted
BWC	Body-worn camera
CAD	Computer Aid System
C	Cooperating
Comp	Complainant
CPL	Corporal
DEF	Defendant
DV	Domestic violence
DVL Screen	Domestic/Dating Violence Lethality Screen for First Responders
EMS	Emergency Medical Service
EST	Emergency Services Team
EVE	Emotional Victim Effect
F	Female
FTO	Field Training Officer
FTP	Field Training Program
GPD	Gainesville Police Department
H	Hispanic
Inj	Injury
LAP	Lethality Assessment Program

LEO	Law Enforcement Officer
M	Male
Multi	Multi Racial
NC	Not Cooperating
NCVS	National Crime Victimization Survey
NIBRS	National Incident-Based Reporting System
Ofc	Officer
Poss	Possible
Subj	Subject
SWAT	Special Weapons and Tactics Unit
UCR	Uniform Crime Reporting
UF	University of Florida
VIC	Victim
W	White
WIT	Witness

List of Tables

1

Police and Battery

Introduction

Police officers serve as gatekeepers of the criminal justice system and are often victims' first point of contact with the criminal justice system after a victimization has occured. The encounter between officers and victims is often a pivotal point for police officers in the process of assessing and perceive victim's credibility and can potentially influence subsequent investigative decisions (Bostaph et al., 2021). Studies also show that the interaction between officers and victims can influence victims' reporting habits and their cooperation with the criminal justice system (Hickman & Simpson, 2003; Xie et al., 2006). By learning more about police officers' perceptions of victims' credibility and their expectations of victims and their behavior, we can learn more about how these perceptions may influence officers' actions toward victims and the information they share with other criminal justice professionals in police reports. This knowledge can highlight potential biases that officers have in the early stages of the case process, that potentially could be shared with other criminal justice professionals, for example in police reports.

M. N. Eliasson, *Who Gets Believed?*, Palgrave's Critical Policing Studies,
https://doi.org/10.1007/978-3-032-22253-4_1

In many states, threats or unwanted physical contact are legally classified as "assaults." However, some states, such as Florida, distinguish between incidents involving physical contact and those that do not. Specifically, in Florida, incidents involving unwanted physical contact are classified as "batteries" while those without physical contact are considered assaults. There are very few studies that explicitly examine batteries separately from assaults. This knowledge gap can lead to misalignment in resource allocation and tailored legal responses needed for incidents that involve physical harm. However, despite often not separating incidents involving physical contact from those with non-physical contact, existing statistics and scholarship on assaults highlight the need to further expand research on domestic and non-domestic battery to understand how various characteristics can impact officers' perceptions and actions in cases where physical violence has occurred (Ask, 2010).

According to the National Crime Victimization Survey (NCVS), assaults and batteries are some of the most common violent crimes that occur in the United States (Tapp & Coen, 2025). However, despite the high rates of assaults and batteries, most existing research examining police officers' perceptions of victims tends to focus on sexual victimization, with only a few studies exploring domestic assaults (Acosta et al., 2013; Cazenave & Zahn, 1992; O'Neal, 2019; O'Neal & Hayes, 2020; Sleath & Bull, 2012, 2017). The focus on sexual victimization and the limited focus on domestic battery have left non-domestic batteries largely overlooked, both when examined independently and in a comparative context. Comparing domestic and non-domestic battery allows us to further understand whether officers rely on similar or distinct factors when assessing credibility. Domestic and non-domestic batteries have similar components as they both include intentional and unlawful physical harm to another person without their consent, as defined under Florida Statutes §784.03. They can also both be classified as either simple battery, felony battery, or aggravated battery. Additionally, they have the same aggravating factors, such as use of a weapon, prior convictions, and the victim's status (e.g., pregnancy), which can elevate charges and penalties. However, they are also distinctly different. For example, in domestic batteries, the victim and offender are household or family members. Non-domestic batteries, on the other hand, can involve a wide range of prior relationships; for example, parties can be acquaintances or friends, but also have no prior relationship and be complete strangers. The existence of a relationship between the victim and offender creates a complex dynamic, impacting not only victims' behaviors and emotions but also the procedures and responses to the incident, which has been highlighted in previous scholarship (DeJong et al., 2008; Felson et al., 1999; Horwitz et al., 2011; Kang & Lynch, 2014; Rollwagen & Jacob, 2018).

Because of the complex nature of batteries, there may be differences in how officers assess not only the incident but also the factors they consider when assessing victim credibility. Scholarship has shown that officers manage domestic and non-domestic batteries differently (Sun, 2006). This could be due to the legal and procedural differences for the two types of batteries. Domestic batteries are subjected to pro-arrest laws (Hirschel et al., 2007) and guidelines which give police officers less discretion in their assessment and actions taken during the initial investigation process (Belknap, 1995; Eitle, 2005; Myhill & Johnson, 2016; Ryan et al., 2022; Strom et al., 2014). However, studies have also underlined other factors such as officers' perception of the victim and case characteristics (Jasinski, 2003) as influencing their actions and perceptions. For example, scholars have emphasized how race and gender (Russell, 2018; Taylor et al., 2009), victim conduct, or emotions can influence officers' perceptions of victims (Ask, 2010; Stewart & Maddren, 1997).

In this book, I investigate how police officers perceive the credibility of domestic and non-domestic battery victims by contrasting multiple points along case development. Specifically, I examine how police officers describe and depict victims and their credibility during the initial encounters, officers' post-incident perceptions, and officers' victim characterization in police reports. The specific aims of the book are to describe how police officers interact with battery victims, to document police officers' initial perceptions of battery victims and contrast them with observational data, and finally, to compare police officers' perceptions in the post-incident interview with how the victim is characterized in police reports. The research questions guiding this book are: (a) How do police officers perceive victim credibility among battery victims? (b) How do police officers describe and depict victim credibility among battery victims in police reports? and (c) What are the similarities and differences between police officers describing victim credibility in reports and after encounters with victims in domestic and non-domestic battery?

Throughout the book, I examine the potential influence of organizational, case and individual-level factors on police officers' perceptions of victims' credibility. I discuss these elements in relation to the Ideal Victim Theory (Christie, 1986) and critical criminological scholarship discussing relationship dynamics and personal characteristics. Additionally, I provide an overview of the police organization, its procedures, and practices when dealing with domestic and non-domestic batteries and describe how these aspects can influence officers' perceptions of victim credibility.

Current Study

During 2022, I spent six months studying police officers working for Gainesville Police Department (GPD) in Gainesville, Florida, conducting over 500 hours of ride-alongs with patrol officers. During this time, I followed 34 domestic and non-domestic battery cases triangulating interviews, observations, police reports, and additional documents with the main objective of understanding more about police officers' perceptions of victim credibility. In this study, a victim is considered the party who was allegedly subjected to a victimization or labeled as the victim by dispatch and officers.

I aimed to provide a "thick" description (Geertz, 2008) and use first-person language to invite readers to visualize the interactions and observations I made while doing my fieldwork. I also triangulated statements made by officers with observations made at the police station, in the patrol car, and at crime scenes. By combining these perspectives with case information from police reports and police department policy documents, I aimed to create a multi-layered immersive reader experience where readers get an insight into the complex encounters and experiences officers have during their day-to-day job.

The context surrounding perceptions is dynamic and can consist of formal and informal rules, organizational structure, power hierarchies, personal belief systems, interpersonal interactions, and social bonds.

Thus, to examine police officers' perception of battery victims' credibility, I needed to study several aspects of the police officers' daily activities, organizational structure, and interactions. Based on these objectives, I decided to conduct a study that relied upon multiple data sources inspired by the methodological frameworks of ethnography by conducting interviews, observations, and analysis of police reports and organizational documents. Early policing scholars have used qualitative and ethnographic methodology to explore various aspects of policing (Bittner, 1970; Cain, 1973; Holdaway, 1983; Punch, 1979; Rubinstein, 1980; Skolnick, 1966; van Maanen, 1973; Westley, 1970). For example, considered classics in the field of policing, Westley's (1970) and Manning and van Maanen's (1975) pieces explored officers' day-to-day activities, use of violence, organizational culture, interpersonal relationships, and normative values. This scholarship was later followed by other important qualitative and ethnographic work by scholars such as Loader and Mulcahy (2003), McLaughlin (2006), Fassin (2013), and Blaustein (2015). Scholars stress the importance of employing ethnographic and qualitative methodology when studying police (Fassin, 2017; Manning, 2015), because of its ability to give insight into the multiple complex and dynamic sets of factors that are involved in policing and that influence officers' conduct.

Relying on this robust body of methodological scholarship exploring policing, qualitative methodology informed by ethnographic frameworks became my primary choice of methodology. However, this book differs from a lot of classic ethnographic studies because it has a specific interest in officers' perceptions of victims' credibility, thus limiting the scope of what is examined in the police organization. Despite this difference, the general methodological approach used in ethnographic research lends useful tools to answer the research questions posed in this book. Perceptions are heavily embedded in and informed by language, concepts, practices, rules, and beliefs that are used by a specific group, which ethnographic frameworks are specifically designed to investigate (Van Maanen, 2011). Thus, by drawing upon ethnographic methodological frameworks, which highlight the need for the researcher to be immersed in the groups and organizations studied, I could explore the context which officers and their perceptions exist within and the factors informing these perceptions.

Data

During my 6 months in the field, I conducted 54 ride-alongs with 28 patrol officers. Of these officers 24 were male and four were women, 14 were White, six were Black, two were Hispanic, one was Asian, and one multi-racial. I rode with 19 of the officers one time, seven officers two times, three officers three times, one officer four times, and one officer eight times. During these ride-alongs I rode in each of the geographical zones 1–3 times, however, I spent 16 of my ride-alongs in two specific zone, which are areas that are known to have a high rate of domestic batteries. Out of the 54 ride-alongs, 22 were day shifts (7.30 am–5.30 pm), 26 were evening shifts (5 pm–3 am), and six midnight shifts (10 pm–7.30 am). On average each ride-along lasted nine to 11 hours. During the first two months of fieldwork, I did three ride-alongs per week, split over different shifts and in the subsequent four months, I did three to four ride-alongs a week either with day or evening shifts as the midnight shift did not subject me to many battery cases during the two first months.

I conducted interviews with four male officers to collect organizational information. Of these four officers, three were White and one was Hispanic, three of the officers were patrol officers and one was a captain. The officers' ages ranged between 26 and 48 years old, and their years of experience ranged between six months and 19 years. I also conducted battery case interviews with 35 officers. Out of these officers, 26 were male and six were female; 22 officers were White, eight Black, three were Hispanic, one was Asian, and one was multi-racial. The age range of the officers was 26–55 years old, and the range of years of experience was two weeks to 27.5 years.

The goal was to collect 20 cases of each type of battery; however, after spending six months in the field, the final sample included 14 non-domestic cases and 20 domestic cases. One important aspect of sampling is knowing when to stop collecting data and a tool that is often used to assess this is saturation (Esterberg, 2002). However, since both domestic and non-domestic batteries can occur in many different contexts and settings it can be difficult to determine when the saturation point is reached. In this sample, I noticed that I reached saturation in the domestic sample, but not in the non-domestic sample. However, due to the time constraint I had, the 14 cases which I collected by the six-month mark would have to be sufficient for the study to ensure I could complete the study on time. I will provide more information about the cases in Chap. 5 and additional information about the analytical procedures can be found in the methodological appendix.

Most of the officers interviewed in this sample were male and White, while many of the victims were female and Black. This demographic composition underscores a significant power dynamic between officers and victims shaped by race/ethnicity and sex/gender. These dynamics are important to consider, as they may influence officers' perceptions of victims and victims' experiences. Moreover, they highlight the broader racialized and gendered experiences that victims and suspects, both male and female, can encounter when interacting with the criminal justice system. Given that the sample was saturated with White male officers and Black female victims, it is essential to recognize that officers' assessments are likely to be informed by their positionality, which is shaped by their own racial, ethnic, and gender identities. Additionally, these dynamics may have influenced victims' behavior during interactions with officers. Victims may have altered their demeanor or level of engagement in response to the racial and gendered context of the encounter, which in turn may have affected how they were perceived and evaluated by officers. However, due to the racial/ethnic and sex/gender distribution of the sample, the racial and gendered influences cannot be in-depth explored. Specifically, due to the limited sample, this book does not present an adequate opportunity for in-depth analysis of the racial and gendered structures that can impact victims in their interactions with the police. To provide an adequate and in-depth analysis of this complex dynamic, the sample must present a wide range of characteristics and demographics, which the sample in this book does not. Additionally, victims would have to be included as interview participants in order to fully explore their experiences and behaviors, which was and element that was not included in this book. Despite this, it is still essential to highlight and recognize the influence race/ethnicity and sex/gender can have on victims' experiences and to note that this books' the lack of engagement with these discourses is not because they are not important, but simply a result of the sample not offering enough demographic variety to provide a proper exploration.

Structure of the Book

The book starts with Chap. 1: Police and Battery, where I outline the role of initial police and victim encounters in shaping investigative decisions and case outcomes, highlight the legal distinction in Florida between assault and battery, and discuss the methodological approach and my positionality statement. Chapter 2: Credibility, Battery, and the Ideal Victim reviews existing literature on how credibility is assessed by criminal justice professionals and introduce Ideal Victim Theory, developed by Nils Christie (1986) as a framework for analyzing how officers construct perceptions of victims. The chapter also presents national statistics on violence to depict the occurrence of domestic and non-domestic battery. In Chap. 3: Gainesville Police Department, I give a detailed overview of the organizational structure, staffing, and patrol operations of the police department. I discuss the department's militarized organizational hierarchy, training programs, and patrol zone assignments, and discuss how these structural elements can shape officers' way of assessing victims and managing investigations. In Chap. 4: Policing Battery, I examine how Florida State Law and Gainesville Police Department's policies guide officers' investigative procedures in domestic and non-domestic battery cases. Specifically, I contrast the general investigative procedures used for non-domestic cases with the more detailed protocols required for domestic cases, which include mandatory arrest policies and victim support guidelines. Chapter 5: Case Facts and Narratives contain a structured overview of the 34 battery cases included in the book, offering demographic, relational, and procedural data to support cross case comparisons. The following chapter, Chap. 6: Attitude, Cooperation, and Story explore how officers assess victim credibility through three interrelated factors: attitude, cooperation, and story. Furthermore. I also highlight how officers evaluate the content and delivery of victims' stories, with narrative coherence and consistency serving as credibility markers. In Chap. 7: Corroboration, I examine the corroborating factors that officers identified as influencing their perceptions of victim credibility. This chapter highlights how corroboration is not limited to physical evidence but includes a range of contextual and relational indicators that officers use to construct credibility. Chapter 8: Help Seeking and Emotional Display, explore how victims' motivations for seeking help and their emotional expressions influence police officers' perceptions of credibility. I discuss how officers construct meaning from victims' behavior and emotions, and how these interpretations are shaped by relational context, institutional norms, and broader social expectations about what a credible victim should look and act like. Finally in Chap. 9: Perceptions and Depictions of Victim Credibility and the Ideal Victims, I combine all the findings throughout the chapters and have an overall discussion of the major take aways and provide answers for the research questions posed in the beginning of the book. I finish the book with a Methodological Appendix outlining the methodological approach and limitations of the study. It details the use of ethnographic methods, including ride-alongs, interviews, and document analysis, and explains how data were triangulated to enhance validity. Finally, I reflect on challenges such as observer effects, and inconsistent data availability across cases.

Positionality and Ethics

I have reflected on my positionality frequently during the process of working on this book. I have considered how my identity may have influenced my experiences in the field and the knowledge produced from those experiences. I am a White, cisgender-presenting woman, born and raised in Sweden in a lower-middle-income blue-collar family. I believe that my external appearance and international status shaped my fieldwork experiences and the knowledge I generated. More specifically, I think my race, gender, and international background contributed to my ability to gain access to the police department and afforded me certain privileges, allowing me to enter a space deeply structured by power hierarchies.

My race aligned with the predominantly White institutional spaces often found in organizations such as the police, while my gender positioned me outside the competitive dynamics of hegemonic masculinity sometimes observed in police departments. Additionally, my international status provided a compelling rationale for my interest in the GPD, as I came from a different cultural and national context, which was something many officers told me they found intriguing. Class and environment also influenced my fieldwork experiences. I encountered environments, interactions, and observations that were unfamiliar to me, including more extensive exposure to drugs, weapons, and poverty than I had previously experienced. This lack of prior exposure shaped my emotional responses, such as fear in certain settings but also prompted reflection on how constant exposure to such conditions might influence the behaviors and attitudes of both officers and the individuals they meet. These reflections were documented in private fieldwork memos after each ride-along.

Another important aspect of my positionality is my prior exposure to and experience with law enforcement. Until his passing in 2020, my father worked as a police officer in Sweden. As a result, I grew up around police officers and was regularly exposed to the profession. I have also conducted ride-alongs and interviews with police officers in the Washington D.C. area and interviewed Swedish officers for previous research projects. These experiences have shaped who I am, my research approach, and the book itself. Growing up as the daughter of a police officer, I was exposed early on to both positive and negative aspects of law enforcement. Due to my race and familial ties to the police, I viewed law enforcement as a source of authority and safety, an experience I recognize may not be shared by others. I have never been subjected to racial profiling or feared for my life during police encounters, which I believe influenced my comfort level around officers. This familiarity also most likely shaped my interactions in the field. Because transparency is a core value in my research, I was open with officers about my background and my father's occupation and I believe this openness facilitated access, as many officers described me as part of the "police family."

In addition to my familial ties to law enforcement, I also had prior experience interacting with victims. I volunteered as a victim advocate, where I accompanied victims to court, depositions, and meetings with prosecutors. I interacted with individuals who had experienced attempted murder, sexual violence, domestic abuse, and other violent crimes. These interactions gave me some insight into some of the trauma victims endure and the diverse ways they can respond to victimization. I drew on this knowledge during my fieldwork and in writing this book, striving to remain sensitive to victims' experiences and to write about them with care and respect.

Overall, I believe that all scholars have personal experiences that can shape their research interests and trajectories. In my case, my background with both police and victims did not only inform the research questions I pursued in this book, but also my experiences and interactions in the field. I have made a conscious effort to remain aware of how my experiences and identity have shaped my perceptions, and to critically examine and challenge my assumptions throughout the research and writing process.

Conclusion

Police officers are often the first point of contact with the criminal justice system for individuals who experience crime, positioning them as critical gatekeepers within the criminal justice system. Their interactions with victims can shape not only how victims perceive the justice process but also influence the early stages of case development. Officers are tasked with determining whether a crime has occurred and whether there is probable cause to make an arrest, which are all decisions that significantly affect the trajectory of a case. Previous scholarship has highlighted that multiple factors, including organizational structures, case-specific details, and individual-level characteristics, influence officers' investigative actions and their perceptions of victims. These perceptions are especially important in cases where physical evidence is limited and credibility assessments carry substantial weight. In this book, I explore these dynamics further by investigating how police officers perceive victim credibility among battery victims.

Battery, defined as an interaction involving unwanted physical contact, is one of the most common violent crimes reported each year. As a result, police officers frequently encounter battery victims and are responsible for investigating these incidents. Although previous scholarship has examined police officers' perceptions of victims more broadly, limited research has focused specifically on officers' perceptions in both domestic and non-domestic battery cases. Several statistical sources have emphasized the high prevalence of violence in both domestic and non-domestic settings, however, despite the widespread occurrence, the academic literature remains limited. Consequently, there is a lack of comprehensive understanding regarding potential differences or similarities in how officers assess victim credibility across these two contexts.

In this book, I used multiple qualitative methodologies informed by ethnographic framework, conducting over 500 hours of ride-alongs with the GPD during a six-month period. I followed 34 cases involving both domestic and non-domestic battery, triangulating interviews, observations, police reports, and additional documents to explore which organizational, case-specific, and individual-level factors informed officers' perceptions of victim credibility. I use the Ideal Victim Theory to conceptualize the notion of credibility and discuss the findings.

References

Acosta, D. F., Gomes, V. L. D. O., & Barlem, E. L. D. (2013). Profile of police reports related to violence against women. *Acta Paulista de Enfermagem, 26*(6), 547–553. https://doi.org/10.1590/S0103-21002013000600007

Ask, K. (2010). A survey of police officers' and prosecutors' beliefs about crime victim behaviors. *Journal of Interpersonal Violence, 25*(6), 1132–1149. https://doi.org/10.1177/0886260509340535

Belknap, J. (1995). Law enforcement officers' attitudes about the appropriate responses to woman battering. *International Review of Victimology, 4*(1), 47–62. https://doi.org/10.1177/026975809500400104

Bittner, E. (1970). *The functions of the police in modern society*. Aronson.

Blaustein, J. (2015). *Speaking truths to power: Policy ethnography and police reform in Bosnia and Herzegovina*. Oxford University Press.

Bostaph, L. G., King, L. L., & Brady, P. Q. (2021). How victim credibility and cooperation influence investigative decision-making: Examining DOJ'S gender bias principles for investigating domestic and sexual violence. *Policing: An International Journal, 44*(4), 612–627. https://doi.org/10.1108/PIJPSM-02-2021-0018

Cain, M. (1973). Society and the policeman's role. *Routledge*. https://doi.org/10.4324/9781315688541

Cazenave, N. A., & Zahn, M. A. (1992). Women, murder, and male domination: Police reports of domestic violence in Chicago and Philadelphia. In E. C. Viano (Ed.), *Intimate violence: Interdisciplinary perspectives* (pp. 83–97). Hemisphere Publishing Corporation.

Christie, N. (1986). The ideal victim. In E. Fattah (Ed.), *From crime policy to victim policy* (pp. 17–30). Palgrave Macmillan. https://doi.org/10.1007/978-1-349-08305-3_2

DeJong, C., Burgess-Proctor, A., & Elis, L. (2008). Police officer perceptions of intimate partner violence: An analysis of observational data. *Violence and Victims, 23*(6), 683–696. https://doi.org/10.1891/0886-6708.23.6.683

Eitle, D. (2005). The influence of mandatory arrest policies, police organizational characteristics, and situational variables on the probability of arrest in domestic violence cases. *Crime & Delinquency, 51*(4), 573–597. https://doi.org/10.1177/0011128705277784

Esterberg, K. G. (2002). *Qualitative methods in social research*. McGraw-Hill.

Fassin, D. (2013). *The moral world of law enforcement* (p. 49). Institute of Advanced Studies.

Fassin, D. (Ed.). (2017). *Writing the world of policing: The difference ethnography makes*. University of Chicago Press.

Felson, R. B., Messner, S. F., & Hoskin, A. (1999). The victim-offender relationship and calling the police in assaults. *Criminology, 37*(4), 931–948. https://doi.org/10.1111/j.1745-9125.1999.tb00510.x

Geertz, C. (2008). Thick description: Toward an interpretive theory of culture. In *The cultural geography reader* (pp. 41–51). Routledge.

Hickman, L. J., & Simpson, S. S. (2003). Fair treatment or preferred outcome? The impact of police behavior on victim reports of domestic violence incidents. *Law & Society Review, 37*(3), 607–634. https://doi.org/10.1111/1540-5893.3703005

Hirschel, D., Buzawa, E., Pattavina, A., & Faggiani, D. (2007). Domestic violence and mandatory arrest laws: To what extent do they influence police arrest decisions. *Journal of Criminal Law and Criminology, 98*(1), 255–298. https://www.jstor.org/stable/40042852

Holdaway, S. (1983). *Inside the British police: A force at work*. Basil Blackwell.

Horwitz, S. H., Mitchell, D., LaRussa-Trott, M., Santiago, L., Pearson, J., Skiff, D. M., & Cerulli, C. (2011). An inside view of police officers' experience with domestic violence. *Journal of Family Violence, 26*(8), 617–625. https://doi.org/10.1007/s10896-011-9396-y

Jasinski, J. L. (2003). Police involvement in incidents of physical assault: Analysis of the redesigned National Crime Victimization Survey. *Journal of Family Violence, 18*, 143–150. https://doi.org/10.1023/A:1023512420703

Kang, J. H., & Lynch, J. P. (2014). Calling the police in instances of family violence: Effects of victim–offender relationship and life stages. *Crime & Delinquency, 60*(1), 34–59. https://doi.org/10.1177/0011128709359655

Loader, I., & Mulcahy, A. (2003). *Policing and the condition of England: Memory, politics and culture*. Oxford University Press.

Manning, P. K. (2015). Researching policing using qualitative methods. In *The Routledge handbook of qualitative criminology* (pp. 265–282). Routledge.

McLaughlin, E. M. (2006). *The new policing*. Sage.

Myhill, A., & Johnson, K. (2016). Police use of discretion in response to domestic violence. *Criminology & Criminal Justice, 16*(1), 3–20. https://doi.org/10.1177/1748895815590202

O'Neal, E. N. (2019). "Victim is not credible": The influence of rape culture on police perceptions of sexual assault complainants. *Justice Quarterly, 36*(1), 127–160. https://doi.org/10.1080/07418825.2017.1406977

O'Neal, E. N., & Hayes, B. E. (2020). "A rape is a rape, regardless of what the victim was doing at the time": Detective views on how "problematic" victims affect sexual assault case processing. *Criminal Justice Review, 45*(1), 26–44. https://doi.org/10.1177/0734016819842639

Punch, M. (1979). *Policing the inner city: A study of Amsterdam's Warmoesstraat*. Springer.

Rollwagen, H., & Jacob, J. C. (2018). The victim–offender relationship and police charging decisions for juvenile delinquents: How does social distance moderate the impact of legal and extralegal factors? *Youth Violence and Juvenile Justice, 16*(4), 378–394. https://doi.org/10.1177/1541204017710315

Rubinstein, J. (1980). *City police*. Macmillan.

Russell, B. (2018). Police perceptions in intimate partner violence cases: The influence of gender and sexual orientation. *Journal of Crime and Justice, 41*(2), 193–205. https://doi.org/10.1080/0735648X.2017.1282378

Ryan, C., Silvio, D., Borden, T., & Ross, N. M. (2022). A review of pro-arrest, pro-charge, and pro-prosecution policies as a response to domestic violence. *Journal of Social Work, 22*(1), 211–238. https://doi.org/10.1177/1468017320979956

Skolnick, J. H. (1966). *Justice without trial: Law enforcement in democratic society*. Wiley.

Sleath, E., & Bull, R. (2012). Comparing rape victim and perpetrator blaming in a police officer sample: Differences between police officers with and without special training. *Criminal Justice and Behavior, 39*(5), 646–665. https://doi.org/10.1177/0093854811434696

Sleath, E., & Bull, R. (2017). Police perceptions of rape victims and the impact on case decision making: A systematic review. *Aggression and Violent Behavior, 34*, 102–112. https://doi.org/10.1016/j.avb.2017.02.003

Stewart, A., & Maddren, K. (1997). Police officers' judgements of blame in family violence: The impact of gender and alcohol. *Sex Roles, 37*, 921–933. https://doi.org/10.1007/BF02936347

Strom, K. J., Warner, T. D., Tichavsky, L., & Zahn, M. A. (2014). Policing juveniles: Domestic violence arrest policies, gender, and police response to child–parent violence. *Crime & Delinquency, 60*(3), 427–450. https://doi.org/10.1177/0011128710376293

Sun, I. Y. (2006). Police response to victims of domestic and non-domestic violence. *Journal of Health and Human Services Administration, 29*(2), 145–172. http://www.jstor.org/stable/25790685

Tapp, S. N., & Coen, E. J. (2025). *Criminal victimization, 2024*. Bureau of Justice Statistics. https://bjs.ojp.gov/document/cv24.pdf

Taylor, T. J., Holleran, D., & Topalli, V. (2009). Racial bias in case processing: Does victim race affect police clearance of violent crime incidents?. *Justice Quarterly, 26*(3), 562–591. https://doi.org/10.1080/07418820802266462

Van Maanen, J. (1973). Working the street; a developmental view of police behavior. In H. Jacobs (Ed.), *Volume III of the annals of criminal justice* (pp. 1–92). Sage Publishing.

Van Maanen, J. (1975). Police socialization: A longitudinal examination of job attitudes in an urban police department. *Administrative Science Quarterly, 20*(2), 207–228. https://doi.org/10.2307/2391695

Van Maanen, J. (2011). *Tales of the field: On writing ethnography*. University of Chicago Press.
Westley, W. A. (1970). *Violence and the police: A sociological study of law, custom, and morality*. MIT Press.
Xie, M., Pogarsky, G., Lynch, J. P., & McDowall, D. (2006). Prior police contact and subsequent victim reporting: Results from the NCVS. *Justice Quarterly, 23*(4), 481–501. https://doi.org/10.1080/07418820600985339

2

Credibility, Battery, and the Ideal Victim

Introduction

In addition to organizational, legal, and situational factors that shape officers' decisions (Cordner, 2017; Sherman, 2020; Skogan, 2006a, 2006b), officers' perceptions of victim credibility can influence decisions and notion such as investigative actions and clearance rates (Bostaph et al., 2021; Campbell et al., 2015; Russell, 2018). Studies show that in the absence of physical evidence, officers often rely on their assessments of victim credibility, among other things, when deciding whether to proceed with an investigation (Alderden & Ullman, 2012; Farrell et al., 2014; LaFree, 1981). Scholars have also found that criminal justice professionals make judgments about cases, for example, prosecutors may label certain victims as "bad" or "good" based on how credible their statements appear to a jury and whether the case is likely to result in a conviction (Frohmann, 1991, 1997). Hence, credibility assessments can shape decisions at multiple stages of the criminal justice process. Since police officers often are the first criminal justice professionals victims encounter, and sometimes the only ones, their perceptions of victim credibility can influence decisions made later

M. N. Eliasson, *Who Gets Believed?*, Palgrave's Critical Policing Studies,
https://doi.org/10.1007/978-3-032-22253-4_2

in the criminal justice process and, in some cases, even potentially affect case outcomes (Bollingmo et al., 2007).

Scholars have conceptualized credibility in multiple ways, including behavioral cues, statement consistency, emotional expression, and perceived moral character. For example, in their investigation of victim credibility among victims of sexual and domestic violence, Bostaph et al. (2021) used variables such as history or active usage of alcohol or drugs, delayed reporting, sexual and criminal history, lack of resistance, homelessness, discrepancies in statements, and memory issues to conceptualize credibility. In another study on sexual victimization, sex crime investigators emphasized credibility factors such as the level of detail and consistency in victims' accounts, cooperation, drug/alcohol use, professional characteristics, moral character, history of lying, criminal history, emotional expression, and age (Campbell et al., 2015). Other scholars have highlighted the emotional victim effect (EVE), which refers to how the emotions victims display influence perceptions of their credibility (Landström et al., 2015). Despite extensive scholarship on credibility in other contexts, very limited research examines how officers assess victim credibility in domestic and non-domestic battery cases. While some insights from sexual assault research can inform the discourse on victim credibility in battery cases, batteries involve distinct social dynamics and require separate analysis. This is not to suggest that previous research on sexual victimization is irrelevant or unimportant, but rather, the separation of sexual victimization and non-sexual violent victimization serves to define the specific scope and focus of the study by in-depth understand the complex nuances of batteries. While empirical findings on how police officers perceive victims of sexual violence may offer insights that are applicable to non-sexual crimes, the goal of this book is not to compare officers' perceptions across these categories. Sexual victimizations differ from batteries. Each type of crime involves distinct contextual dynamics, varying levels and forms of stigmatization, and different responses from society and the criminal justice system. Hence, to provide a detailed understanding of the specific circumstances surrounding batteries, this book will concentrate on scholarship that explores domestic and non-domestic victimization, or similar non-sexual offenses.

In 2024, NCVS recorded slightly over three million incidents of stranger violence and just over one million incidents of domestic violence, with 782,900 of those involving intimate partners. Although there have been slight fluctuations, these rates have remained relatively stable over the past four years, indicating the persistent prevalence of violence in both domestic and non-domestic settings. Among the total number of violent incidents reported in 2024, 75.6% involved male perpetrators and 19.3% involved female perpetrators. In terms of victim demographics, 50.3% of victims were male and 49.7% were female. Regarding offenders' racial demographics, 46.9% were White, 27.7% Black, 16.1% Hispanic, 2.7% Asian/Native Hawaiian/Other Pacific Islander, and 2.1% identified as other. Among victims, 56.3% were White, 19.1% Hispanic, 12.7% Black, 3.8% Asian/Native Hawaiian/Other Pacific Islander, and 8% identified as other. Additionally, according to NCVS, only 47.7% of domestic violence incidents and 44.9% of stranger violence incidents were reported to the police (Tapp & Coen, 2025). Altogether, these numbers highlight that a broad segment of the population is subjected to violent incidents each year. Given the high prevalence of violent crimes occurring in both domestic and non-domestic contexts and the of individuals affected, it is essential to further explore how officers perceive victim credibility and the factors that influence these perceptions. Doing so may uncover potential biases that shape investigative decisions and outcomes.

Non-domestic Battery

According to Florida Law, Statute 784.03, a person commits a simple battery if they "(1) Actually and intentionally touches or strikes another person against the will of the other; or (2) Intentionally causes bodily harm to another person" (2025a). A battery that does not occur in a domestic setting, here known as a non-domestic battery, is a form of violent crime that can occur across a range of social contexts. For example, it may include workplace violence (Barling, 1996; Neuman & Baron, 1998; Pich & Roche, 2020; Piquero et al., 2013), violence between friends and acquaintances (Hessick, 2007; Waasdorp et al., 2009), stranger violence (Petherick & Turvey, 2009; Phillips & de Roos, 2022; Riedel, 2017), and street or gang-related violence (Anderson, 2000; Faragher, 2016; Johnson et al., 2000; Stewart & Simons, 2010; Vigil, 2003).

Research directly examining credibility in non-domestic battery cases is sparse. However, studies exploring factors that influence police officers' perceptions of victims of non-specified violent crimes show some overlap with studies examining credibility in domestic battery cases (Bostaph et al., 2021; Campbell et al., 2015; Epstein & Goodman, 2018; Landström et al., 2015). For example, Ask (2010) emphasizes the importance of victims' behavior, specifically highlighting how non-verbal and emotional expressions are linked to perceived truthfulness. Studies that investigate officers' perceptions of victims, without limiting the scope to a specific type of victimization, offer valuable insights into how extra-legal factors influence officer decision making (Ask, 2010; Eliasson, 2022; Watson et al., 2004). For example, Watson et al. (2004) demonstrated that victims' mental health status can affect officers' perceptions, while Eliasson (2022) found that officers consider victims' choices and perceived role in their victimization when assessing culpability. Together, these studies highlight the wide range of extra-legal factors such as behavior, mental health, and perceived responsibility that shape officers' perceptions of victims, and may influence assessments of credibility. These dynamics could be also be applicable in non-domestic battery cases, where victims do not always align with familiar cultural narratives of vulnerability. However, because these current studies do not specifically examine violent crime in non-domestic contexts, further research is necessary to explore the applicability to non-domestic battery cases.

Not only do statistics show a high prevalence of violence in non-domestic settings (Tapp & Coen, 2025), but previous research also suggests that police responses to non-domestic battery differ in important ways from responses to domestic battery. For instance, Sun (2006) found that officers were less likely to take the initiative to respond in non-domestic battery cases compared to domestic cases, indicating a potential disparity in engagement and intervention. Research has also shown that incidents involving injury and female victims are more likely to result in police involvement (Jasinski, 2003). These findings emphasize how factors such as social relationships and gender can influence law enforcement's responses. Additionally, while the domestic violence literature has advanced understanding of female victimization, it has contributed less to knowledge about violence in non-domestic settings. Men, in particular, represent a population frequently exposed to non-domestic battery (Tapp & Coen, 2025), yet their experiences remain fairly underexplored compared to women in certain contexts of violence.

One body of literature that addresses police officers' perceptions and responses to non-domestic batteries emerges from studies on street and gang violence, often exploring the dynamic and complex experiences of street crime and violence (Aspholm, 2020; Baskin, 2018). For instance, Contreras (2013) examined interactions between youth involved in drug sales and police in New York City, highlighting that youth who are victims of violent crime often choose not to report their victimization to law enforcement. Similarly, Anderson (2000) emphasized the informal rules that shape how victims of street and gang violence navigate their interactions with police. Kwak et al. (2019) further explored how these informal norms, along with prior experiences with law enforcement, influence the likelihood of reporting violent victimization. Their findings suggest that among Black victims of violence, the likelihood of reporting decreases as perceptions of police ineffectiveness increase, underscoring the complexity of police-community dynamics, especially in the context of violent crimes. Additionally, the study found that factors such as weapon use, severity of injuries, victim gender, and the relationship between victim and offender significantly impact the likelihood of reporting. In his ethnographic study of Latino youth and police interactions, Rios (2017) observed that officers often exerted dominance and masculinity over young men encountered on the street and noted that Latino youth were frequently targeted by law enforcement. He emphasized that race plays a significant role in shaping these encounters, a point echoed by Bachman (1994), who also highlighted racial dynamics in police interactions with victims of non-domestic violence. Altogether, this scholarship stress that individuals exposed to street and gang violence may develop negative perceptions of the criminal justice system, which in turn can influence their willingness to report victimization. It also suggests that officers may hold biases against individuals from certain environments, potentially affecting how victims are treated during police encounters and how they are being perceived. Finally, this research highlights how factors such as gender, race, and prior experiences with law enforcement play a significant role in shaping victims' interactions with police.

Domestic Battery

In addition to defining battery in a non-domestic setting, Florida Law also makes a distinction of batteries that are committed in a domestic context. Statute 741.28 provides a definition of domestic violence which states:

> "Domestic violence" means any assault, aggravated assault, battery, aggravated battery, sexual assault, sexual battery, stalking, aggravated stalking, kidnapping, false imprisonment, or any criminal offense resulting in physical injury or death of one family or household member by another family or household member. (Fla. Stat. § 741.28, 2025b)

The Statute also further defines what constitutes a family or household member:

> "Family or household member" means spouses, former spouses, persons related by blood or marriage, persons who are presently residing together as if a family or who have resided together in the past as if a family, and persons who are parents of a child in common regardless of whether they have been married. With the exception of persons who have a child in common, the family or household members must be currently residing or have in the past resided together in the same single dwelling unit. (Fla. Stat. § 741.28, 2025b)

One important distinction between domestic and non-domestic batteries is the presence of a household or relational tie between the parties, which is something that has a significant impacts on law enforcement's and the criminal justice system's responses. For example, individuals found guilty of battery in a domestic setting are subject to different legal penalties compared to those convicted of battery in non-domestic contexts. Domestic battery convictions often carry mandatory sanctions, such as participation in and completion of a Batterers' Intervention Program. However, the definitions, procedures, and sanctions may vary from state to state.

Domestic violence has previously been studied, with decades of research shaping current legal and policy frameworks. Both early (Benson et al., 2003; Buzawa & Austin, 1993; Finn & Stalans, 1997; Saunders & Size, 1986) and more recent studies (DeJong et al., 2008; Fleming & Franklin, 2021; García et al., 2011; Goodson, 2020; Hirschel et al., 2007; Horwitz et al., 2011; Myhill & Johnson, 2016; Pahl, 2016; Russell, 2018) have emphasized the importance of understanding police officers' perceptions of domestic violence and their responses to victims. The existing body of scholarship has significantly contributed to the development of policies and practices aimed at improving law enforcement responses to domestic violence, including mandatory arrest policies and specialized training programs. One of the most influential studies in this area is the Minneapolis Domestic Violence Experiment conducted by Sherman and Berk (1984), which found that arrest was more effective in reducing future violence than alternatives such as counseling or temporarily separating the involved parties. Following the publication of this study, many states, including Florida, adopted mandatory or pro-arrest policies for domestic violence incidents (Buzawa et al., 2015). These legal reforms have significantly shaped officers' discretionary power, requiring them to arrest suspects when probable cause exists (Tatum & Pence, 2015). A key implication of reduced discretion in domestic violence cases is that officers may manage these incidents differently than non-domestic cases. For example, mandatory arrest policies can often lead to higher arrest rates in domestic incidents. The legal requirements may also influence officers' reporting practices, potentially resulting in more thorough documentation due to the increased number of reports generated under pro-arrest mandates. Therefore, when examining domestic violence cases, it is essential to consider the legal frameworks that guide officer behavior, as they directly inform decision making and procedural conduct.

Beyond legal mandates, scholars have also emphasized the role of extra-legal factors can have in shaping officers' responses, particularly in arrest decisions. Waaland and Keeley (1985) and Buzawa and Austin

(1993) found that factors such as the presence of witnesses or children during the incident can increase the likelihood of arrest. Hence, officers' actions are influenced not only by statutory obligations but also by situational dynamics and perceived social cues. Research has also shows that victims' emotional expressions and conduct significantly influence officers' perceptions of credibility, especially in domestic violence cases. For example, Landström et al. (2015), found in their study of Swedish police officers, that victims who displayed certain emotional responses were perceived as more credible than those who remained neutral. El Sayed et al. (2022) further expanded the discourse by examining how various factors such as victim statements, physical trauma, witness credibility, prior family violence calls, and victim involvement in substance use or illegal activity affect officers' perceptions of credibility. The study also considered how officer characteristics including age, rank, gender, and years of experience influenced these assessments. The authors found that older and more experienced officers were less influenced by victim-related factors than younger or less experienced officers. Additionally, male officers were more likely than female officers to believe that victims could easily leave abusive relationships and placed greater emphasis on physical evidence when evaluating credibility. Male officers also tended to view victim involvement in substance abuse and criminal activity more negatively than female officers. These findings highlight the complex interplay between victim behavior, case characteristics, and officer demographics ithat can impact credibility assessments. However, the findings also reinforce the importance of examining how discretionary judgments and assessments are informed not only by legal mandates but by subjective interpretations rooted in personal and cultural biases and perceptions.

Scholars have also extensively examined how victims' and suspects' race, gender, and sexual orientation shape police officers' conduct, decision making, and perceptions of domestic battery victims (Franklin et al., 2019; Huisman et al., 2005; Russell & Sturgeon, 2019; Sokoloff & Dupont, 2005; Storey & Strand, 2017; Younglove et al., 2002). For instance, Finn and Stalans (1997) found that gender influences officers' perceptions of victim culpability, with male victims often viewed as more responsible for their victimization due to assumptions about their greater control over behavior. Similarly, Russell (2018) explored how gender and sexual orientation affect assessment of credibility and found that in cases with male perpetrators the victims were considered more credible compared to victims in cases with female perpetrators. The study also revealed that victims in cases with heterosexual male and lesbian perpetrators were more likely to be perceived by officers as exhibiting signs of mental illness. Additionally, female victims were generally viewed as more credible than male victims in domestic violence cases.

In addition to gender and sexual orientation, race has also been shown to impact officers' assessments of blameworthiness. Harrison and Esqueda (2000) found that when alcohol was involved, Black victims were perceived as more responsible for their victimization than White victims. Altogether, these findings highlight the importance of further examining the role extra-legal factors such as race and ethnicity have in shaping officers' discretionary decisions and their perceptions of victims. Understanding police officers' perceptions of domestic battery victims' credibility is especially critical when considering the potential influence of racial biases. For example, prior research has shown that Black and Hispanic women are more likely to report domestic violence to law enforcement (Lipsky et al., 2009; Pearlman et al., 2003). This raises important questions about whether these victims are subject to differential treatment based on race or ethnicity, which could shape their experiences with the criminal justice system. If victims perceive bias or unfair treatment, this may negatively affect their trust in law enforcement and reduce the likelihood of reporting future victimizations (Coulter et al., 1999; Hickman & Simpson, 2003).

While much of the existing literature focuses on domestic violence, the influence of victim demeanor, substance use, and officer characteristics on credibility assessments may also extend to non-domestic battery cases. However, this area remains underexplored. Given that officers rely on a combination of legal mandates and subjective interpretations when evaluating victims, biases could shape their responses in non-domestic contexts. Unlike domestic cases, where pro-arrest policies and structured interventions guide officer conduct, non-domestic battery incidents often afford greater discretionary latitude. This raises important questions about whether victims in both types of settings are treated equally and whether their credibility is assessed through similar extra-legal lenses.

The Ideal Victim

The notion that victims may be perceived differently by others is highlighted by Nils Christie (1986) in his discussion of victim legitimacy. Christie's Ideal Victim Theory outlines specific characteristics of victims and their victimizations that influence societal perceptions of their legitimacy. This framework offers a useful lens when exploring police officers' perceptions of victims as it can help determine whether police officers adhere to the same normative perceptions of victim credibility as those held by the general public about legitimacy. According to the Merriam-Webster dictionary credibility is defined as "the quality or power of inspiring belief" (Merriam-Webster, 2025a), whereas legitimacy is the quality or state of being legitimate which is defined as "being exactly as intended or presented: neither spurious nor false" and "being an actual example of something specified" (Merriam-Webster, 2025b). Legitimacy and credibility are two concepts that in this book are linked together to refer to the believability of individuals who potentially have been subjected to violence and the factors that are taken into consideration when making this assessment. Both concepts are interrelated as they enhance each other in the assessment of credibility. One of the goals of this book is to understand if the factors used to assess victim legitimacy in the Ideal Victim Theory can be extended to perceptions of credibility by providing a robust conceptual framework that offers a structured description of various dynamic factors related to the victim and victimization.

Christie (1986) argued that victims that exhibit certain characteristics are more likely to be perceived by society as legitimate in their claim to the victim label. To illustrate this concept further, Christie used the example of the "little old lady," representing the archetype of the most legitimate victim in the eyes of society.

> The little old lady on the way home in the middle of the day after having cared for her sick sister. If she is hit on the head by a big man who thereafter grabs her bag and uses the money for liquor or drugs-in that case. (Christie, 1986, p. 36)

Through this example, Christie further conceptualized the Ideal Victim by developing the following six characteristics that he argued described Ideal Victims:

1. The victim is weak.
2. The victim is carrying out a respectable activity.
3. The victim could not be blamed for the location they are in.
4. The offender is "big and bad."
5. There is no prior personal relationship between the victim and the offender.
6. The victim is powerful enough to make his/her case known without threatening strong countervailing vested interests.

Rainer Strobl (2004) later added two additional characteristics to supplement the six developed by Christie (1986), which state:

7. The victim should not have behaved provocatively toward the offender.
8. The victim should cooperate perfectly with the criminal justice system.

This framework raises the question of whether similar characteristics shape police officers' assessments of credibility in battery cases. This book's specific focus on domestic and non-domestic battery also provides a compelling context for discussing Christie's (1986) Ideal Victim Theory, particularly in relation to victim credibility among women who experience domestic violence. Christie argues that women subjected to domestic violence are not traditionally viewed as Ideal Victims. Women who experience domestic battery may face greater challenges in attaining legitimacy compared to those who experience non-domestic battery, largely because their abusers are individuals they know. However, Christie (1986) contends that it is not solely the familiarity with the perpetrator that complicates the attainment of Ideal Victim status. He also emphasizes the role of the abuser's actions in shaping perceptions. Specifically, domestic abusers often construct narratives that portray the female victim as someone who provoked the abuse, framing the abuse as "discipline" or an expression of anger and frustration. As a result, victims may not even seek to claim the victim label, as they may not recognize their experiences as victimization, which can be an issue less prevalent in cases of non-domestic battery.

Although Christie (1986) asserts that women who experience domestic violence are less likely to be perceived as Ideal Victims, he also acknowledges that societal changes specifically related to women's status influence these perceptions. As women gain independence and agency, they are better positioned to claim the victim label. Christie argues that the progression of women's rights has reshaped normative perceptions of victims, particularly female victims, and by extension, potentially the perceptions held by police officers. However, he also notes that increased agency can introduce new barriers to legitimacy. For instance, as women become more capable of leaving abusive relationships, they may be blamed for choosing to stay, thereby undermining their victim status. The Ideal Victim, according to Christie, is perceived as weak and subordinate, and the empowerment of women that challenges this discourse can make it more difficult for victims of domestic battery to be seen as legitimate victims.

Beyond gender, race is another critical factor in discussions of the Ideal Victim. Scholars have highlighted that non-White victims often face racial biases that affect how they are perceived. For example, Dukes and Gaither (2017) found that Black male victims were more likely to be viewed as blameworthy than White victims in cases of police violence. One of the few studies examining race in relation to the Ideal Victim (Wilson & O'Brien, 2016) conceptualized race as a proxy for weakness, one of Christie's key characteristics, though it did not explore racial dynamics in depth. While Christie (1986) did not include race as a factor in his original framework, scholars such as Long (2021) have emphasized the need to incorporate racial dynamics into discussions of victim legitimacy.

The characteristics developed by Christie (1986) and Strobl (2004) offer a valuable lens for examining police officers' perceptions of victim credibility in cases of domestic and non-domestic battery. These characteristics include not only the victim's traits but also those of the suspect, the environment, and the victim's behavior. Previous scholarship has underscored the relevance of the Ideal Victim Theory, particularly in European studies of genocide, war crimes (Basic, 2015; Schwöbel-Patel,

2018; Van Wijk, 2013), cybercrime (Black et al., 2019), and racialized victimizations (Fohring, 2018; Jägervi, 2014; Long, 2021). More recently, scholars in other regions of the world have begun applying the concept (Duggan, 2018; Lewis et al., 2019; Schwöbel-Patel, 2018; Wilson & O'Brien, 2016). For example, several studies have examined how criminal justice professionals perceive victims and how these perceptions align with the Ideal Victim Theory (Alexius, 2020; Törnqvist, 2022). However, few have specifically explored police officers' views (Black et al., 2019; Inzunza, 2022). The few existing studies suggest that officers in various countries hold perceptions of victims that reflect the characteristics outlined by Christie (1986) and Strobl (2004), demonstrating the theory's relevance across diverse victimizations and geographic contexts.

In reviewing empirical literature, it is evident that Christie's and Strobl's characteristics have been conceptualized in varied ways, with no standardized approach to measurement. For instance, Törnqvist (2022, p. 269) defines weakness as "old age, cognitive disability, and being broken due to a longer period of intimate partner violence," while Wilson and O'Brien (2016, p. 37) conceptualize it based on "age, sex, and ethnicity." Few studies provide detailed justifications for their conceptual frameworks. Inzunza (2022, p. 5), for example, notes that "items were developed based on the characteristics that were considered feasible to operationalize," and were assessed for clarity and content validity. The lack of consensus and rationale in operationalizing these characteristics leaves room for scholarly interpretation, which this book will aim to address by drawing on prior applications and inductive analysis of the study's findings.

This book contributes to the existing scholarship by explicitly focusing on police officers' perceptions of victim credibility, a topic that has received limited attention in Europe and the United States (Black et al., 2019; Cross, 2018; Ricciardelli et al., 2020). By applying the Ideal Victim Theory to both domestic and non-domestic battery cases, this book expands its empirical scope to include understudied populations such as male victims and victims without prior relationships to their offenders. The Ideal Victim Theory offers a robust framework for this study for several reasons. Christie (1986) and Strobl (2004) emphasize the importance of considering factors beyond the victim, including the offender's characteristics, the victim-offender relationship, and the context of the victimization (Ask & Landström, 2010). These elements align with broader criminological scholarship (Ask, 2010; Engel et al., 2000; Lee et al., 2013) and provide a structured approach to understanding officers' decision making and perceptions, especially when assessing credibility, which is heavily integrated with factors beyond the victim. Moreover, the Ideal Victim Theory complements critical frameworks by focusing on battery, a form of victimization often overlooked in victimological research, specifically batteries in a non-domestic setting. While concepts such as victim-blaming have generated victimization-specific frameworks (e.g., battered spouse syndrome), the Ideal Victim Theory can enrich these discussions by offering a broader lens for examining victim credibility.

Finally, the concept's emphasis on societal norms makes it particularly relevant for analyzing police officers' perceptions. Christie (1986) and Strobl (2004) argue that their characteristics reflect societal beliefs about victim legitimacy. In this study, these norms will be used to explore how officers, despite their professional training, may internalize and act upon societal perceptions of victims. Although the Ideal Victim Theory will not be empirically tested, it provides a valuable framework for discussing normative beliefs in relation to organizational practices, procedures, and individual-level factors that shape officers' perceptions of victims.

Conclusion

This chapter has explored how officers' perceptions of victim credibility are shaped by a combination of legal mandates, case-specific, and extra-legal factors. Although domestic violence cases have received significant scholarly attention, similar dynamics may also apply to non-domestic battery cases, which remain less studied. The influence of victim demeanor, substance use, and officer characteristics appears to extend beyond domestic contexts and opens up for further investigation.

In non-domestic battery cases, where officers have greater freedom to exercise discretion, the potential for bias may be even more pronounced.

Without the procedural constraints present in domestic violence cases, officers may depend more heavily on personal judgments, which can result in inconsistent or unequal treatment of victims. This raises important concerns about fairness and the equitable application of justice across different types of violent incidents.

In domestic violence cases, structured interventions and pro-arrest policies guide officer conduct and reduce discretionary decision making. However, even within these frameworks, officers' assessments are shaped by subjective interpretations related to gender, race, sexual orientation, and perceived lifestyle. These biases affect not only arrest decisions but also how officers evaluate victim credibility, particularly when physical evidence is limited. Officer demographics such as age, gender, rank, and experience also play a role in shaping credibility assessments. Research suggests that male officers and those with less experience may be more influenced by victim-related factors, while older and more experienced officers may rely less on these cues. These findings highlight the importance of understanding how individual-level traits interact with broader institutional and cultural contexts. Finally, the chapter addresses how the Ideal Victim Theory can lend a hand in conceptualizing credibility and how it is perceived by officers.

References

Alderden, M. A., & Ullman, S. E. (2012). Creating a more complete and current picture: Examining police and prosecutor decision-making when processing sexual assault cases. *Violence Against Women, 18*, 525–551. https://doi.org/10.1177/1077801212453867

Alexius, K. (2020). The exposed child in a qualitative study of cases at the Swedish schools inspectorate. An ideal or not-so-ideal victim? *Pedagogy, Culture & Society, 28*(3), 367–382. https://doi.org/10.1080/14681366.2019.1649296

Anderson, E. (2000). *Code of the street: Decency, violence, and the moral life of the inner city*. WW Norton & Company.

Ask, K. (2010). A survey of police officers' and prosecutors' beliefs about crime victim behaviors. *Journal of Interpersonal Violence, 25*(6), 1132–1149. https://doi.org/10.1177/0886260509340535

Ask, K., & Landström, S. (2010). Why emotions matter: Expectancy violation and affective response mediate the emotional victim effect. *Law and Human Behavior, 34*(5), 392–401. https://doi.org/10.1007/s10979-009-9208-6

Aspholm, R. (2020). *Views from the streets: The transformation of gangs and violence on Chicago's south side*. Columbia University Press.

Bachman, R. (1994). Victim's perceptions of initial police responses to robbery and aggravated assault: Does race matter? *Journal of Quantitative Criminology, 12*, 363–390. https://doi.org/10.1007/BF02354424

Barling, J. (1996). The prediction, experience, and consequences of workplace violence. In G. R. VandenBos & E. Q. Bulatao (Eds.), *Violence on the job: Identifying risks and developing solutions* (pp. 29–49). American Psychological Association. https://doi.org/10.1037/10215-001

Basic, G. (2015). Constructing "ideal victim" stories of Bosnian war survivors. *Social Inclusion, 3*(4), 25–37. https://doi.org/10.17645/si.v3i4.249

Baskin, D. (2018). *Casualties of community disorder: Women's careers in violent crime*. Routledge.

Benson, M. L., Fox, G. L., DeMaris, A., & Van Wyk, J. (2003). Neighborhood disadvantage, individual economic distress and violence against women in intimate relationships. *Journal of Quantitative Criminology, 19*(3), 207–235. https://doi.org/10.1023/A:1024930208331

Black, A., Lumsden, K., & Hadlington, L. (2019). 'Why Don't you block them?' Police officers' constructions of the ideal victim when responding to reports of interpersonal cybercrime. In K. Lumsden & E. Harmer (Eds.), *Online othering* (pp. 355–378). Palgrave Studies in Cybercrime and Cybersecurity). Springer International Publishing. https://doi.org/10.1007/978-3-030-12633-9_15

Bollingmo, G. C., Wessel, E. O., Eilertsen, D. E., & Magnussen, S. (2007). Credibility of the emotional witness: A study of ratings by police investigators. *Psychology, Crime & Law, 14*, 29–40. https://doi.org/10.1007/s10979-006-9024-1

Bostaph, L. G., King, L. L., & Brady, P. Q. (2021). How victim credibility and cooperation influence investigative decision-making: Examining DOJ's gender bias principles for investigating domestic and sexual violence. *Policing: An International Journal, 44*(4), 612–627. https://doi.org/10.1108/PIJPSM-02-2021-0018

Buzawa, E. S., & Austin, T. (1993). Determining police response to domestic violence victims: The role of victim preference. *American Behavioral Scientist, 36*(5), 610–623. https://doi.org/10.1177/0002764293036005006

Buzawa, E. S., Buzawa, C. G., & Stark, E. D. (2015). *Responding to domestic violence: The integration of criminal justice and human services*. Sage Publications.

Campbell, B. A., Menaker, T. A., & King, W. R. (2015). The determination of victim credibility by adult and juvenile sexual assault investigators. *Journal of Criminal Justice, 43*(1), 29–39. https://doi.org/10.1016/j.jcrimjus.2014.12.001

Christie, N. (1986). The ideal victim. In E. Fattah (Ed.), *From crime policy to victim policy* (pp. 17–30). Palgrave Macmillan. https://doi.org/10.1007/978-1-349-08305-3_2

Contreras, R. (2013). *The stickup kids: Race, drugs, violence, and the American dream*. University of California Press.

Cordner, G. (2017). Police culture: Individual and organizational differences in police officer perspectives. *Policing: An International Journal, 40*(1), 11–25. https://doi.org/10.1108/PIJPSM-07-2016-0116

Coulter, M. L., Kuehnle, K., Byers, R., & Alfonso, M. (1999). Police-reporting behavior and victim-police interactions as described by women in a domestic violence shelter. *Journal of Interpersonal Violence, 14*(12), 1290–1298. https://doi.org/10.1177/088626099014012004

Cross, C. (2018). Denying victim status to online fraud victims: The challenges of being a "non-Ideal Victim". In M. Duggan (Ed.), *Revisiting the ideal victim concept* (pp. 243–262). Policy Press. https://doi.org/10.1332/policypress/9781447338765.003.0015

DeJong, C., Burgess-Proctor, A., & Elis, L. (2008). Police officer perceptions of intimate partner violence: An analysis of observational data. *Violence and Victims, 23*(6), 683–696. https://doi.org/10.1891/0886-6708.23.6.683

Duggan, M. (2018). *Revisiting the ideal victim': Developments in critical victimology*. Policy Press. https://doi.org/10.1332/policypress/9781447338765.001.0001

Dukes, K. N., & Gaither, S. E. (2017). Black racial stereotypes and victim blaming: Implications for media coverage and criminal proceedings in cases of police violence against racial and ethnic minorities. *Journal of Social Issues, 73*(4), 789–807. https://doi.org/10.1111/josi.12248

El Sayed, S. A., DeShay, R. A., Davis, J. B., Knox, K. N., & Kerley, K. R. (2022). A blue step forward: An exploratory study of law enforcement perceptions of intimate partner violence in the southern United States. *Journal of Interpersonal Violence, 37*(9–10), 6514–6534. https://doi.org/10.1177/0886260520966675

Eliasson, M. N. (2022). A qualitative examination of Swedish police officers' perceptions of victim culpability. *Victims & Offenders, 19*(2), 160–178. https://doi.org/10.1080/15564886.2022.2091069

Engel, R. S., Sobol, J. J., & Worden, R. E. (2000). Further exploration of the demeanor hypothesis: The interaction effects of suspects' characteristics and demeanor on police behavior. *Justice Quarterly, 17*(2), 235–258. https://doi.org/10.1080/07418820000096311

Epstein, D., & Goodman, L. A. (2018). Discounting women: Doubting domestic violence survivors' credibility and dismissing their experiences. *University Pennsylvania Law Review, 167*, 399.

Faragher, J. M. (2016). *Eternity street: Violence and justice in frontier Los Angeles*. WW Norton & Company.

Farrell, A., Owens, C., & McDevitt, J. (2014). New laws but few cases: Understanding the challenges to the investigation and prosecution of human trafficking cases. *Crime, Law and Social Change, 61*, 139–168. https://doi.org/10.1007/s10611-013-9442-1

Finn, M. A., & Stalans, L. J. (1997). The influence of gender and mental state on police decisions in domestic assault cases. *Criminal Justice and Behavior, 24*(2), 157–176. https://doi.org/10.1177/0093854897024002002

Fleming, J. C., & Franklin, C. A. (2021). Predicting police endorsement of myths surrounding intimate partner violence. *Journal of Family Violence, 36*(4), 407–416. https://doi.org/10.1007/s10896-020-00178-w

Florida Senate. (2025a). *Fla. stat. Chapter 784.03*. Florida Senate. https://www.leg.state.fl.us/statutes/index.cfm?App_mode=Display_Statute&Search_String=&URL=0700-0799/0784/Sections/0784.03.html

Florida Senate. (2025b). *Fla. stat. Chapter 741.28*. Florida Senate https://www.leg.state.fl.us/statutes/index.cfm?mode=View%20Statutes&SubMenu=1&App_mode=Display_Statute&Search_String=741.28&URL=0700-0799/0741/Sections/0741.28.html

Fohring, S. (2018). Revisiting the non-ideal victim. In M. Duggan (Ed.), *Revisiting the 'ideal victim': Developments in critical victimology* (pp. 195–210). https://doi.org/10.1332/policypress/9781447338765.003.0012

Franklin, C. A., Goodson, A., & Garza, A. D. (2019). Intimate partner violence among sexual minorities: Predicting police officer arrest decisions. *Criminal Justice and Behavior, 46*(8), 1181–1199. https://doi.org/10.1177/0093854819834722

Frohmann, L. (1991). Discrediting victims' allegations of sexual assault: Prosecutorial accounts of case rejections. *Social Problems, 38*, 213–226. https://doi.org/10.2307/800530

Frohmann, L. (1997). Convictability and discordant locales: Reproducing race, class, and gender ideologies in prosecutorial decision-making. *Law and Society Review, 31*, 531–555. https://doi.org/10.2307/3054045

García, E., García, F., & Lila, M. (2011). Police attitudes toward policing partner violence against women: Do they correspond to different psychosocial profiles? *Journal of Interpersonal Violence, 26*(1), 189–207. https://doi.org/10.1177/0886260510362892

Goodson, A. J. (2020). *Heterosexual and same-sex intimate partner violence: Police attributions of victim culpability*. Doctoral dissertation, Sam Huston State University. https://hdl.handle.net/20.500.11875/2758

Harrison, L. A., & Esqueda, C. W. (2000). Effects of race and victim drinking on domestic violence attributions. *Sex Roles, 42*, 1043–1057. https://doi.org/10.1023/A:1007040701889

Hessick, C. B. (2007). Violence between lovers, strangers, and friends. *Washington University Law Review, 85*(2), 343–407. https://openscholarship.wustl.edu/law_lawreview/vol85/iss2/3

Hickman, L. J., & Simpson, S. S. (2003). Fair treatment or preferred outcome? The impact of police behavior on victim reports of domestic violence incidents. *Law & Society Review, 37*(3), 607–634. https://doi.org/10.1111/1540-5893.3703005

Hirschel, D., Buzawa, E., Pattavina, A., & Faggiani, D. (2007). Domestic violence and mandatory arrest laws: To what extent do they influence police arrest decisions. *Journal of Criminal Law and Criminology, 98*(1), 255–298. https://www.jstor.org/stable/40042852

Horwitz, S. H., Mitchell, D., LaRussa-Trott, M., Santiago, L., Pearson, J., Skiff, D. M., & Cerulli, C. (2011). An inside view of police officers' experience with domestic violence. *Journal of Family Violence, 26*(8), 617–625. https://doi.org/10.1007/s10896-011-9396-y

Huisman, K., Martinez, J., & Wilson, C. (2005). Training police officers on domestic violence and racism: Challenges and strategies. *Violence Against Women, 11*(6), 792–821. https://doi.org/10.1177/1077801205276110

Inzunza, M. (2022). The significance of victim ideality in interactions between crime victims and police officers. *International Journal of Law, Crime and Justice, 68*, 1–12. https://doi.org/10.1016/j.ijlcj.2021.100522

Jägervi, L. (2014). Who wants to be an ideal victim? A narrative analysis of crime victims' self-presentation. *Journal of Scandinavian Studies in Criminology and Crime Prevention, 15*(1), 73–88. https://doi.org/10.1080/14043858.2014.893479

Jasinski, J. L. (2003). Police involvement in incidents of physical assault: Analysis of the redesigned National Crime Victimization Survey. *Journal of Family Violence, 18*, 143–150. https://doi.org/10.1023/A:1023512420703

Johnson, B., Golub, A., & Dunlap, E. (2000). The rise and decline of hard drugs, drug markets, and violence in inner-city New York. In A. Blumstein & J. Wallman (Eds.), *The crime drop in America* (pp. 164–206). Cambridge University Press.

Kwak, H., Dierenfeldt, R., & McNeeley, S. (2019). The code of the street and cooperation with the police: Do codes of violence, procedural injustice, and police ineffectiveness discourage reporting violent victimization to the police? *Journal of Criminal Justice, 60*, 25–34. https://doi.org/10.1016/j.jcrimjus.2018.11.001

LaFree, G. D. (1981). Official reactions to social problems: Police decisions in sexual assault cases. *Social Problems, 28*, 582–594. https://doi.org/10.2307/800232

Landström, S., Ask, K., & Sommar, C. (2015). The emotional male victim: Effects of presentation mode on judged credibility. *Scandinavian Journal of Psychology, 56*(1), 99–104. https://doi.org/10.1111/sjop.12176

Lee, J., Zhang, Y., & Hoover, L. T. (2013). Police response to domestic violence: Multilevel factors of arrest decision. *Policing: an International Journal of Police Strategies & Management, 36*(1), 157–174. https://doi.org/10.1108/13639511311302524

Lewis, J. A., Hamilton, J. C., & Elmore, J. D. (2019). Describing the ideal victim: A linguistic analysis of victim descriptions. *Current Psychology*, (9), 1. https://doi.org/10.1007/s12144-019-00347-1

Lipsky, S., Caetano, R., & Roy-Byrne, P. (2009). Racial and ethnic disparities in police-reported intimate partner violence and risk of hospitalization among women. *Women's Health Issues, 19*(2), 109–118. https://doi.org/10.1016/j.whi.2008.09.005

Long, L. J. (2021). The ideal victim: A critical race theory (CRT) approach. *International Review of Victimology, 27*(3), 344–362. https://doi.org/10.1177/0269758021993339

Merriam-Webster. (2025a). *Credibility*. In Merriam-Webster.com dictionary. Retrieved October 15, 2025, from https://www.merriam-webster.com/dictionary/credibility

Merriam-Webster. (2025b). *Legitimacy*. In Merriam-Webster.com dictionary. Retrieved October 15, 2025, from https://www.merriam-webster.com/dictionary/legitimacy?src=search-dict-box

Myhill, A., & Johnson, K. (2016). Police use of discretion in response to domestic violence. *Criminology & Criminal Justice, 16*(1), 3–20. https://doi.org/10.1177/1748895815590202

Neuman, J. H., & Baron, R. A. (1998). Workplace violence and workplace aggression: Evidence concerning specific forms, potential causes, and preferred targets. *Journal of Management, 24*(3), 391–419. https://doi.org/10.1016/S0149-2063(99)80066-X

Pahl, J. (2016). *Private violence and public policy: The needs of battered women and the response of the public services*. Routledge. https://doi.org/10.4324/9781315562100

Pearlman, D. N., Zierler, S., Gjelsvik, A., & Verhoek-Oftedahl, W. (2003). Neighbor-hood environment, racial position, and risk of police-reported domestic violence: A contextual analysis. *Public Health Reports, 118*(1), 44–58. https://doi.org/10.1093/phr/118.1.44

Petherick, W. A., & Turvey, B. (2009). *Forensic victimology: Examining violent crime victims in investigative and legal contexts*. Elsevier.

Phillips, A., & de Roos, M. S. (2022). Gender stereotypes and perceptions of stranger violence: Attributions of blame and motivation. *International Journal of Offender Therapy and Comparative Criminology, 69*(1), 43–61. https://doi.org/10.1177/0306624X221124849

Pich, J., & Roche, M. (2020). Violence on the job: The experiences of nurses and midwives with violence from patients and their friends and relatives. *Healthcare, 8*(4), 1–12. https://doi.org/10.3390/healthcare8040522

Piquero, N. L., Piquero, A. R., Craig, J. M., & Clipper, S. J. (2013). Assessing research on workplace violence, 2000–2012. *Aggression and Violent Behavior, 18*(3), 383–394. https://doi.org/10.1016/j.avb.2013.03.001

Ricciardelli, R., Spencer, D. C., & Dodge, A. (2020). "Society wants to see a true victim": Police interpretations of victims of sexual violence. *Feminist Criminology, 16*(2), 216–235. https://doi.org/10.1177/1557085120970270

Riedel, M. (2017). A perspective on stranger violence. In W. Laufer & F. Adler (Eds.), *The criminology of criminal law* (pp. 29–52). Routledge. https://doi.org/10.4324/9781315131535

Rios, V. M. (2017). *Human targets: Schools, police, and the criminalization of Latino youth*. University of Chicago Press. https://doi.org/10.7208/chicago/9780226091044.001.0001

Russell, B. (2018). Police perceptions in intimate partner violence cases: The influence of gender and sexual orientation. *Journal of Crime and Justice, 41*(2), 193–205. https://doi.org/10.1080/0735648X.2017.1282378

Russell, B., & Sturgeon, J. A. (2019). Police evaluations of intimate partner violence in heterosexual and same-sex relationships: Do experience and training play a role? *Journal of Police and Criminal Psychology, 34*(1), 34–44. https://doi.org/10.1007/s11896-018-9279-8

Saunders, D. G., & Size, P. B. (1986). Attitudes about woman abuse among police officers, victims, and victim advocates. *Journal of Interpersonal Violence, 1*(1), 25–42. https://doi.org/10.1177/088626086001001003

Schwöbel-Patel, C. (2018). The 'ideal' victim of international criminal law. *European Journal of International Law, 29*(3), 703–724. https://doi.org/10.1093/ejil/chy056

Sherman, L. W. (2020). Targeting American policing: Rogue cops or rogue cultures? *Cambridge Journal of Evidence Based Policing, 4*, 77–88. https://doi.org/10.1007/s41887-020-00046-z

Sherman, L. W., & Berk, R. A. (1984). The specific deterrent effects of arrest for domestic assault. *American Sociological Review, 49*(2), 261–272. https://doi.org/10.2307/2095575

Skogan, W. G. (2006a). *Police and community in Chicago: A tale of three cities*. Oxford University Press. https://doi.org/10.1093/acprof:oso/9780195154580.001.0001

Skogan, W. (2006b). Asymmetry in the impact of encounters with police. *Policing and Society, 16*(2), 99–126. https://doi.org/10.1080/10439460600662098

Sokoloff, N. J., & Dupont, I. (2005). Domestic violence at the intersections of race, class, and gender: Challenges and contributions to understanding violence against marginalized women in diverse communities. *Violence Against Women, 11*(1), 38–64. https://doi.org/10.1177/1077801204271476

Stewart, E. A., & Simons, R. L. (2010). Race, code of the street, and violent delinquency: A multilevel investigation of neighborhood street culture and individual norms of violence. *Criminology, 48*(2), 569–605. https://doi.org/10.1111/j.1745-9125.2010.00196.x

Storey, J. E., & Strand, S. (2017). The influence of victim vulnerability and gender on police officers' assessment of intimate partner violence risk. *Journal of Family Violence, 32*(1), 125–134. https://doi.org/10.1007/s10896-016-9905-0

Strobl, R. (2004). Constructing the victim: Theoretical reflections and empirical examples. *International Review of Victimology, 11*(2–3), 295–311. https://doi.org/10.1177/026975800401100206

Sun, I. Y. (2006). Police response to victims of domestic and non-domestic violence. *Journal of Health and Human Services Administration, 29*(2), 145–172. http://www.jstor.org/stable/25790685

Tapp, S. N., & Coen, E. J. (2025). *Criminal victimization, 2024*. Bureau of Justice Statistics. https://bjs.ojp.gov/document/cv24.pdf

Tatum, K. M., & Pence, R. (2015). Factors that affect the arrest decision in domestic violence cases. *Policing: An International Journal of Police Strategies & Management, 38*(1), 56–70. https://doi.org/10.1108/PIJPSM-07-2014-0075

Törnqvist, N. (2022). Drizzling sympathy: Ideal victims and flows of sympathy in Swedish courts. *International Review of Victimology, 28*(3), 263–285. https://doi.org/10.1177/02697580211035586

Van Wijk, J. (2013). Who is the 'little old lady 'of international crimes? Nils Christie's concept of the ideal victim reinterpreted. *International Review of Victimology, 19*(2), 159–179. https://doi.org/10.1177/0143034312472770

Vigil, J. D. (2003). Urban violence and street gangs. *Annual Review of Anthropology, 32*(1), 225–242. https://doi.org/10.1146/annurev.anthro.32.061002.093426

Waaland, P., & Keeley, S. (1985). Police decision making in wife abuse: The impact of legal and extralegal factors. *Law and Human Behavior, 9*(4), 355–366. https://doi.org/10.1007/BF01044476

Waasdorp, T. E., Bagdi, A., & Bradshaw, C. P. (2009). Peer victimization among urban, predominantly African American youth: Coping with relational aggression between friends. *Journal of School Violence, 9*(1), 98–116. https://doi.org/10.1080/15388220903341372

Watson, A. C., Corrigan, P. W., & Ottati, V. (2004). Police officers' attitudes toward and decisions about persons with mental illness. *Psychiatric Services, 55*(1), 49–53. https://doi.org/10.1176/appi.ps.55.1.49

Wilson, M., & O'Brien, E. (2016). Constructing the ideal victim in The United States of America's annual trafficking in persons reports. *Crime, Law and Social Change, 65*(1–2), 29–45. https://doi.org/10.1007/s10611-015-9600-8

Younglove, J. A., Kerr, M. G., & Vitello, C. J. (2002). Law enforcement officers' perceptions of same sex domestic violence: Reason for cautious optimism. *Journal of Interpersonal Violence, 17*(7), 760–772. https://doi.org/10.1177/0886260502017007004

3

Gainesville Police Department

Introduction

Previous research highlighting that organizational hierarchy, occupational norms, practices and procedures, funding, and policing strategies or tactics all influence officers' attitudes, perceptions, and conduct (Braga et al., 2019; Cordner, 2017; Demirkol & Nalla, 2020; Ingram et al., 2018; Reiner, 2017; Sherman, 2020; Skogan, 2006; Skogan & Hartnett, 1999). These organizational features impact how officers make decisions in the field and influence both investigative practices and interactions with the public.

Perceptions of the organization itself can also influence officers' behavior. Wolfe and Piquero (2011) found that officers who perceived their organization as fair were less likely to engage in misconduct. Similarly, Myhill and Bradford (2013) found that organizational justice was associated with more positive attitudes toward the public. This association was mediated by officers' commitment to community policing and their overall satisfaction with the organization. Other scholars have also emphasized the role of police culture and the "code of silence," where officers protect each other by for example not reporting officer

M. N. Eliasson, *Who Gets Believed?*, Palgrave's Critical Policing Studies,
https://doi.org/10.1007/978-3-032-22253-4_3

misconduct, as influential on officers' conduct and perceptions (Crank, 2014; Loftus, 2009; Westmarland, 2005). Critical criminological scholarship highlights that these organizational norms are shaped by broader social constructs such as gender and race, with masculinity norms being particularly influential (Brown, 2007; Rios, 2017).

In addition to these organizational factors, individual level factors also influence officers' attitudes and conduct. These factors include officers' personal characteristics, social dynamics among officers, and training. For example, a longitudinal study found that officers' attitudes toward their job and occupational behavior changed over time (Garner, 2005) and that additional training can improve officers' empathy and behavior toward victims and suspects (Cunha et al., 2022; Patterson, 2004). Furthermore, race/ethnicity and sex/gender can shape how officers perceive their roles and behave in the field (Ba et al., 2021; Martin, 1994; Poteyeva & Sun, 2009; Sun & Payne, 2004). LeCount (2017) found that White officers were more likely than Black officers to express racial resentment and to perceive Black individuals as violent. Additionally, Sun and Payne (2004) found that Black officers were more coercive than White officers when handling conflict, and that White officers were less likely to engage in supportive activities in Black neighborhoods. However, the authors found no racial differences in officers' participation in racially diverse neighborhoods.

It is essential to recognize that officers' conduct, perceptions, and decisions are shaped by dynamic contexts and are influenced by organizational, legal, case, and individual-level factors. For example, despite the existence of occupational norms and practices guiding police report writing, officers still exercise discretion in determining what to include (Fisher, 1993; Myhill & Johnson, 2016). Thus, officers' actions are informed by a combination of organizational procedures, individual discretion, and legal mandates. In this chapter, I will provide an overview of the organizational structure of the GPD, describe staffing and patrol operations, and offer insight into the day-to-day work conducted by officers. The goal is to give the reader background and contextual information on how the police department operates, the organizational challenges officers face, and the internal dynamics that influence their interactions with victims and other citizens, as well as how they manage case investigations.

Organizational Structure and Staffing

After graduating from the police academy and being hired at GPD, officers attend a four-week internal training program known as the "mini-academy," where they are introduced to GPD's policies, computer systems, and expectations. After completing the mini-academy, officers enter a 16-week Field Training Program (FTP), during which they are paired with Field Training Officers (FTOs). This training is divided into four phases, with officers rotating among different FTOs for varying durations. Upon successful completion of the program, officers begin "riding solo," indicating that they are no longer under direct supervision and are considered fully trained.

GPD adheres to the militarized ranking structure common among police agencies in the United States (Kraska, 1996). Officers begin their careers as patrol officers and may be promoted to the ranks of corporal, sergeant, lieutenant, and captain. Additionally, officers may apply for specialized units such as Special Weapons and Tactics Unit (SWAT), Emergency Services Team (EST), FTO, K-9 Unit, or the detective division. According to officers, the promotion criteria, including required competencies and years of experience, varies depending on the position and are often influenced by internal departmental politics. GPD's organizational structure is hierarchical, with divisions and specialized units reporting through a chain of command that is overseen by the Police Chief. Two Assistant Police Chiefs support the Police Cheif, with one one supervising the Personnel Division, while the other oversees the Fiscal Division, Patrol Operations, Investigations Bureau, and the Training and Education Division. There is also a Youth and Community Service Bureau Director who manages units such as the Youth Resources Unit, High-Risk Diversion Unit, and Citizens on Patrol. GPD also has a dedicated detective unit responsible for investigating specific types of crimes, including domestic violence and sexual assault cases. These detectives are located on the second floor of the police station, which patrol officers commonly refer to as "upstairs." For instance, officers may say, "the investigation will be dealt with upstairs," indicating that the case will be handled by detectives. The second floor also houses other personnel and victim advocates who support victims in certain cases.

Staff Demographics

According to the GPD website, the department has its origin in the late 1800s to early 1900s. In 1922, GPD consisted of three officers, who during the next 13 years increased to 10 officers. In 1946, the first African American officer joined GPD. In 1970, the first sworn female officer joined the department as a detective. In 1975, the two first female patrol officers joined the force. During the mid-1970s, the department had grown to have 101 sworn officers and 97 civilian staff members (Gainesville Police Department, 2022). Table 3.1 describes GPD's self-generated staff statistics from March 2022, describing the gender, race, ethnicity, and rank among current officers.

These data show that GPD employs approximately four times as many male as female officers, which is consistent with the sex/gender demographics of female and male officers at a national level according to

Table 3.1 Gainesville Police Department staff demographics, March 2022

	Male 80.1% (*n* = 198)				Female 19.9% (*n* = 49)				Total
Race	B	W	H	O	B	W	H	O	
Rank									
Chief	1								1
Assistant chief	1	1							2
Chief inspector						1			1
Captain		2			2				4
Lieutenant	4	5	1		2	3	1		16
Sergeant	4	27			2	3	1		37
Corporal	4	22	3		1	8			38
Officer	33	74	7	4	3	18	1	2	142
Non-certified	5					1			6
Total	52	131	11	4	10	34	3	2	

Data were obtained from the Gainesville Police Department in an email request to department staff

Uniform Crime Report (UCR) data from 2019 (Federal Bureau of Investigation, 2019). Furthermore, the racial and ethnic demographics of the officers at GPD show that 56.8% (n = 165) of the officers are White, 25.1% (n = 62) are Black, 5.6% (n = 14) are Hispanic, and 2.4% (n = 6) are categorized as other among officers. The predominantly White male demographic of GPD is consistent with the racial and ethnic demographic of policing agencies across the United States, which, although becoming slightly more racially and ethnically diverse during the last few years, still reflects that most of the officers are White (Leatherby & Oppel, 2020).

Census data reveals that of the 143,611 individuals residing in Gainesville in 2023, 54.3% were non-Hispanic or Latino White, 21.1% Black or African American, 6.12% Asian, 4.91% Hispanic or Latino White, and 4.48% identified as two races including other and Hispanic (Data USA, 2023). The racial and ethnic demographics of officers working for GPD resemble the racial and ethnic demographics of the population of Gainesville, with the exception of a lower rate of Black officers working for GPD.

Staffing Shortage

Staffing shortages represent a significant organizational challenge that have been explored previously by policing scholarship, particularly exploring its impact on departmental operations and the practices of individual officers. Numerous police agencies across the United States report being understaffed and lists a wide range of factors as causing or contributing to the staffing issues (Wilson, 2012). During my six-month fieldwork with GPD, multiple observations and statements made by officers and leadership the department's ongoing challenges with staffing constraints, particularly among patrol officers. Throughout my time in the field, several officers left their positions due to promotions, resignations, or transitioning into other roles, while new officers joined the department which resulted in a dynamic turnover. In a conversation with the Captain, he acknowledged the staffing issue stating: "So every shift has…ideally, budgeted we would have 18 officers per shift…we are well below staffing." His statement mirrored a reality I faced while in the field, none of the shifts I observed during ride-alongs were fully staffed. On average, only 11 to 13 officers were present per shift, not counting officers who did overtime.

While some scholars have attributed staffing shortages in part to the COVID-19 pandemic (Stogner et al., 2020), officers at GPD did not identify the pandemic as a primary cause. Instead, during interviews and informal conversations, officers mentioned factors such as retirement, internal politics, low pay, and heavy workloads as major contributing factors, which are findings that align with pre-pandemic scholarship (Ricciardelli, 2018). However, this does not entirely rule out the pandemic's potential influence on recruitment and retention but rather reflect officers' perceptions. One officer, formerly involved in recruitment efforts at GPD, described several initiatives aimed at attracting new personnel. He shared that these initiatives included sign-on bonuses and a program in which GPD funded recruits' police academy training, contingent upon a three-year service commitment. However, he noted that despite these efforts, GPD continued to experience an officer shortage.

Staffing shortages emerged as a central theme during my fieldwork, as I observed its effects in officers' day-to-day activities. Several officers reported that being understaffed influenced their decision making during investigations and constrained their ability to perform essential duties. For example, Officer Young stated: "So the biggest challenge is that we're short-staffed…not having the proper amount of backup to handle certain situations we get put in daily." Other officers also noted that staffing shortages affected their discretion regarding paperwork and arrests. In some cases, they stated that they opted not to arrest individuals or file police reports to remain available for emergency calls or to support fellow officers, which is something I witnessed during my time in the field in battery cases and other types of crimes. For example, one officer, Officer Miller, explained his decision not to arrest a man for possessing heroin residue during a night when a University of Florida (UF) sports team was playing a home game:

> "I sometimes think about what I do because taking him to jail would have meant me not being available here…it would take me off the streets, which on a night like this would not be good."

Later that same evening, while responding to a non-domestic battery incident outside a bar, Officer Miller chose not to file a police report or make an arrest, stating: "This is how we deal with these down here…we don't have time to take everyone to jail, especially down here." The officers' mention of "down here" was in reference to his zone which was one of the zones close to the town center and that had the highest number of bars and patrons being students from UF, making the zone a very busy zone, especially during evenings, nights, and weekends. The statement Officer Miller shared with me alluded to that, in certain context, officers can exercise discretion based on staffing levels, particularly in certain types of crimes such as non-domestic battery incidents, where procedural flexibility is greater compared to certain types of crimes.

The Operations of Gainesville Police Department Patrol Units

There are many "moving parts" in the day-to-day responsibilities of patrol officers, involving multiple individuals across various ranks and roles. Officers are required to make numerous decisions during each shift and must navigate a complex range of protocols and guidelines that shape how they perform their duties. This section outlines the operational structure of the GPD, focusing on the routine activities of patrol officers. Rather than providing an exhaustive list of daily tasks, my goal is to offer some contextual insight into how officers carry out their responsibilities, both from their own perspectives and through my observations as a researcher.

Shifts, Zones, and Sectors

The patrol unit at GPD is divided into two shift rotations named Alpha and Bravo, each working four days of the week with one overlapping day per shift during which both Alpha and Bravo rotations work. There are three shifts, day shift (7.30 am and 5 pm), evening shift (5 pm–3 am), and midnight shift (10 pm and 8 am) and for each shift, one officer is supposed to be assigned to each of the geographical 18 zones in Gainesville. The zones cover the main part of the city of Gainesville, with some exceptions such as the University of Florida (UF) campus and Santa Fe College campus which have their own police enteties. When asked about how the zones were organized and created Captain Smith stated:

> So, what we try to base them on is it calls for service and population, oh, really go hand in hand. The higher the population, the higher the number of calls. So, we tried to do it that way, with some consideration of geographic boundaries to another way, we don't want an officer, that has a zone where the roadways don't allow for him to easily travel into a zone... So that's another consideration we take into consideration. But this was created, actually, we set up a committee, and this was created and presented by a group of officers.

As explained by the Captain, patrol zones are determined based on the types and frequency of calls for service, as well as the mobility of officers within each zone. As a result of this, certain types of crimes are often more prevalent in certain zones. Several officers I rode with confirmed this observation, noting that zones such as "Juliet" and "Whiskey" are more prone to domestic battery cases, whereas zones covering the downtown or midtown areas, such as "Mike", tend to experience a higher volume of non-domestic battery incidents.

These patterns have important implications for officers' exposure or inexposure to certain types of crimes. Officers assigned to zones with higher rates of domestic or non-domestic batteries may be more likely to have investigated and handled such cases, potentially more frequently than their counterparts in zones where other types of crimes are more typical. This repeated exposure may influence officers' practices, as they become more familiar with individuals who have previously reported battery incidents and they may develop specific approaches to handling cases based on their frequent exposure or lack thereof. Variation in exposure to certain crimes can also be related to officers' years of experience and seniority, as newer officers lack the experience more senior officers have. Thus, zone assignment and years on the job, are notions that can impact the level of exposure officers may have to domestic and non-domestic batteries which may influence the familiarity they have with certain procedures and how they approach battery investigations. During my ride-alongs, some officers expressed "not having worked" domestic cases recently which often meant that they had not been the "primary" officers on a battery cals in a long time. Not being the "primary officer" referred to that they were not the officer who made the main investigative decisions in the case nor the one who wrote the police report. The officers who expressed that they had not worked domestic cases recently, were often assigned to zones that had many commercial buildings, had a limited number of residential households, or had only been working as an officers for a few months.

The patrol zones in Gainesville were, at the time of my study, organized into three sectors, each with its own team and chain of command responsible for overseeing operations within that sector. As Captain Smith explained: "Each district is divided up into three sectors. Each sector has a lieutenant, and there is a zone within that sector… each sector has three zones and that has a sergeant." This structure ensured that each shift included not only patrol officers but also sergeants and a lieutenant, providing a consistent supervisory presence across all three shifts. Consequently, there was always a higher-ranking officer available to assist patrol officers during their shift. This organizational framework also shaped working relationships, as patrol officers tended to interact more frequently with specific sergeants and lieutenants in their assigned zones. These assignments established clear protocols regarding which supervisor serveed as the primary point of contact during a given shift. Patrol officers were typically assigned to a specific zone, often referred to as "their zone" and as the primary officer for that area, they were responsible for writing police reports for incidents occurring within it. However, officers also provide backup to other zones within their sector and, when necessary, may respond to calls in zones outside their assigned sector. In cases where the primary officer for a zone was unavailable, another patrol officer would be tasked with writing the report.

Beyond call frequency and officer mobility, Captain Smith highlighted two additional factors that influenced how zones are managed, one pertaining to individual-level considerations and the other to organizational-level decision making. According to the Captain, staffing zones presented ongoing challenges, particularly regarding whether officers should be rotated between zones or remain assigned to the same zone for extended periods. This issue has been the subject of repeated discussions among upper-level management within GPD, reflecting broader concerns about balancing consistency, officer familiarity with their zones, and operational flexibility.

> We don't want officers to only experience certain parts of the city. As you can imagine that Mike and Delta (zones) are very busy. Officers can get burned out, especially if you work night shift, bar closing, weekend after weekend. And then the other thing you don't do when the officers who were way out in the southwest, or we have an alpha zone, don't get that experience. And they may have to go to that zone (Mike or Delta). So, we had talks, you know, many years ago of kind of expanding to larger zones to have more experience…we had for a while we did basically where instead of the three zones, like you know Bravo, Charlie, that was like one zone with three officers assigned…So they would have to travel within a larger geographic area. Yeah. But then there's the concern of you know, that that model of community policing is that they kind of have an understanding of their neighborhood and their zone, and they know their business owners. And, you know, they know the issues going on in the neighborhood. So, it's almost like that.

According to the Captain, patrol zones influenced officers' levels of stress, their exposure to specific types of crimes, and the volume of calls they responded to. These factors, in turn, shaped how officers engaged in policing. One of the key benefits of maintaining consistent zone assignments, as noted by Captain Smith, was the development of specialized knowledge and expertise, particularly in handling high-frequency offenses such as drug-related crimes. This accumulated experience was viewed as a form of specialty competence that enhanced operational effectiveness. Additionally, consistent zone assignments facilitated relationship-building between officers and community members. The Captain emphasized that rotating officers between zones could hinder the development of these relationships, as officers then would not remain in a neighborhood long enough to establish trust or familiarity. As such, the question of whether to rotate officers or maintain fixed zone assignments became a recurring topic of discussion within the department.

Conclusion

In this chapter I have examined the organizational structure, operational routines, and discretionary practices of patrol officers within GPD by highlighting how organizational and individual-level factors intersect to shape the everyday duties of patrol work. Officers operate within a highly structured environment defined by militarized ranking systems, formal training protocols, and a division of labor that assigns them to specific geographic zones. These zones, determined by call frequency, mobility, and crime type, served as both spatial and symbolic anchors for officers, who often referred to their assigned area as "their zone."

Additionally, the chapter discussed how staffing shortages represented a persistent challenge for GPD, particularly within the patrol division. Although national scholarship has attributed such shortages in part to the COVID-19 pandemic, officers at GPD identified alternative causes, including retirement, internal politics, low pay, and heavy workloads. These perceptions align with pre-pandemic research and highlight the importance of examining the various types of organizational strain an police department may experience. The impact of understaffing is not only logistical but also directly influenced officers' decision making in the field. For example, officers described modifying their investigative practices, opting not to arrest individuals or file reports in certain cases, to remain available for emergency calls or to support fellow officers.

References

Ba, B. A., Knox, D., Mummolo, J., & Rivera, R. (2021). The role of officer race and gender in police-civilian interactions in Chicago. *Science, 371*, 696–702. https://doi.org/10.1126/science.abd8694

Braga, A. A., Brunson, R. K., & Drakulich, K. M. (2019). Race, place, and effective policing. *Annual Review of Sociology, 45*, 535–555. https://doi.org/10.1146/annurev-soc-073018-022541

Brown, J. (2007). From cult of masculinity to smart macho: Gender perspectives on police occupational culture. *Sociology of Crime, Law and Deviance, 8*(1), 205–226. https://doi.org/10.1016/S1521-6136(07)08008-6

Cordner, G. (2017). Police culture: Individual and organizational differences in police officer perspectives. *Policing: An International Journal, 40*(1), 11–25. https://doi.org/10.1108/PIJPSM-07-2016-0116

Crank, J. P. (2014). *Understanding police culture.* Routledge. https://doi.org/10.4324/9781315721255

Cunha, O., Carvalho, F., de Castro Rodrigues, A., Cruz, A. R., & Gonçalves, R. A. (2022). Attitudes of police recruits towards offenders: The impact of the police training on attitudinal change. *Journal of Police and Criminal Psychology, 37*(1), 162–172. https://doi.org/10.1007/s11896-021-09484-5

Data USA. (2023). *Gainesville, Florida about.* https://datausa.io/profile/geo/gainesville-fl/

Demirkol, I. C., & Nalla, M. K. (2020). Police culture: An empirical appraisal of the phenomenon. *Criminology & Criminal Justice, 20*(3), 319–338. https://doi.org/10.1177/1748895818823832

Federal Bureau of Investigation. (2019). *Full-time law enforcement employees by population group, percent male and female.* https://ucr.fbi.gov/crime-in-the-u.s/2019/crime-in-the-u.s.-2019/topic-pages/tables/table-74

Fisher, S. Z. (1993). Just the facts, ma'am: Lying and the omission of exculpatory evidence in police reports. *New England Law Review, 28*(1), 1–62. https://scholarship.law.bu.edu/faculty_scholarship/906

Gainesville Police Department. (2022, December). *Staffing records.* Retrieved from Gainesville Police Department.

Garner, R. (2005). Police attitudes: The impact of experience after training. *Applied Psychology in Criminal Justice, 1*(1), 56–70.

Ingram, J. R., Terrill, W., & Paoline, E. A., III. (2018). Police culture and officer behavior: Application of a multilevel framework. *Criminology, 56*(4), 780–811. https://doi.org/10.1111/1745-9125.12192

Kraska, P. B. (1996). Enjoying militarism: Political/personal dilemmas in studying US police paramilitary units. *Justice Quarterly, 13*(3), 405–429. https://doi.org/10.1080/07418829600093031

Leatherby, L., & Oppel, R. A. (2020). Which police departments are as diverse as their communities. *New York Times*, 23.

LeCount, R. J. (2017). More black than blue? Comparing the racial attitudes of police to citizens. *Sociological Forum, 32*(1), 1051–1072. https://doi.org/10.1111/socf.12367

Loftus, B. (2009). *Police culture in a changing world.* Oxford Academic. https://doi.org/10.1093/acprof:oso/9780199560905.001.0001

Martin, S. E. (1994). "Outsider within" the station house: The impact of race and gender on black women police. *Social Problems, 41*(3), 383–400. https://doi.org/10.2307/3096969

Myhill, A., & Bradford, B. (2013). Overcoming cop culture? Organizational justice and police officers' attitudes toward the public. *Policing: an International Journal of Police Strategies & Management, 36*(2), 338–356. https://doi.org/10.1108/13639511311329732

Myhill, A., & Johnson, K. (2016). Police use of discretion in response to domestic violence. *Criminology & Criminal Justice, 16*(1), 3–20. https://doi.org/10.1177/1748895815590202

Patterson, G. T. (2004). Evaluating the effects of child abuse training on the attitudes, knowledge, and skills of police recruits. *Research on Social Work Practice, 14*(4), 273–280. https://doi.org/10.1177/1049731503262390

Poteyeva, M., & Sun, I. Y. (2009). Gender differences in police officers' attitudes: Assessing current empirical evidence. *Journal of Criminal Justice, 37*(5), 512–522. https://doi.org/10.1016/j.jcrimjus.2009.07.011

Reiner, R. (2017). Is police culture cultural? *Policing: A Journal of Policy and Practice, 11*(3), 236–241. https://doi.org/10.1093/police/paw046

Ricciardelli, R. (2018). "Risk it out, risk it out": Occupational and organizational stresses in rural policing. *Police Quarterly, 21*(4), 415–439. https://doi.org/10.1177/1098611118772268

Rios, V. M. (2017). *Human targets: Schools, police, and the criminalization of Latino youth.* University of Chicago Press. https://doi.org/10.7208/chicago/9780226091044.001.0001

Sherman, L. W. (2020). Targeting American policing: Rogue cops or rogue cultures? *Cambridge Journal of Evidence Based Policing, 4*, 77–88. https://doi.org/10.1007/s41887-020-00046-z

Skogan, W. G. (2006). *Police and community in Chicago: A tale of three cities*. Oxford University Press. https://doi.org/10.1093/acprof:oso/9780195154580.001.0001

Skogan, W. G., & Hartnett, S. M. (1999). *Community policing, Chicago style*. Oxford University Press.

Stogner, J., Miller, B. L., & McLean, K. (2020). Police stress, mental health, and resiliency during the COVID-19 pandemic. *American Journal of Criminal Justice, 45*(4), 718–730. https://doi.org/10.1007/s12103-020-09548-y

Sun, I. Y., & Payne, B. K. (2004). Racial differences in resolving conflicts: A comparison between black and white police officers. *Crime & Delinquency, 50*(4), 516–541. https://doi.org/10.1177/0011128703259298

Westmarland, L. (2005). Police ethics and integrity: Breaking the blue code of silence. *Policing and Society, 15*(2), 145–165. https://doi.org/10.1080/10439460500071721

Wilson, J. M. (2012). Articulating the dynamic police staffing challenge: An examination of supply and demand. *Policing: An International Journal of Police Strategies & Management, 35*(2), 327–355. https://doi.org/10.1108/13639511211230084

Wolfe, S. E., & Piquero, A. R. (2011). Organizational justice and police misconduct. *Criminal Justice and Behavior, 38*(4), 332–353. https://doi.org/10.1177/0093854810397739

4

Policing Battery

Introduction

Police officers operate under a wide range of laws and policies that govern how they conduct investigations, make arrest decisions, and exercise discretion in report writing. One of the primary frameworks guiding officers' procedures in both domestic and non-domestic battery cases is Florida State Law. However, in addition to complying with state law, officers at GPD follow departmental policies that distinguish procedures between domestic and non-domestic battery investigations. These policies do not only align with state mandates but also offer more detailed procedural guidance tailored to the department's operational context. When investigating crimes, officers are required to adhere to GPD's General Investigation Procedures (Gainesville Police Department General Order 42.2, 2023c), which outline the steps for conducting preliminary investigations and provide detailed instructions on identifying and collecting relevant information. To address specific types of crimes, for example, domestic batteries, GPD supplements the general protocols with specialized directives. For domestic violence incidents, this supplement is called the General Investigation Procedures for Domestic and Dating

M. N. Eliasson, *Who Gets Believed?*, Palgrave's Critical Policing Studies,
https://doi.org/10.1007/978-3-032-22253-4_4

Violence (Gainesville Police Department General Order 40.6, 2023b) which offers additional guidance on managing the unique dynamics of domestic violence cases, such as victim support, documentation requirements, and arrest decision making.

Several studies have emphasized the importance of laws and policies in shaping officers' conduct and decision making, particularly in victimization cases where mandatory or pro-arrest laws have been implemented, such as in domestic violence cases (Belknap, 1995; Ryan et al., 2022). For example, Eitle (2005) found that mandatory arrest policies in domestic violence cases predicted arrest outcomes and modestly reduced the influence of race as a predictor. Similarly, Strom et al. (2014) found that such policies increased arrest rates for both male and female juveniles accused of assaulting a parent. Juveniles were more likely to be arrested in states with mandatory or pro-arrest policies than in those where officers had greater discretion.

In this chapter, I examine how these legal and institutional directives influence officers' conduct, focusing specifically on the procedures for investigating battery incidents, the decision-making processes surrounding arrest and documentation, and the interaction they have with victims. Drawing on Florida Statutes and GPD's internal policies, I outline the formal expectations placed on officers when responding to battery calls. Specifically, I discuss how officers navigate the complexities of report writing, evidence collection, and discretionary judgment in both domestic and non-domestic battery cases.

Call Classification: The Emergence of a Battery

When GPD receives a call of a suspected battery, the incident is initially grouped with assaults in the Computer Aided Dispatch (CAD) system and labeled as S29 Assault/Battery. If the incident is domestic in nature, it is classified as S29D Domestic Battery. Despite this initial grouping, officers distinguish clearly between assault and battery, emphasizing the legal and evidentiary differences between the two. Officer Brown explained:

> In assaults, there has to be a threat of physical violence by a person who has the capacity and means to inflict the violence. However, in a battery actual physical contact has to be made between the two parties.

This distinction emphasizes that physical touch is a necessary element for a battery charge. Officer Willson further elaborated, stating:

> Assaults are much harder to prove because of the lack of evidence, it's often a 'he said - she said', batteries are easier that way because there are usually marks. It is very rare that assaults go anywhere.

Officer Willson's insights highlighted how officers can perceive and navigate the evidentiary challenges of assault versus battery cases, with physical evidence playing a central role in determining case viability. Thus, while assault and battery may be grouped administratively in CAD systems, officers operationally differentiate between them based on legal definitions and other extra-legal factors.

In addition to calls explicitly being classified as battery by 911 dispatchers, incidents may initially be labeled under a variety of other categories, such as S22 Disturbance, S22A Armed Disturbance, S22D Domestic Disturbance, or S22F Physical Fight. This variability in classification reflects the complexity of interpreting limited information during emergency calls. Specifically, the formation of a battery case is often contingent on the circumstances surrounding the call and the information available at the time of dispatch.

My observations from the ride-alongs revealed multiple pathways through which a battery case can emerge. In some instances, dispatchers classify a call based on the caller's report, which may lack details about physical violence. Upon arrival, officers may uncover new information such as witness statements or visible injuries that prompt a reclassification of the incident from a disturbance to a battery. Conversely, a call initially labeled as a battery may be reclassified if parties at the scene retract their statements or if no physical contact is confirmed. In some cases, a battery may even occur while officers are present on scene, further complicating the classification. These different pathways highlight the dynamic nature of case formation and the pivotal role of both dispatcher input and officer discretion.

It is essential to emphasize the role that access to information plays before officers arrive on scene, as it influences how officers prepare for and approach the situation they are walking into. Meanwhile, information gathered on-site can reshape the legal framing of the incident the fluidity has implications for how battery cases are documented, investigated, and ultimately processed within the criminal justice system. For example, in cases where officers have very limited access to information prior to arrival, their understanding of the incident is often based solely on what has been relayed to 911. As a result, one of their primary objectives upon arrival is to gather information about what has occurred in order to determine whether a crime has taken place. If minimal information is relayed to 911 and officers are unable to obtain details from parties on scene or if there is little to no physical evidence, it can significantly influence the course of the investigation.

Investigation

Once officers are on scene, they are tasked with investigating whether a crime has occurred. Depending on the agency and the type of crime officers are investigating, there are different policies that inform the investigation procedures officers utilize. The distinction between various investigation policies is critical to understanding how officers are instructed to respond differently depending on the nature of the crime. For non-domestic battery cases, GPD officers follow the General Investigation Procedures (Gainesville Police Department General Order 42.2, 2023c), which provide broad guidance on evidence collection, victim and witness interviews, and report writing. In contrast, domestic battery cases require adherence to the General Investigation Procedures for Domestic and Dating Violence (Gainesville Police Department General Order 40.6, 2023b). While both sets of procedures share foundational elements, such as the importance of documenting physical evidence and obtaining statements, they differ in key areas. For example, the domestic violence procedures emphasize victim safety, mandatory arrest protocols, and referrals to support services, reflecting the heightened legal and social sensitivity surrounding these cases. According to GPD, both sets of procedures are designed to ensure a "thorough investigation," with a strong emphasis on generating and processing information related to the incident. However, the way these procedures are framed and prioritized differs depending on whether the battery is domestic or non-domestic in nature. Given the length and detail of both documents, I will not provide an exhaustive description of every instruction, instead, I will offer a brief overview of each set of procedures and a comparative discussion of their key similarities and differences.

Both the *General Investigative Procedures* and the *General Investigation Procedures for Domestic and Dating Violence* instruct GPD officers to assess the conditions of the event when arriving at the scene. The assessment includes observing the physical environment and the interactions between the victim and suspect. Officers are also need to identify and interview potential witnesses, secure the scene to prevent evidence tampering, and ensure that no further volatile or violent interactions occur between involved parties. Evidence collection is emphasized in both sets of procedures, with officers being instructed to photograph injuries, document physical damage, and arrange for the collection of potential weapons such as knives. In cases with multiple witnesses, both policies acknowledge that while interviewing all parties on scene is ideal, follow-up interviews may be necessary to complete the investigation.

The *General Investigation Procedures for Domestic and Dating Violence* reflect additional legal and procedural requirements informed by Florida State Laws on domestic and dating violence. These procedures enforce stricter guidelines for arrest and provide officers with definitions of qualifying relationships. Specifically, they outline what constitutes a family or household member, describe the criteria for identifying a dating relationship, and specify the duration and nature of the relationship required for it to be classified as domestic or dating violence. These distinctions are critical, as they determine whether the enhanced legal protections and mandatory arrest policies apply. Compared to the *General Investigation Procedures,* the *General Investigation Procedures for Domestic and Dating Violence* offer more detailed guidance on the actions officers should take at the scene. Officers are directed to assess the degree of trauma and fear experienced by victims and witnesses, determine whether children were present during the incident, separate the involved parties, ensure the safety of children, elderly individuals, or other third parties, de-escalate the situation, provide medical assistance if needed, and summon an interpreter when necessary. These directives go beyond the scope of the general procedures, which primarily focus on identifying and collecting information relevant to the investigation.

Additionally, the *General Investigation Procedures for Domestic and Dating Violence* also provide more detailed guidance on how and when officers should contact victim advocates. While the instructions state that officers should reach out to advocates "when applicable," they list six specific factors to consider in making this determination. These factors include the presence of children, the extent of injuries, whether an arrest has been made, the level of trauma observed, and the presence of a "neutral" third party at the scene. The procedures also offer practical resources for contacting victim advocates and instruct officers to notify the shift commander, who then can determine whether a detective should be dispatched to the scene. In contrast, the *General Investigative Procedures* do not include any guidance on contacting victim advocates. Thus, the domestic violence policies not only acknowledge the importance of advocacy but also attempt to standardize the decision-making process by listing relevant factors to consider for the determination. However, the use of the phrase "when applicable" introduces a level of discretion, as the policies do not specify clear thresholds or mandatory conditions under which officers must contact a victim advocate. The discretion allows officers to interpret the applicability of advocacy support based on their own judgment of the six factors listed in the procedures.

In line with the *General Investigation Procedures*, the *General Investigation Procedures for Domestic and Dating Violence* provide guidance for initial investigations. However, the domestic violence procedures offer significantly more detailed instructions, particularly regarding the documentation of past, present, and potential future violence or threats. Officers are instructed to record indicators such as prior abuse, substance use (alcohol and/or drugs), life stressors, and unusual behavior, elements not addressed in the general procedures. Additionally, officers are directed to make detailed notes on the demeanor of both victims and suspects, as well as any damage or out-of-place items in the surrounding environment.

In domestic battery cases, officers are also required to conduct more thorough assessments of injuries and the nature of the relationship between the involved parties. The procedures include specific instructions for collecting victim statements, emphasizing the importance of capturing emotional tone, behavioral cues, and contextual details. Furthermore, officers are instructed to administer the Lethality Assessment Program (LAP) and the Domestic/Dating Violence Lethality Screen for First Responders (DVL Screen). These screening tools help identify high-risk cases and, depending on the assessment score, guide officers in initiating additional support measures, such as direct phone contact with domestic violence program counselors.

In summary, despite sharing similarities, GPD's investigative procedures for domestic and non-domestic battery cases differ in scope and detail. For example, while both the *General Investigative Procedures* and the *General Investigation Procedures for Domestic and Dating Violence* instruct officers to secure the scene, collect evidence, and interview witnesses, the domestic violence protocols include more comprehensive guidance. These include assessing trauma, separating involved parties, ensuring the safety of vulnerable individuals, and prioritizing rapid response. Officers investigating domestic cases are also directed to document past and potential future threats, evaluate relationship dynamics, and use screening tools like the *LAP* and *DVL Screen* to identify high-risk situations. Furthermore, domestic violence procedures provide criteria for contacting victim advocates, though they leave room for officer discretion by using the phrase "when applicable."

The Reality of Investigating Batteries

When observing how officers followed organizational procedures, several important patterns emerged, particularly regarding the use of body-worn cameras (BWCs), which are not explicitly addressed in GPD's investigative policy guidelines. During field observations, I observed that all officers consistently wore their BWCs and the officers explained to me that they were required to activate them during interactions with individuals at incident scenes. Officers routinely turned on their cameras when entering a scene, with only rare instances of oversight or technical malfunction leading to them not being turned on. After each incident, officers were instructed to "tag" their footage by attaching the incident number ensuring that the video was properly uploaded to the evidence storage cloud. Officers with excessive untagged videos tended to be verbally reprimanded by sergeants or lieutenants. When I asked officers what the repercussions for repeated noncompliance would be, they stated that it could lead to formal disciplinary action or informal punishment such as being the one who was assigned to host the ride-along for the shift, which during my fieldwork often meant me. During my ride-alongs, several officers expressed that BWCs enhanced their sense of safety and served as a valuable tool for report writing, with several officers using the footage to review details from the scene before completing their police reports. Although BWCs are not mentioned in any of the policy guidelines for investigations, it became evident throughout the ride-alongs that they play an important role in how officers manage investigations. The cameras offered an opportunity to capture specific case details that could help officers with their report writing and they provide a formal process to document interactions with some victims, even when those interactions do not result in a written police report.

Another observation I made regarding the application of GPD's domestic and non-domestic battery policies in day-to-day practice relates to the role of information. As mentioned earlier in this chapter, officers relied heavily on the details provided by dispatchers, which were based on what was communicated during the initial 911 call. As a result, the amount and quality of information officers received before arriving at a scene could vary significantly. In some cases, officers were informed that they were responding to a domestic battery, while in others, they were only told that a physical altercation had occurred, or, in some instances, received no clear indication of violence at all. In multiple instances did I witness how variations in access to information influenced how officers prepared for and approached the scene.

Both the *General Investigative Procedures* and the *General Investigation Procedures for Domestic and Dating Violence* instruct officers on how to gather information upon arrival, particularly to determine whether a battery has occurred. However, this initial fact-finding is also critical for identifying whether the incident qualifies as a domestic battery, which in turn dictates which set of investigative and arrest procedures officers had to follow. Hence the officers did not only investigate the facts of the incident but also assessed the nature of the relationship between the involved parties to determine the appropriate procedural path. Hence, based on my field observations and the review of GPD's investigative policies, one of the most critical factors officers must determine at the outset of an investigation is the relationship between the involved parties. In some cases, this information was available prior to arrival because it hade been apart of the information given by the 911 caller. However, in many cases, officers arrived at the scene with limited or no knowledge of the nature of the relationship between parties, which meant that one of the central things officers officers were tasked with, in addition to investigate whether a crime occurred, was to obtain information about relationship status between the victim and suspect so they could follow the appropriate investigatory procedures.

To better understand how officers interpreted and applied investigative procedures, I asked several officers about their approach to conducting investigations and making decisions in the field. Officer Willson emphasized the importance of state statutes and laws as the primary guiding framework when responding to a crime scene. He explained that while departmental policies provide structure, it was ultimately the legal definitions and requirements outlined in Florida Law that shaped his decision-making process. He stated:

> So, it reverts back to state statute and the law. So, I have to determine if there's probable cause to make an arrest. If I don't have enough probable cause, I won't make an arrest. I will document why I didn't make the arrest and move on from there. But if I have enough probable cause, I have to determine that situation whether or not somebody goes to jail if it's domestic, I don't have a lot of choices. State law says if I have probable cause somebody goes to jail. Nine times out of 10, I can ask, "How do you want

> this resolved?" And that generally works. They will. They'll tell me what they want to see happen. And if it's within my legal capability, then we'll make that happen.

Officer Willson described one of his critical tasks at the scene as determining whether there was probable cause for a crime, a decision guided primarily by Florida State Statutes. Establishing probable cause was central to deciding whether a suspect should be arrested, and many of the steps taken during a preliminary investigation were aimed at making that determination. He noted that while officers generally have discretion in how they assess and respond to incidents, this discretion is significantly limited in certain types of crimes, particularly domestic violence cases. In these situations, officers are bound by stricter legal and departmental mandates, which reduce their flexibility in deciding whether to arrest or how to resolve the situation. During my time in the field, several other officers echoed this sentiment, emphasizing that domestic violence investigations impose more constraints on their discretionary power compared to non-domestic cases.

In addition to discussing the impact Florida State Statutes have on the actions officers take, Officer Williams emphasized the inputs of other officers or senior colleagues when he was unsure of how to manage investigations or parties at an incident:

> The easiest and most efficient way…is to either ask another officer who's on the scene, if available, that's been doing this for a long time and get their opinion on it. Or the even better way to do that is if you're unsure what decision needs to be made at the time…is to either contact your supervisor by phone, or on the radio, just run by him everything that you see, everything that's in front of you, everything you have, and talk to him and say here's what I got, here's what I'm thinking. And he'll kind of guide you in the right direction from there. So yeah, we try not to ever make insecure decisions on our own without reaching out for help, which is the good part about working at this agency. Somebody is always willing to help you and guide you in the right direction for making a decision.

Officer Williams, who had only been "on the job" for a few months, described how he regularly sought guidance from colleagues and supervisors when uncertain about how to proceed at a scene. This practice was not unique to him. Nearly all the officers I rode with engaged in some form of consultation, whether to clarify investigative steps or to keep others informed about the status of the incident and investigation strategy. On multiple occasions, especially in batteries, I observed officers discussing potential courses of action with one another, sometimes explicitly asking how others would handle a situation. In cases involving violent crimes, sergeants frequently arrived on scene to oversee the investigation. When sergeants were present, the primary officer almost always made a point to discuss their investigative approach with the sergeants. This finding is something that supports previous literature that emphasizes the significant role hierarchy and peer relationships play for officers when investigating crime (Glomseth et al., 2007). The findings suggest that while GPD's formal policies provide a foundational framework for investigations, officers also rely heavily on Florida Statutes, peer input, and supervisory guidance to navigate complex and evolving situations.

Arrest and Report

Officers are provided with distinct legal and procedural instructions for making arrest decisions in domestic and non-domestic battery cases. Under Florida Law, officers may arrest individuals without a warrant for felony offenses, however, in cases involving misdemeanor offenses, a warrant is generally required unless the incident is classified as domestic in nature. In domestic battery cases, an exception is made that permits warrantless arrests under specific conditions. According to Florida Statute 901.15(7), officers are authorized to make a warrantless arrest for a misdemeanor domestic battery if they have probable cause to believe that the person committed the offense.

Officers are specifically instructed to make an arrest in domestic battery cases if:

> There is probable cause to believe that the person has committed an act of domestic violence, as defined in s. 741.28, or dating violence, as provided in s. 784.046. The decision to arrest shall not require the consent of the victim or consideration of the relationship of the parties. It is the public policy of this state to strongly discourage arrest and charges of both parties for domestic violence or dating violence on each other and to encourage the training of law enforcement and prosecutors in these areas. A law enforcement officer who acts in good faith and exercises due care in making an arrest under this subsection, under s. 741.31(4) or s. 784.047, or pursuant to a foreign order of protection accorded full faith and credit pursuant to s. 741.315, is immune from civil liability that otherwise might result by reason of his or her action. (Fla. Stat. § 901.15(7), 2025)

Hence, in domestic batteries, officers are instructed to arrest the offender if they establish probable cause for a crime, regardless of whether the offense is classified as a felony or a misdemeanor. In contrast, for non-domestic battery cases, although officers can arrest without a warrant, they have a higher level of discretion in the arrest decisions. For domestic cases officers have to establish who the primary aggressor is and find probable cause for the arrest, whereas in non-domestic cases officers do not have to establish who the primary aggressor is and can rely more heavily on department policy guidelines on preferred arrest decisions.

Additionally, Florida Statute §741.29 provides additional directives specific to domestic violence incidents. It mandates that officers assist victims in obtaining medical treatment when necessary and inform them about local domestic violence centers that offer support services. The statute also outlines specific procedures for arrest decisions and report writing in domestic cases. Officers are required to:

> When a law enforcement officer investigates an allegation that an incident of domestic violence has occurred, the officer shall handle the incident pursuant to the arrest policy provided in s. 901.15(7), and as developed in accordance with subsections (3), (4), and (5). Whether or not an arrest is made, the officer shall make a written police report that is complete and

> clearly indicates the alleged offense was an incident of domestic violence. Such report shall be given to the officer's supervisor and filed with the law enforcement agency in a manner that will permit data on domestic violence cases to be compiled. (Fla. Stat. § 741.29, 2025)

Furthermore, the following instructions are given in what officers should include in the police reports:

> (a) A description of physical injuries observed, if any. (b) If a law enforcement officer decides not to make an arrest or decides to arrest two or more parties, the officer shall include in the report the grounds for not arresting anyone or for arresting two or more parties. (c) A statement which indicates that a copy of the legal rights and remedies notice was given to the victim. (Fla. Stat. § 741.29, 2023)

Officers are legally required to manage domestic and non-domestic battery cases differently, with particularly notable distinctions in arrest protocols. Altogether these differences are reflected in the guidelines for navigating arrest decisions giving officers less discretion in non domestic batteries but can also impact officers procedures dealing with injuries. However, Florida Statue § 741.29 emphasizes another important thing, which is potential differences in report writing.

Report Discretion: "If there is no victim, there is no crime"

Police officers occupy positions of authority, and this authority gives credibility to the information they document in their reports (Dorfman, 1999). Existing literature on police reporting has primarily focused on discrepancies between victim accounts and police documentation (Averdijk & Elffers, 2012), patterns in how domestic victimization is reported (Acosta et al., 2013; Cazenave & Zahn, 1992; Tjaden & Thoennes, 2000), and the overall accuracy of reports (Beehr et al., 2004; Kassin et al., 2017). While these studies offer valuable insights, few have examined how officers learn to write reports and how reporting practices are shaped during the initial stages of case processing. These reports are not only internal records but also serve as foundational documents for a wide range of criminal justice professionals throughout the legal process (Miller & Pomerenke, 1989). Consequently, the content of police reports can significantly influence decisions made at various stages of case processing and may ultimately affect case outcomes.

Officers are trained to follow Florida Statues that mandates certain elements in their reports, which for example can be seen in § 741.29, and departmental guidelines, such as those outlined in GPD's General Investigations Procedures and General Orders, to ensure consistency and completeness in their documentation. However, I was interested in exploring whether officers also learn reporting practices through other avenues, such as during their time at the police academy or through GPD's mini academy. To investigate this further, I asked one of the newer officers, Officer Williams, how he learned to write reports:

> Before we start on the road, we have our mini-academy, which is about three months long. I had several classes on the structure of police reports, what is crucial to be in those police reports and also how to gather what is needed to be in those police reports. And then also, on-the-road training, you get shown little tips and tricks on how to write police reports easier. And you know, what you need to gather when you're on the scene, you get more of that once you start on the road in training.

His statement suggested that report writing is not solely guided by legal statues or departmental guidelines, but also by the informal norms and practical advice shared by experienced colleagues. The influence of both training and peer mentorship on officers' reporting habits has been emphasized by previous research, specifically highlighting how learning continues beyond formal education and is shaped by organizational culture and interpersonal dynamics (Yu & Monas, 2020).

According to GPD policies on police reports and report writing, officers should, but are not to be limited to, write reports on: "All citizens' request for services, incidents resulting in an employee being dispatched or assigned, to include follow-ups and non-criminal cases initiated by law enforcement officers, incidents involving arrest, and citations or ordinance violation citations" (Gainesville Police Department General Order 26.1, 2023a). As I started doing my ride-alongs, I discovered that police reports were not written for every incident officers go to. While officers per GPD policy always have to write a report if a citizen requests one or if they arrest someone, officers can also choose not to write a report in certain cases where they have more discretion, such as non-domestic batteries. In non-domestic battery incidents, officers noted that staffing levels, workload, and the victim's willingness to participate in the investigation influenced their decision to document the event. When asked what influences their decisions to write a police report, particularly in situations where they are not legally or organizationally required to do so, officers described several victim-related factors. In follow-up conversations, I asked more about these factors and discovered some patterns.

First, according to the officers, the absence of a victim or uncertainty about who the victim was could significantly impact the decision. There were not always guarantees that the alleged victims would be on scene when officers arrived, and if officers did not have the victim's contact information, and the 911 caller was a witness who did not know the victim or failed to respond to follow-up calls, officers sometimes perceived the incident as "victimless." For example, one night during one of my first few ride-alongs I observed Officer Miller respond to a possible battery call in Midtown. A restaurant employee had called 911 to report that a woman entered the establishment and said that a random man had grabbed and threatened her. When Officer Miller arrived, he spoke with the caller, who explained that the woman had left and that he did not know her nor witnessed the incident. After speaking to the 911 caller, Officer Miller searched the local area but was unable to locate the victim. When I asked him if he would write a report, he responded, "No, I have no victim here, so therefore I have no crime." This was a statement that several officers echoed "If there is no victim, there is no crime" which illustrates how the absence of a victim at the scene can have a significant impact on whether or not a police report is written, especially in non-domestic cases.

A second notion officers mentioned was whether victims "wanted to be victims" which appeared especially prevalent in non-domestic cases. During one of my ride-alongs, Officer Taylor was dispatched to a possible battery in Midtown. Upon arrival at the scene, located behind several bars frequented by undergraduate students, he observed a White male in his late 20s (suspect) being escorted to a police car and another White male in his early 20s (victim) standing with a few other officers. Officer Taylor approached the victim and asked what had occurred. The victim explained that he worked as a bouncer at one of the bars and that the suspect had approached him "trying to start a fight." The victim stated that he attempted to de-escalate the situation because he was working and did not want to engage in a physical altercation. He also added that he did not see himself as a victim and did not want to make a report because he did not want to cause issues for the suspect. After a few minutes, Officer Taylor and I returned to his patrol car. When I asked what would happen with the case, he explained that he had more discretion in non-domestic battery incidents and that many individuals who are victimized do not "want to be victims." He stated: "What we often do is ask if they want to press charges. If neither of them wants to do that, we ask them to just go their separate ways. It is very rare that people want to be victims." Thus, the notion of "not wanting to be a victim" appeared to reflect victims' unwillingness to participate in the legal process or file charges, which officers interpret as a reason not to write a police report. I asked the same officer whether he relied solely on victims to determine what actions should be taken. He responded, "No, for DV cases it is obviously different because of the laws, and if there are non-domestic cases with extensive injuries or arrests then we write a report." This response reinforced findings from previous scholarship that emphasize the importance of victim cooperation and victims' preferences for outcomes in shaping police decision making in non-sexual violent victimizations (Balenovich et al., 2008; Serrano-Montilla et al., 2023).

Despite GPD policies directing officers to write reports whenever they take any action on scene or when a citizen requests one, I observed that officers frequently did not document incidents. In some cases, officers made no contact with victims, suspects, or witnesses, which, according to policy, could justify not writing a report, as no citizen had made a request. However, I also noted numerous interactions between officers and victims, suspects, and witnesses that were not documented in a police report, even though they were recorded on body-worn cameras. This often occurred when officers responded to a violent crime that was non-domestic in nature and the victim declined to participate or, in the officers' words, did not "want to be a victim." There were also a handful of situations where victims asked for a report but none was written; however, this was not a common occurance throughout my time in the field. Based on these observations, it appears that in cases where Florida Statues grants officers greater discretionary power, GPD's guidelines for report writing may not always be followed. One of the possible implications of this is that fewer reports might be written in non-domestic cases, where officers have more discretion, compared to domestic cases, where officers' level of discretion is more constrained.

Thus, there were examples of when officers did not follow the guidelines and policies that they are governed by in both non-domestic and domestic cases, which was specifically visible in report writing. According to Statute 741.29:

> Whether or not an arrest is made, the officer shall make a written police report that is complete and clearly indicates the alleged offense was an incident of domestic violence. Such report shall be given to the officer's supervisor and filed with the law enforcement agency in a manner that will permit data on domestic violence cases to be compiled. (Fla. Stat. § 741.29, 2023)

If officers consistently followed Florida Statutes and departmental provisions, almost all domestic cases in this book would result in a police report. However, in this book, 25% of domestic cases did not have a report. This not only reflects gaps in policy adherence but also highlights the number of victimizations that go unrecorded in official statistics. This issue was even more pronounced in non-domestic battery cases, where 57% of incidents did not result in a report. While the guidelines for non-domestic batteries are less stringent than those for domestic cases, the implication of this discretionary power is that fewer reports are written which means that the incidents may be excluded from official data. It is essential to emphasize that in some cases, officers made an assessment based on their investigation, that a crime did not occur or that they did not have enough evidence to establish probable cause. This should not be viewed as an example of officers failing to follow guidelines or neglecting their duties, but rather the opposite.

However, officers' reporting discretion presented an interesting point of discussion for the formal recording of crime, particularly in crime types where officers exercised a higher level of discretion. Traditional statistical outlets and scholarly research often rely on cases that have been formally documented through police reports. As a result, a substantial number of battery cases, particularly non-domestic ones, may be omitted from datasets such as the UCR and the National Incident-Based Reporting System (NIBRS). Officers' decisions not to write reports can therefore directly influence which cases are represented in these datasets. Although this study includes a limited number of cases, the inclusion of cases that did not lead to a report offers a rare insight into cases that are not included in official data outlets due to not resulting in a police report or any other effort to document the case.

Officer Conduct Policy

When investigating and interacting with victims and other parties on a potential crime scene, police officers are subject to normative expectations and organizational rules that define acceptable and unacceptable conduct. One of GPD's primary documents for conduct is titled *Rules of Conduct*, which is part of the General Order and outlines departmental policies and regulations for personnel (Gainesville Police Department General Order 26.1, 2023a). In addition to the *Rules of Conduct*, personnel are also governed by the collective bargaining agreement, the City of Gainesville Personnel Policies and Procedures, and the code of ethics outlined in Administrative Procedures Number G-2.

The *Rules of Conduct* include a broad range of policies that articulate how GPD expects its officers to behave. These policies include general principles and specific directives addressing officers' interactions with the public, relationships with fellow personnel, and individual conduct on and off duty. Officers are expected to fulfill general policing responsibilities such as upholding the law, preventing crime, maintaining public peace, and demonstrating impartiality. Furthermore, they are required to be courteous, orderly, attentive, and patient in their interactions with the public. Beyond these general expectations, the *Rules of Conduct* also provide more detailed guidance on appropriate behavior. These include standards for public engagement as well as conduct in non-public settings. For instance, officers are explicitly instructed to avoid prejudice based on personal characteristics or group identity and to refrain from using language that is coarse, violent, profane, or insolent.

The conduct policies provided to officers by GPD are significant not only because they outline expected and prohibited behaviors, but also because they reflect the department's organizational stance on the responsibilities officers hold toward one another and the broader community. For instance, GPD explicitly discourages differential treatment and prejudice toward individuals encountered in the line of duty, indicating an institutional effort to adopt practices aligned with procedural justice. Hence, GPD's conduct policies can be seen as part of a broader initiative to promote department-wide standards for policing and justice, as well as to encourage the adoption of professional norms of behavior.

Officer and Victim Encounter

The *Rules of Conduct in the General Order*, the *General Investigation Procedures*, and the *General Investigation Procedures: Domestic and Dating Violence* did not provide guidance on how officers should offer supportive responses to victims at the scene. For example, the policies do not address the use of appropriate body language or specify the terminology and tone officers should employ when officers are interacting with involved parties. However, within the *General Investigation Procedures*, there is a section outlining the steps officers must follow when collecting statements from victims and witnesses. Officers were, for example, required to document what victims and witnesses observed or experienced, including the presence and use of weapons and the injuries sustained. Additionally, officers had to report the specific language used by victims and witnesses to describe the incident and assess any potential biases among those providing statements. Hence, the instructions provided guidance on the types of information officers are expected to document or inquire about when taking statements from victims and witnesses at the scene and during subsequent stages of the investigation. While these procedures specify what information should be obtained, they do not offer explicit guidance on how officers should interact with victims or witnesses. Instead, the focus remained on the actions officers take to in order generate information relevant to the preliminary or general investigation. When I reviewed GPD's policies it revealed a clear emphasis on officer conduct as it pertains to determining whether a crime has occurred and conducting the investigation thereafter. However, the guidelines did not directly address the interpersonal dynamics of officer-victim interactions, suggesting that officers instead rely on other forms of training, informal norms, or external guidelines to inform their approach to victim interactions.

The instructions for taking statements from victims and witnesses apply broadly across all types of crimes encountered by GPD officers, including non-domestic crimes such as battery. However, additional guidelines exist for cases involving domestic violence. Specifically, GPD policy states: "Domestic Violence Victims/Witnesses: State statute requires, whenever possible, that investigating officers obtain a written statement from the victims and witnesses of alleged domestic violence incidents" (Gainesville Police Department General Order 42.2, 2023c). In these cases, GPD provided more detailed instructions regarding the collection of statements. Florida Statutes mandate that, when feasible, officers should obtain written statements from victims and witnesses in domestic violence investigations. However, beyond these instructions, there is no further in-depth guidance on victim and witness interaction.

Normative Assessments of Legitimacy

Like professionals in other fields, police officers exhibit varying attitudes toward their work and develop distinct habits during their shifts. One such habit is related to how officers manage battery calls, particularly their response behavior. Previous empirical research has highlighted that officers may delay responses to certain calls or actively avoid them as they are dispatched (Sherman et al., 1992). In my observations, a few patterns emerged, specifically, officers made normative assessments of calls prior to arriving at the scene and, second, there was a tendency among some officers to avoid specific calls, which are findings that align with earlier studies (Bowker, 1982; Hirschel et al., 1992; Sherman et al., 1992). These observations are important because they suggest that officers may, in certain battery cases, deviate from the conduct and investigative procedures outlined by GPD policy, highlighting a potential gap between formal guidelines and actual practice.

When a battery call was dispatched, I observed officers often making an initial normative assessment of the call. Within GPD, officers commonly categorized calls as either "legit" or "bullshit." These assessments typically occurred when a battery call first appeared on the CAD system. Officers would review the information provided in the CAD and then determine whether the call was considered legitimate. When I asked officers about the factors influenced their assessment, they identified several aspects. First, if the CAD notes indicated that the caller did not wish to have contact with the police upon arrival, officers interpreted this as a potential sign that the call was "bullshit." Second, if neither the victim nor the suspect was present at the scene, the call was similarly viewed with skepticism. Third, officers expressed doubt about callers reporting incidents that occurred the previous day or several days earlier. Officer White explained: "Well, why didn't they report it yesterday, like why did they not report it right away?" Officers also noted that prior familiarity with the caller influenced their assessment. If the caller's name was recognized from previous incidents that were deemed false or unfounded, the current call was more likely to be dismissed as "bullshit." In some cases, officers explicitly referenced a history of inaccurate or misleading reports from the same individual as justification for their negative perception of the legitimacy of the call.

The assessments officers made of incoming calls appeared to influence their responsiveness, particularly in cases they labeled as "bullshit" calls. For many of these calls, I observed that officers would not voluntarily respond to the call unless they were formally dispatched, even if the call fell within their assigned patrol zone. Although several officers engaged in this normative assessment, not all used the term "bullshit." Some expressed skepticism or negative attitudes in more subtle ways. For instance, Officer Jackson remarked that the call "will not turn into something," referring to situations where officers anticipated that no parties would be present upon arrival, and therefore no action would be required.

While I documented officers' assessments of calls as they came in, the data did not allow for a comprehensive exploration of how these assessments influenced their behavior toward the involved parties. In most cases, officers maintained a neutral tone during interactions. However, due to the scope of the data and the volume of calls officers receive daily, the relationship between call assessment and officer behavior was something that I could not fully examine. Nonetheless, these findings align with previous empirical research indicating that officers may evaluate the legitimacy of calls and respond differently based on those judgments (Bowker, 1982; Hirschel et al., 1992).

The normative assessments made by officers are particularly interesting given that GPD policies explicitly instruct personnel not to exhibit prejudice toward individuals they encounter. However, the practice of evaluating a call's legitimacy based solely on CAD notes prior to arriving at the scene suggests that officers may hold negative attitudes toward certain types of incidents, particularly non-domestic battery calls. This judgment can influence officers' conduct and mindset before they engage with parties at the scene. For instance, when a call is deemed "bullshit" or "not legit," officers could potentially be less invested in following investigative procedures than in cases they perceive as legitimate. This predetermined belief about a call's validity could introduce potential bias toward the involved parties, particularly victims and their credibility.

Avoiding Battery Calls

On several occasions, I observed officers actively avoiding battery calls. While the reasons varied, there was often one common denominator for these cases, which was that the calls originated from Grace Market Place. Grace Market Place is a location on the outskirts of town known for housing a significant portion of the homeless population in Gainesville. This finding echoes previous research that emphasizes the influence of notions such as socioeconomic composition of neighborhoods on officers' actions. These actions could, for example, be decisions to downgrade call classifications (Lum, 2011) or, like in the context of this book, be the avoidance of taking calls. The finding also underscores the importance of call location as a factor that shaped officers' perceptions and case management. Although officers that I observed generally preferred to remain within their assigned zones, many expressed a willingness to cover other areas, except for "Golf" zone, which included Grace Market Place. Battery calls from Grace Market Place were frequently dismissed or deprioritized. Officers commonly referred to the area as "a shit hole," expressing frustration over being flagged down for additional incidents unrelated to the original call, which they viewed as burdensome. This sentiment seemed to contribute to a broader reluctance to engage with calls from the area. Officers often attempted to respond to other calls instead or waited to be formally dispatched, rather than volunteering to go. As one male officer stated, he was "hoping that someone else would be dispatched."

Another strategy officers employed to avoid responding to certain battery calls was referred to as "sitting on a call." This practice involved remaining logged into a previous call in the computer system, even after the incident had concluded. Officers justified this behavior in different ways. Some remained on a call to complete follow-up tasks on previous calls, such as writing reports or transporting individuals to jail, actions that were generally accepted among officers as valid reasons to stay logged in. However, others used this strategy to avoid taking on new calls. One evening, I rode with Officer Nelson who was assigned to a zone he described as "not a busy zone." After responding to a battery call that resulted in the suspect being taken for involuntary commitment to a mental health facility, Officer Nelson parked in a business center parking lot to finish the report he had started earlier at the hospital. While working on the report, several new calls appeared in the CAD system, including another battery call. Officer Nelson said: "Even though I am done with my report I am not going to go to this call, it is not in my zone…but no one else is available and I do not want to take another report tonight." This was not an isolated incident. I observed multiple occasions where officers remained logged into calls longer than they seemingly, according to my assessment, were actively engaged in the case or report writing.

These findings align with previous scholarship indicating that officers' response times can vary depending on the shift and the timing of the call (James et al., 2018).

During another ride-along with Officer Moore, I raised the topic of "sitting on calls" while we were on scene with another officer who was serving as an FTO. When they asked me what I had learned so far during my time at GPD, I mentioned that I had observed officers "sitting on calls." Both officers smiled and laughed while verbally acknowledging that this practice was common. Officer Walker, the FTO, stated that they were actively trying to discourage new officers from engaging in this behavior, emphasizing that it did not only impact community members but also placed additional strain on fellow officers. The officers' reactions, combined with my frequent observations of officers "sitting on calls," indicate that this was a informal practice recognized by several officers at GPD.

The avoidance of certain calls could carry significant implications for battery cases. Delayed responses could endanger the involved parties and increase the likelihood that individuals would leave the scene before officers arrive. Additionally, scholars have found a strong causal relationship between delayed response time and the likelihood of an incident causing injury in violent incidents, especially among female victims. Hence delayed response times could have a significant impact on domestic battery victims, whom often are female (DeAngelo et al., 2023). Overall delayed response times does not only hinder the ability to gather timely evidence and statements but also compromise the safety of those involved. According to GPD's investigative guidelines, officers are instructed to "promptly" assist citizens in need and when officers intentionally delay or avoid responding, they fail to uphold this directive.

Conclusion

In this chapter, I have discussed several dimensions of the organizational context that shape officers' conduct, practices, and attitudes in battery cases. Rather than offering an exhaustive list of all possible organizational, policy, and legal factors influencing, the goal of this chapter has been to illustrate how officers' conduct, practices, and attitudes are embedded within a broader organizational framework. This context informs their perceptions of credibility and guides the actions they take in battery investigations. When examining the organizational factors that influence officer behavior, this study highlights the presence of both formal and informal guidelines provided by GPD and state legislation, particularly in relation to domestic and non-domestic battery cases. Officers are instructed through GPD's "General Investigation Procedures," which apply broadly to all crimes, including non-domestic batteries. In contrast, investigations involving domestic and dating violence are governed by more specific protocols outlined in the "General Investigation Procedures for Domestic and Dating Violence." These differentiated guidelines reflect the distinct legislative frameworks: Florida Statute §784.03 addresses non-domestic battery, and Florida Statute §784.041 pertains to domestic battery. The most notable difference in these guidelines is the emphasis on a pro-arrest policy in domestic violence cases, which limits officer discretion and mandates more structured investigative procedures. In non-domestic battery cases, officers retain greater discretion, particularly in decisions related to arrest and report writing. This discretion was evident in officers' reporting habits, where many chose not to file a report unless a citizen explicitly requested one or an arrest was made. Officers often justified this by stating that cases lacking a "willing victim" were difficult to investigate and unlikely to result in charges. These findings support previous scholarship, such as Fisher (1993), which emphasizes that despite the presence of formal organizational rules, officers exercise discretion in determining when and how to document incidents. This discretionary power can significantly influence how battery cases are constructed and whether they are formally recorded.

Another key finding is that the geographical zones officers were assigned influenced their exposure to different types of crime. Some zones experienced higher rates of battery, which could result in varying levels of familiarity with domestic and non-domestic battery cases among officers. The potential implication of this is that some officers may have limited knowledge and experience of the specific procedures that are in effect for domestic and non-domestic batteries, compared to other crimes. Additionally, GPD officers are governed by a broad set of conduct policies that emphasize impartiality and the prompt assistance to victims. However, findings from this study suggest that these policies were not always upheld. Officers' normative assessments of call legitimacy, made prior to arriving on scene, and their avoidance of battery calls involving the homeless population indicate instances where officers did appear biased, which can shape officers' responsiveness and engagement with certain communities.

References

Acosta, D. F., Gomes, V. L. D. O., & Barlem, E. L. D. (2013). Profile of police reports related to violence against women. *Acta Paulista de Enfermagem, 26*(6), 547–553. https://doi.org/10.1590/S0103-21002013000600007

Averdijk, M., & Elffers, H. (2012). The discrepancy between survey-based victim accounts and police reports revisited. *International Review of Victimology, 18*(2), 91–107. https://doi.org/10.1177/0269758011432955

Balenovich, J., Grossi, E., & Hughes, T. (2008). Toward a balanced approach: Defining police roles in responding to domestic violence. *American Journal of Criminal Justice, 33*, 19–31. https://doi.org/10.1007/s12103-007-9028-5

Beehr, T. A., Ivanitskaya, L., Glaser, K., Erofeev, D., & Canali, K. (2004). Working in a violent environment: The accuracy of police officers' reports about shooting incidents. *Journal of Occupational and Organizational Psychology, 77*(2), 217–235. https://doi.org/10.1348/096317904774202153

Belknap, J. (1995). Law enforcement officers' attitudes about the appropriate responses to woman battering. *International Review of Victimology, 4*(1), 47–62. https://doi.org/10.1177/026975809500400104

Bowker, L. H. (1982). Police services to battered women: Bad or not so bad? *Criminal Justice and Behavior, 9*(4), 476–494. https://doi.org/10.1177/0093854882009004005

Cazenave, N. A., & Zahn, M. A. (1992). Women, murder, and male domination: Police reports of domestic violence in Chicago and Philadelphia. In E. C. Viano (Ed.), *Intimate violence: Interdisciplinary perspectives* (pp. 83–97). Hemisphere Publishing Corporation.

DeAngelo, G., Toger, M., & Weisburd, S. (2023). Police response time and injury outcomes. *The Economic Journal, 133*(654), 2147–2177. https://doi.org/10.1093/ej/uead035

Dorfman, D. N. (1999). Proving the lie: Litigating police credibility. *American Journal of Criminal Law, 26*(3), 455–504. http://digitalcommons.pace.edu/lawfaculty/533/

Eitle, D. (2005). The influence of mandatory arrest policies, police organizational characteristics, and situational variables on the probability of arrest in domestic violence cases. *Crime & Delinquency, 51*(4), 573–597. https://doi.org/10.1177/0011128705277784

Fisher, S. Z. (1993). Just the facts, ma'am: Lying and the omission of exculpatory evidence in police reports. *New England Law Review, 28*(1), 1–62. https://scholarship.law.bu.edu/faculty_scholarship/906

Florida Senate. (2023). Fla. Stat. Chapter 741.29. Florida Senate. https://www.flsenate.gov/laws/statutes/2023/741.29

Florida Senate. (2025). Fla. Stat. Chapter 901.15. Florida Senate. https://www.leg.state.fl.us/Statutes/index.cfm?App_mode=Display_Statute&URL=0900-0999/0901/Sections/0901.15.html

Gainesville Police Department. (2023a). General Order 26.1 Rules Of Conduct. https://public.powerdms.com/GPD/tree/documents/265

Gainesville Police Department. (2023b). General Order 40.6 General Investigation Procedures for Domestic and Dating Violence. https://public.powerdms.com/GPD/tree/documents/313

Gainesville Police Department. (2023c). General Order 42.2 General Investigation Procedures. https://public.powerdms.com/GPD/tree/documents/325

Glomseth, R., Gottschalk, P., & Solli-Saether, H. (2007). Occupational culture as determinant of knowledge sharing and performance in police investigations. *International Journal of the Sociology of Law, 35*(2), 96–107. https://doi.org/10.1016/j.ijsl.2007.03.003

Hirschel, J. D., Hutchison, I. W., Dean, C. W., & Mills, A. M. (1992). Review essay on the law enforcement response to spouse abuse: Past, present, and future. *Justice Quarterly, 9*(2), 247–283. https://doi.org/10.1080/07418829200091361

James, L., James, S., & Vila, B. (2018). The impact of work shift and fatigue on police officer response in simulated interactions with citizens. *Journal of Experimental Criminology, 14*, 111–120. https://doi.org/10.1007/s11292-017-9294-2

Kassin, S. M., Kukucka, J., Lawson, V. Z., & DeCarlo, J. (2017). Police reports of mock suspect interrogations: A test of accuracy and perception. *Law and Human Behavior, 41*(3), 230–243. https://doi.org/10.1037/lhb0000225

Lum, C. (2011). The influence of places on police decision pathways: From call for service to arrest. *Justice Quarterly, 28*(4), 631–665. https://doi.org/10.1080/07418825.2010.526130

Miller, M., & Pomerenke, P. (1989). Police reports must be reader based. *Law and Order, 37*(9), 66–69. https://www.ojp.gov/pdffiles1/Digitization/120641NCJRS.pdf

Ryan, C., Silvio, D., Borden, T., & Ross, N. M. (2022). A review of pro-arrest, pro-charge, and pro-prosecution policies as a response to domestic violence. *Journal of Social Work, 22*(1), 211–238. https://doi.org/10.1177/1468017320979956

Serrano-Montilla, C., Lozano, L. M., Alonso-Ferres, M., Valor-Segura, I., & Padilla, J. L. (2023). Understanding the components and determinants of police attitudes toward intervention in intimate partner violence against women: A systematic review. *Trauma, Violence, & Abuse, 24*(1), 245–260. https://doi.org/10.1177/15248380211029398

Sherman, L. W., Schmidt, J. D., & Rogan, D. P. (1992). *Policing domestic violence*. The Free Press.

Strom, K. J., Warner, T. D., Tichavsky, L., & Zahn, M. A. (2014). Policing juveniles: Domestic violence arrest policies, gender, and police response to child–parent violence. *Crime & Delinquency, 60*(3), 427–450. https://doi.org/10.1177/0011128710376293

Tjaden, P., & Thoennes, N. (2000). The role of stalking in domestic violence crime reports generated by the Colorado Springs Police Department. *Violence and Victims, 15*(4), 427–441. https://doi.org/10.1891/0886-6708.15.4.427

Xie, M., Pogarsky, G., Lynch, J. P., & McDowall, D. (2006). Prior police contact and subsequent victim reporting: Results from the NCVS. *Justice Quarterly, 23*(4), 481–501. https://doi.org/10.1080/07418820600985339
Yu, H., & Monas, N. (2020). Recreating the scene: An investigation of police report writing. *Journal of Technical Writing and Communication, 50*(1), 35–55. https://doi.org/10.1177/0047281618812441

5

Case Facts and Narratives

Introduction

To give a nuanced understanding of the chapters that follow, I, in this chapter introduce general descriptive statistics related to key demographic variables and relationship characteristics across the 34 cases. Additionally, brief case summaries that capture both the factual context and the perspectives of those present at the scene is provided. These depictions serve as reference points, providing a foundation for the analysis throughout the remainder of this book. My goal is to ensure that the complexity of each case remains accessible for ongoing reference, without the need to repeat the description of the case every time it is mentioned in subsequent chapters. I also present tables summarizing critical demographic and relational variables for each case.

I encouraged readers to consult this data as they engage with the detailed narratives and analyses throughout the remaining chapters, as it can provide additional insights to the dynamics and interactions discussed. The tables (Tables 5.1, 5.2, and 5.3) include variables such as victim and suspect gender and race, the nature of their relationship, and the length of that relationship. This overview provides readers with a clear and organized snapshot of the cases, laying the groundwork for deeper

M. N. Eliasson, *Who Gets Believed?*, Palgrave's Critical Policing Studies,
https://doi.org/10.1007/978-3-032-22253-4_5

Table 5.1 Case characteristics

Case	Location	911 Caller	Witness	Victim injury	Alcohol	Arrest
Non-domestic Batteries						
Non-report Yielding Cases						
5	Hotel	3rd party	Yes (C)	No	Yes	No
6	Public	Vic	No	No	Yes	No
7	Vic res	Vic	Yes (C)	No	No	No
8	Public	Vic	Yes (C)	No	No	No
15	Public	Vic	No	Yes	No	No
26	Public	Vic	No	No	No	No
27	Shared res	3rd party	Yes (NC)	Yes	Yes	No
34	Public	Vic	Yes (C)	No	Yes	No
Report Yielding Cases						
10	Public	3rd party	Yes (NC)	Yes	No	No
12	Public	Vic	Yes (C)	No	No	Yes
14	Hotel	Vic	Yes (C)	No	No	No
21	Vic res	3rd party	Yes (NC)	No	No	No
23	Public	Vic	No	No	Yes	No
28	Shared res	Vic	Yes (C)	Yes	No	BA
Domestic Batteries						
Non-report Yielding Cases						
1	Public	3rd party	Yes (C)	Yes	Unknown	No
13	Shared res	3rd party	No	No	Yes	No
16	Vic res	3rd party	No	No	Unknown	No
22	Shared res	3rd Party	No	No	Unknown	No
32	Vic res	3rd Party	No	No	No	No
Report Yielding Cases						
2	Vic res	Vic	No	Yes	Unknown	Yes
3	Public	3rd Party	Yes (C)	Yes	Yes	Yes
4	Shared res	3rd Party	No	Yes	No	BA
9	Shared res	Vic	Yes (C)	No	Yes	No
11	Shared res	Vic	No	Yes	No	Yes
17	Vic res	3rd Party	No	No	Yes	No
18	Shared res	Vic	Child	Yes	Yes	No
19	Susp res	3rd Party	Child	No	Unknown	Yes
20	Shared res	Vic	No	Yes	No	Yes
24	Public	Vic	Child	No	No	No
25	Vic res	Vic	Child	No	No	No
29	Vic res	3rd Party	Child	No	No	Yes
30	Shared res	3rd Party	No	Yes	No	Yes
31	Vic res	Vic	No	No	No	No
33	Shared res	Vic	No	No	Yes	No

C = Cooperating, NC = Not Cooperating, Res = Residence, BA = Baker Acted

Table 5.2 Victim and offender characteristics

Case	Victim gender	Victim race	Suspect gender	Suspect race	Type of relationship	Relationship length
Non-domestic Batteries						
Non-report Yielding Cases						
5	F	W	M	W	Unknown	Unknown
6	F	W	F	H	Stranger	Unknown
7	M	B	F	B	Friends	Unknown
8	F	B	M	B	Neighbors	Unknown
15	F	B	F	B	Stranger	Unknown
26	F	B	M	B	Stranger	Unknown
27	F	W	F	W	Co-patient	Unknown
34	F	W	F	B	Stranger	Unknown
Report Yielding Cases						
10	M	W	M	B	Stranger	Unknown
12	F	B	F	W	Stranger	Unknown
14	M	B	M	B	Stranger	Unknown
21	F	B	M	UNK	Unknown	Unknown
23	F	B	F	W	Stranger	Unknown
28	F	B	F	W	Staff	Unknown
Domestic Batteries						
Non-report Yielding Cases						
1	F	W	M	B	Rom	Unknown
13	F	B	M	B	Prior Rom	Unknown
16	F	B	M	B	Rom	Unknown
22	F	B	M	B	Rom	Unknown
32	M	B	F	B	Rom	Unknown
Report Yielding Cases						
2	M	H	F	B	Prior Rom	3 months
3	F	W	M	W	Rom	Unknown
4	F	B	M	B	Rom	10 years
9	F	H	M	H	Rom	Unknown
11	M	B	F	W	Rom	6 months
17	F	W	M	B	Rom	8 months
18	F	B	M	B	Rom	Unknown
19	F	B	M	B	Rom	Unknown
20	F	A	M	A	Rom	6 months
24	F	B	M	B	Rom	2 years
25	F	H	M	H	Rom	9 months
29	F	B	M	B	Rom	10 years
30	M	B	F	B	Rom	2 years
31	F	B	M	B	Rom	Unknown
33	F	B	M	B	Rom	1 year

Table 5.3 Case officer characteristics

Case	Gender	Race	Age	Experience	Rank	Officers Interviewed (Tot. Officers on Scene)
Non-domestic Batteries						
Non-report Yielding Cases						
5	F	W	36	3	Ofc	1(3)
6	F	W	38	14.5	Cpl	1(2)
7	M	B	30	3	Ofc	1(2)
8	M	H	32	6	Cpl	1(1)
15	M	W	33	0.5	Ofc	1(2)
26	M, M	W, B	29, 42	0.5, 15	Ofc, Cpl	2(2)
27	M	W	29	0.5	Ofc	1(5)
34	M,F	B, W	26, 28	1.5, 6	Ofc, Ofc	2(3)
Report Yielding Cases						
10	M	W	48	3	Ofc	1(2)
12	M	H	32	6	Cpl	1(2)
14	M	W	33	0.5	Ofc	1(2)
21	M, M	W, W	48, 45	3, 15	Ofc, Ofc	2(4)
23	M, M	W, W	33, 55	0.5, 27.5	Ofc, Ofc	2(4)
28	M	W	29	0.5	Ofc	1(2)
Domestic Batteries						
Non-report Yielding Cases						
1	F	W	36	3y	Ofc	1(4)
13	M	W	33	6m	Ofc	1(2)
16	M	W	48	3y	Ofc	1(2)
22	M	W	27	1y	Ofc	1(2)
32	M	W	48	3y	Ofc	1(1)
Report Yielding Cases						
2	M	W	48	3y	Ofc	1(1)
3	M, M, F	B, W, W	26, 26, 28	6m, 1.5y, 5.5y	Ofc,Ofc,Cpl	3(10)
4	M, F	B, W	30, 38	3y, 14.5y	Ofc,Cpl	2(2)
9	M	W	43	19.5y	Ofc	1(2)
11	M, M	W, B	31, 28	3y, 3y	Ofc, Ofc	2(3)
17	M	W	27	4y	Ofc	1(2)
18	M	H	40	12y	Ofc	1(2)
19	M	B	33	3y	Ofc	1(8)
20	M	H	32	6y	Cpl	1(2)
24	M	W	31	2w	Ofc	1(2)
25	M	W	31	2w	Ofc	1(3)
29	M	Mult	46	5y	Ofc	1(3)
30	M, M	W, W	29, 29	6m, 6m	Ofc, Ofc	2(2)
31	M	W	33	6m	Ofc	1(1)
33	M, M	A, B	28, 29	3y, 6m	Ofc, Ofc	2(2)

exploration of patterns and themes that emerge across the dataset. For example, by grouping cases according to categories such as domestic batteries and incidents that did not result in a report, I hope that readers can more easily navigate the many complex layers of analysis and characteristics that could be taken into consideration when diving deeper into the next few chapters.

Beyond characteristics I also provide a table below with the officers' aliases and their characteristics (Table 5.4). To protect the officers' identity, I changed a few characteristics, such as removed or added 1–3 years to their age and gave them aliases which reflects the list of the most common last names in the United States. To further enhance the utility of this data, the tables are organized to allow straightforward identification of demographic trends among officers. Overall, I hope that this chapter provides transparency in the data presentation and analytical process (Esterberg, 2002).

Non-domestic Battery Case Demographic Information

In total I collected 14 non-domestic battery cases. Table 5.1 provides case details on the situational context of the victimization. In all cases but three, the victim was female. Among the suspect eight were female and six were male. Thus, in this sample it was more common to have female-on-female violence (seven) compared to male-on-male violence (two) and opposite-gender violence (five). In the cases of opposite-gender violence women were more often victims (four) compared to men (one). In nine cases, the victims were Black and in five cases the victims were White. Additionally, in seven cases the suspect was Black, in five cases the suspect was White, in one case the suspect was Hispanic and in one case race/ethnicity was unknown. Out of the 14 cases, there were seven cases in which the victim and suspect were either both Black (five) or both White (two). When looking across the 14 cases Black females were more common as victims (seven cases) and White females were slightly more common as suspects (four cases) compared to Black men (three cases).

Table 5.4 Officer aliases and characteristics

Alias	Gender	Race	Age	Years of experience	Rank
Smith	M	W/Hisp	42	19y	Captain
Johnson	M	W	55	19y	Corporal
Williams	M	W	29	6months	Patrol Ofc
Brown	M	W	26	1.5y	Patrol Ofc
Willson	M	W	48	3y	Patrol Ofc
Miller	M	W/Hisp	21	1y	Patrol Ofc
Davis	M	W	38	3y	Patrol Ofc
Anderson	M	B	36	11.5y	Corporal
Taylor	M	W	42	10y	Patrol Ofc
Moore	F	W	36	3y	Patrol Ofc
Thomas	F	W	28	5.5y	Corporal
Garcia	M	A	28	3y	Patrol Ofc
Jackson	M	B	26	6months	Patrol Ofc
Martin	M	B	30	3y	Patrol Ofc
Lee	F	W	38	14.5y	Corporal
Thompson	M	Hisp/Latino	32	6y	Corporal
White	M	W	43	19.5y	Patrol Ofc
Perez	M	W	26	1y	Patrol Ofc
Harris	M	W	31	3y	Patrol Ofc
Sanchez	M	B	28	3y	Patrol Ofc
Clark	M	W	33	6months	Patrol Ofc
Lewis	M	W	27	4y	Patrol Ofc
Robinson	M	B	33	3y	Patrol Ofc
Walker	M	Hisp	40	12y	Patrol Ofc
Young	M	W	43	12	Patrol Ofc
King	M	W	27	1y	Patrol Ofc
Wright	M	B	26	1.5y	Patrol Ofc
Scott	M	B	28	2	Patrol Ofc
Torres	M	W	31	2weeks	Patrol Ofc
Hill	M	B	44	15y	Corporal
Green	M	Multi Racial	46	5y	Patrol Ofc
Adams	M	B	35	2y	Patrol Ofc
Nelson	M	W	29	6months	Patrol Ofc
Baker	M	W	55	27.5 Y	Patrol Ofc
Rivera	M	W	33	1y	Patrol Ofc
Mitchell	M	B	29	6months	Patrol Ofc
Campbell	F	W	28	6y	Patrol Ofc

When comparing the race and gender characteristics of the cases that resulted in a report with GPD's statistics of non-domestic batteries that occurred during 2022, the gender demographic for victims in my sample is not in line with the statistics GPD provided. The GPD statistics reflect the combined number of simple batteries, simple batteries with other weapons, and aggravated batteries that were non-domestic in nature. The sample in this study was oversaturated with female victims, whereas in the GPD statistics the gender demographic of the cases with reports is more evenly distributed between genders. However, the gender distribution among suspects in this study is in line with GPD statistics. When looking at race, the sample in this study had a higher number of Black victims compared to the GPD statistics and slightly more White suspects than the statistics provided by GPD. It is important to highlight that GPD only could provide statistics for cases with reports, hence the accuracy of the gender and race distribution in cases that did not yield reports cannot be compared. However, when looking at the demographics of the cases that did not yield reports in my study, they are similar to the demographics that yielded reports.

When looking at prior or current relationships between the parties, the most common type of relationship was the victim and suspect being strangers (eight cases). In two cases, the victim and suspect were co-patients at a care facility, in two cases the relationship was unknown, in one case the victim and suspect were friends and in one case they were acquaintances. In more than half of the cases the victimization occurred in a public space, in two cases in the victim's residence, in two cases it occurred in a shared residence, and in two cases at a hotel. In this sample stranger violence was more likely to occur in public spaces, and the violence between parties with a previous non-romantic relationship was more likely to occur in a private space, such as a residence or hotel room.

In most cases (10) the victim reported not having an injury, compared to four cases where the victim had an injury. In these four cases, three of the victims went to the emergency room for medical treatment and in the other case, the victim refused medical attention. In the majority of cases (10) no alcohol or drugs was reportedly involved, however in three cases either the victim or suspect was reportedly intoxicated, and in one case there was no information reported on drugs or alcohol. In one case a suspect was arrested, in one case the suspect was baker acted and in 12 cases, no arrest was made. Additionally, six cases yielded police reports and in eight cases no police report was written. Thus, in the majority of cases officers made decisions not to write police reports. None of the cases involved strangulation and one case involved a pregnant victim.

The classification of the battery could only be collected in cases that yielded reports because officers did not specify the offense in the non-report-yielding cases. Hence, out of the six cases that yielded a report all batteries were simple batteries with no aggravating circumstances and thus were classified as misdemeanor offenses.

Domestic Battery Case Demographic Information

Out of the 20 domestic battery cases, five cases did not yield a police report, and 15 cases yielded a report which can be seen in Table 5.2. Out of the 20 domestic battery victims, 16 were female and four were male, and amongst the 20 suspects 16 were male and four were female. It was more common that women were subjected to violence by men compared to the opposite. There was no same-gender domestic battery in my data. Among the victims, the most common race was Black (13) with the second and third being White (three) and Hispanic (three), and the fourth being Asian (one). As for the suspects, 15 were Black, two were White, two were Hispanic, and one was Asian. In all cases except three the victim had the same race or ethnicity as the suspect. Thus, the most common race and gender among victims were Black females and among suspects it was Black men.

In nine cases, I observed that the suspect was located and talked to by officers on scene. In 11 cases I did not observe that the suspect was not located, however, some of these suspects were located after the fact, which I found out from either the original police report or supplemental notes made to the police report. At the scene I observed four suspects admitted perpetration, four suspects denied and in 12 cases, the suspect's view was unknown. In 12 cases, there was no arrest made, in seven cases an arrest was made either at the scene or at a later stage, and in one case the suspect was Baker Acted.

In 18 of the domestic battery cases, the victim and suspect were in a domestic partnership or romantic relationship and in two cases they had a prior romantic relationship. In the 10 cases where the length of the relationship was known, the relationship had lasted less than a year in half of the domestic battery cases. In the other half of cases, the relationships were longer than one year: three relationships had been ongoing for one to three years and two relationships had been ongoing for ten years. Additionally, nine of the domestic occurred in shared residences, seven in the victims' residence, three in a public space, and one in the suspect's residence. In 11 cases, a third-party called 911 and in nine cases the victim was the 911 caller. All the non-report-yielding cases had a third-party caller, whereas in more than half of the report-yielding cases, the domestic battery victim was the 911 caller. Three cases had witnesses present that cooperated, 12 cases had no witnesses present, and five cases had children present during the victimization. Alcohol was noted to be involved in six cases; however, the involvement of alcohol was either unknown (five) or not involved (nine) in the majority of the cases. Eight of the victims reported having some type of injury because of the victimization, and 12 victims reported not having an injury.

Furthermore, none of the cases involved strangulation and no case involved a pregnant victim. Out of the 16 cases that yielded a report, three cases were classified as felony, 12 as misdemeanor and one was not classified due to the suspect being baker acted. In line with the non-domestic cases, the classification of the offense was not specified by officers in the domestic cases that did not yield a report.

Officer Characteristics Domestic Cases

In the 20 domestic battery cases I observed that there was a total of 56 officers present on scene. The number of officers present on the scene ranged from one to ten, with the median number of 2.8 officers as can be seen in Table 5.3. All cases but two, two to four officers were present. In the two other cases had 8 and 10 officers present, in both cases there was a weapon involved in the battery.

There was a total of 23 officers interviewed for the 20 domestic battery cases. In 15 cases, one officer was interviewed, in four cases two officers were interviewed, and in one case three officers were interviewed. In the five cases where more than one officer was interviewed, one of the officers interviewed was assigned to the case as the primary officer. In all the cases where only one officer was interviewed, the officer interviewed was assigned as primary officer to the case. One officer was interviewed for three of the cases, and one officer was interviewed for two cases; the rest of the officers were only interviewed for one case each. One officer wrote two police reports, however, all the other reports were written by different officers.

Out of the 23 officers, 20 were men and three were women. Fourteen officers identified as White, five as Black, two as Hispanic, one as Asian, and one as multi-racial. Thus, overall, the sample of officers was heavily saturated with White males. The age of the officers ranged between 26 and 48, with a mean age of 32.6. Additionally, the years of experience ranged from two weeks to 19.5 years, with a mean of four years. Most of the officers were patrol officers (20), and three had the rank of corporal.

Officer Characteristics Non-domestic Cases

I observed several different officers who were present on scene. The number of officers on scene varied between one and five, with the average number of officers on scene being 2.5. Furthermore, a total of 12 officers were interviewed for the 14 cases included in this study, specific information about each officer can be found in Table 5.3. Out of the 12 officers interviewed, four were interviewed in more than one case, with two of the officers being interviewed for two cases and the two other officers being interviewed for three cases. Out of the 14 cases, 10 cases had one officer interviewed, nine of which were primary officers for the case, the other primary officer declined to be interviewed and thus another officer who interacted with the victim was interviewed. In the remaining four cases, two officers were interviewed with one of them being the primary officers and the second being officers who fit the inclusion requirement of being present on the scene and I observed them interacting with the victim.

Out of the 12 officers interviewed, nine were male and three were female. Officers interviewed were White (eight), Black (three), and Hispanic (one). Nine officers were ranked as patrol officers while three of them were corporals. The age range of the officers was 26–55 years with a mean age of 36.8 years. The range of years of experience was 6 months–27.5 years with a mean of 6.8 years, with 2 officers having less than 1 year of experience, 5 officers having 1–5 years of experience, 1 with 6–10 years of experience, 3 officers with 11–15 years of experience, and 1 had more than 12 years of experience.

Out of the six cases that generated police reports, two reports were written by a White male officer with three years of experience and with the rank of police officer. Of the other four cases that yielded police reports, two officers had less than a year of experience and were White males at the rank of police officer; one was a White male officer with 27.5 years of experience with the rank of police officer; and one was a Hispanic officer with six years of experience at the rank of corporal.

Case Narratives

The descriptive narratives are based on 911 call logs, observations of interactions at the scene, and police reports. These accounts are not derived from officers' post-scene interview statements, but rather from publicly available facts about each incident. Certain details have been removed to protect the identities of victims, suspects, and witnesses.

Domestic Case 1: A third-party caller contacted 911, reporting that a female had been kicked by a male and was lying unconscious outside a hotel. Several officers responded to the scene and contacted the victim (White female), who stated that she did not want to be a victim and that nothing had happened. A witness at the scene identified the victim's boyfriend (Black male) as the alleged suspect. However, he was not present at the scene and could not be located. Upon speaking with the witness, officers learned that the reported victimization had occurred a week prior to the call and not on the day of the call. The identity of the third-party caller could not be determined, and officers were not able to obtain more information from the caller. The officers learned from the witness that the alleged incident took place outside the responding officers' jurisdiction, and thus, the case was transferred to another police agency. No police report was written.

Domestic Case 2: The victim (Hispanic male) came to the police station to file a report against the suspect (Black female). He stated that the suspect had struck him with a stick and that they had previously been in a romantic relationship lasting three months, though they were no longer romantically involved. The victim reported that there had been several prior violent interactions between them and that the suspect had violated an injunction. The responding officer acknowledged knowing about the prior violent interactions between the victim and the suspect. According to the victim, the most recent violent incident occurred outside his residence, which is where the suspect struck him with a stick. He expressed a desire for police to help him, stating that he wanted the suspect's violent behavior to stop. He also stated that because he did not have a phone, he walked to the police station to file the report. The victim reported having multiple injuries and visible marks, however he declined EMS assistance but said he would go to the hospital later. Officers photographed his injuries and provided him with paperwork outlining victims' rights and available resources. The victim later submitted a sworn complaint form. A police report was completed, and a warrant was issued for the suspect, who was arrested a few days later.

Domestic Case 3: A third-party caller contacted 911, reporting that the victim (White female) had been struck by the suspect (White male) outside a bar. Multiple officers responded and located the victim sitting at the back of the establishment. The victim was not willing to give any information to the police about the alleged incident and stated that nothing had happened, although officers observed visible marks on her cheek. The victim expressed concern for the suspect, whom she was in a relationship with and while officers were speaking with her, the suspect called her multiple times. Officers obtained the suspect's information and learned that he was currently on parole for a separate offense. Several witnesses at the scene confirmed the victim being struck by the suspect and reported that he had fled by car. Although the suspect was not located while officers were on scene and no arrest was made, a police report was written.

Domestic Case 4: A third-party caller contacted 911, reporting that a female had been stabbed and threatened with a knife by a man. Officers arrived on scene and spoke with the victim (Black female), who stated that she was married to the suspect (Black male). She reported that the suspect had previously been violent toward her and that police had responded to their residence in the past. Officers photographed the victim's injuries and interviewed witnesses. Upon walking into the shared residence, officers stated that they saw multiple signs of a struggle, including a disheveled carpet. EMS arrived and assessed the victim's injuries, but she declined being transported to the hospital. She said that she was scared and stated that she wanted her husband to receive help because the suspect had Alzheimer's which affected his mental state and behavior. Officers attempted to assess the suspect's cognitive status by questioning him, but he was unable to answer questions about the incident or demonstrate awareness of his mental condition. This prompted officers to consult with their sergeant regarding next steps. The suspect was transported to the hospital by one of the officers, and a police report was completed.

Non-domestic Case 5: A third-party caller contacted 911, reporting that they had heard a female yelling, "Stop hitting me," from a hotel room. One officer spoke with the victim (White female), who denied that anything had happened and stated that she and the suspect (White male) only had been arguing. She explained that she and the suspect were in a domestic partnership and were currently staying at the hotel only as roommates. The suspect was found sitting outside the hotel smoking. Another officer spoke with him, and he also denied that any incident had occurred. Officers also spoke with the witness who had called 911 and was staying a few rooms away from the victim's room. The witness maintained that they heard the victim yelling, "Stop hitting me." Officers consulted with a sergeant who responded to the scene. No arrest was made, and no police report was written.

Non-domestic Case 6: The victim (White female) called 911 and reported that she had been slapped by the suspect (White female) on a street downtown. The officers met the victim in a parking lot downtown e few streets over from multiple bars. The victim stated that she also witnessed the suspect being abusive toward her boyfriend and clarified that she did not know either the suspect or her boyfriend prior to the incident. The victim expressed that she did not want to press charges and simply wished to go home. Officers attempted to locate the suspect, however, was unsuccessful. No police report was written and no arrest was made.

Non-domestic Case 7: The victim (White male) called 911, reporting that the suspect (White female) had hit him after he asked her to leave his house following a party, and she refused. Upon arrival, two officers spoke with the victim outside a house in a residential neighborhood. The victim stated that he and the suspect were friends, that there had been a history of violence between them, and he also expressed that he did not wish to press charges. A witness at the scene noted that the victim had been antagonizing the suspect. Officers looked up the suspect's information in their system however they did not attempt to contact or locate the suspect. No police report was written and no arrest was made.

Non-domestic Case 8: The victim (Black female) called 911 and reported that she and her sons had been attacked by a group of boys (Black males) who lived in their apartment complex. Several officers responded to the scene and while some officers remained with the victim, others attempted to locate the suspects but were unsuccessful. When officers spoke to the victim, she stated that her family, along with others in the complex, had been harassed by this group of boys for a long time, but that no one else was willing to call the police. The victim explained that her sons are minors with disabilities and that she wanted help to stop the ongoing harassment. Upon further conversation with the victim, officers determined that no physical contact had occurred during the incident, contrary to what was initially reported to 911. The officers left the scene, no arrests were made, and no police report was written.

Domestic Case 9: The victim (Hispanic female) called 911, reporting that her boyfriend (Hispanic male) had pushed her during an argument the previous day. When officers spoke with her, she stated that during the altercation, she had pushed a table against him, and he responded by hitting her. She disclosed that there had been prior incidents of violence during arguments and that both she and the suspect had come to Florida for work. The victim mentioned that there were witnesses to the incident but noted that they were her boyfriend's friends and were likely to support him. Officers located the witnesses in a closed-off abandoned building, however, they stated that they had not observed anything. The victim showed officers marks she claimed were from the push, but officers reported that they could not see any visible injuries. She also stated that she had video footage of the incident, which officers reviewed but said did not clearly show the incident. The victim then expressed a desire to leave Florida, so one of the officers offered to take her to the airport, which she agreed to. A police report was written, but no arrests were made, and the suspect was not located.

Non-domestic Case 10: The victim (White male) flagged down a Sheriff's Officer and reported that he had been attacked the previous evening, stating that he blacked out after being punched in the head. He also reported that his medications were stolen during the incident. The victim said he did not know the suspect (Black male) personally but had seen him before outside a convenience store. The victim also disclosed that he was homeless and had a medical condition that caused seizures. The officer spoke with a man who confirmed witnessing an altercation between two individuals the night before but declined to be a witness in the investigation. The victim reported injuries from the attack, including a lost tooth and a sore lip. Officers photographed the victim's injuries, and EMS transported him to the emergency room. One officer followed EMS to the hospital to provide the victim with paperwork and to return his belongings. The officer then went to the convenience store where the incident allegedly occurred to search for witnesses and surveillance footage. The store clerk informed the officer that the cameras did not face the area where the incident occurred and therefore would not have captured the incident. The suspect was not located and no arrest was made but a police report was written.

Domestic Case 11: The victim (Black male) called 911, reporting that his girlfriend (White female) was throwing objects at him and had struck him with an ashtray. When officers arrived on scene, the victim declined to cooperate. He stated that he had changed his mind about calling and did not want his girlfriend to be charged, he simply just wanted to stop the fighting. The victim refused to have photos taken of his potential injuries and did not wish to complete a sworn complaint. When officers spoke with the suspect, she admitted to throwing the ashtray at her boyfriend. During the conversation, she screamed and swore at the victim in front of the officers. Both parties confirmed that police had previously responded to their residence for arguments. The suspect stated that in prior incidents where the victim had attacked her, officers had not taken him to jail. The officers on scene consulted with a sergeant regarding the appropriate course of action. The female suspect was arrested, and a police report was written.

Non-domestic Case 12: The victim (Black female) called 911 to report that a customer, the suspect (White female), had chest-bumped her at the restaurant where she was working. Upon arrival, officers spoke with the victim, who stated that she and the suspect had engaged in a verbal altercation, during which the suspect chest-bumped her. The victim noted that although she had been trained in physical defense, she chose to control her response to de-escalate the situation. The suspect was located outside the restaurant. She explained that she had arrived with a friend who claimed that someone inside the restaurant had been looking at her butt. The suspect demanded to speak with a staff member (the victim), to request a refund, which was granted. The interaction then escalated between the suspect and the victim. The suspect stated that she did not recall chest-bumping the victim, but added that if she had done so, it was not intentional. Several witnesses were present at the scene, including restaurant staff and individuals accompanying the suspect. Officers reviewed camera footage of the incident, which showed a broken bottle of drink on the floor in the area where the altercation occurred. The suspect was arrested, transported to jail and a police report was written.

Domestic Case 13: A third-party caller contacted 911, reporting that one of their patients may have been battered by her boyfriend. Upon arrival, the officer spoke with the victim (Black female), who stated that she had sought medical care for an injury and that the suspect (Black male) had been violent. She expressed fear of the suspect, with whom she lived and had previously been in a romantic relationship that ended two months prior. The victim described a history of verbal abuse and explained that the suspect, who had nowhere else to live, had moved in with her and her daughter. However, she later clarified that the injury for which she sought medical attention was not related to the violence she had experienced, and that the incident had occurred outside the responding officer's jurisdiction. The officer consulted with the police agency responsible for that jurisdiction, but they stated they could not assist since there had been no violent encounter. The officer encouraged the victim to seek help and to have the suspect removed from her residence. The officer did not attempt to contact the suspect, no arrest was made and no police report was written.

Non-domestic Case 14: The victim (Black male) called 911, reporting that he had been pushed by the suspect (Black male) during a dispute over money the suspect had borrowed. When officers arrived at the apartment complex, the victim explained that he had previously loaned the suspect money to buy drugs. When he returned to collect the debt, the suspect was unable to repay him. According to the victim, during the argument, the suspect stood up and pushed the victim with both hands to the chest. The victim stated that he knew the suspect typically carried a gun, so he "backed off" and called the police. The victim completed a sworn statement and requested that the suspect be charged. Officers then spoke with the suspect, who said the victim had come to demand money and began yelling and "aggressively got into his face." The suspect admitted to pushing the victim, stating that he did so out of fear for his safety. Both parties indicated that there were witnesses to the incident, but when officers approached one of them, the individual declined to participate and claimed not to have seen anything. One of the officers informed the victim that there was insufficient evidence to proceed, noting that neither party had visible injuries and that the case amounted to "word against word." No arrest was made, but a police report was written.

Non-domestic Case 15: The victim (Black female) called 911 requesting EMS, stating that she had been hit in the head while trying to get a ride. An officer met with the victim in the parking lot of a local gas station. During the conversation, the victim explained that she and her girlfriend were visiting town and that she had attempted to get a ride from the suspect (Black male), whom she did not know prior to the encounter. She stated that during the ride, the suspect struck her in the head with an object. Initially, the victim expressed a desire to file a report but changed her mind after speaking with her mother on the phone. Her girlfriend was also present at the scene. The victim held her head and reported having a bump, requesting EMS to assess her injuries. When EMS arrived, she declined transport to the ER, stating that her girlfriend would take her to the hospital instead. The officer attempted to gather more details from the victim and her girlfriend but reported that the information provided was confusing and inconsistent. After speaking with both the victim and EMS personnel, the officer noted that the story did not make sense and that something seemed off about the account. The suspect was not located, and no police report was written.

Domestic Case 16: A third-party caller contacted 911, reporting that a man (Black) was hitting a woman (Black) inside an apartment. The caller also stated that the parties had a child together and that there was a history of prior violence between them. Upon arrival, officers listened outside the apartment door to determine if any fighting could be heard but heard nothing. They then contacted the victim, who lived in the apartment, by knocking on the door. She stated that nothing had happened and explained that she had been crying due to the recent death of a relative. She also claimed that the neighbor had made similar false reports to police in the past. The suspect was not located, no arrest was made, and no police report was written.

Domestic Case 17: A third-party caller contacted 911, reporting that a woman (White) had been battered by her boyfriend (Black). The caller stated that the victim had attempted to call 911 herself, but the call was disconnected, and the suspect had taken her phone. Dispatch confirmed the attempted 911 call. Upon arrival, officers spoke with both the caller and the victim. The victim reported that during their relationship, the suspect had been physically and emotionally abusive. She said she was scared and stated that she wanted help. She also stated that there had been prior contact with police regarding the suspect but said she had not received assistance at that time. The victim described the suspect performing a "maneuver" on her, though she could not give a detailed explanation of what had occurred during the maneuver. She expressed concern that the suspect had a military background and could seriously harm her. Officers observed redness on the left side of the victim's face. Officers confirmed that he lived at the same residence as the victim and had a prior conviction for a violent crime. The suspect was not located at the scene and no arrest was made. The victim completed a sworn complaint, and officers photographed her injuries. A police report was written.

Domestic Case 18: The victim (Black female) called 911 reporting that a child was bleeding and that a domestic battery had occurred. Upon arrival, officers found the suspect (Black male) bleeding at the scene. The victim stated that both she and the suspect had been drinking and that an argument had escalated into mutual shoving. She could not recall who initiated the physical contact. She explained that the suspect was walking toward the kitchen while yelling at her when he fell over a glass table, resulting in an injury to his face. The victim and suspect lived together and shared a child. She reported a history of arguments and substance abuse issues in the relationship, noting her past struggles with alcohol and the suspect's ongoing drinking problem, for which he had not sought treatment. Inside the residence, officers observed a shattered glass table, shards of glass on the floor, and drops of blood. The victim was provided a sworn complaint form to complete and return. Officers photographed the suspect, who had visible injuries and was bleeding from his face. He was transported to the ER under a trauma alert due to the head injury. At the hospital, officers interviewed the suspect, who stated that he did not remember the incident but confirmed that an argument had occurred. He denied any physical altercation, saying he did not recall falling over the table or what happened afterward. He emphasized that he was a former boxer and would never touch the victim, as he could seriously hurt her. The officer noted that he could not determine a primary aggressor. No arrest was made, but a police report was written.

Domestic Case 19: A child called 911 reporting that their father was hitting their mother. Multiple officers responded to the scene, and the children ran out of the apartment where the incident occurred. Inside the residence, the suspect (Black male) was present with two victims (Black females), both of whom he had children with. Once officers surrounded the residence, the victims and the suspect exited the apartment. One of the victims stated that she had been hit by the suspect and wanted to press charges. The other victim declined to press charges. The victim who wished to pursue charges reported that she and the suspect had gotten into a verbal argument, during which the suspect pushed her to the ground. After she got up, she stated that the suspect pulled a gun from his waistband and held it at his side. She expressed that she was in fear for her life during this moment. Officers noted that the suspect had a felony record and was prohibited from possessing firearms. A search of the residence revealed a firearm and drugs hidden in the kitchen. The suspect did not make any statements to police, he was arrested, taken to jail, and a police report was written.

Domestic Case 20: The victim (Asian female) called 911 and reported that her boyfriend (Asian male), whom she had been in a romantic relationship with for six months and lived with, had hit her during an argument. Upon arrival, officers spoke with the victim, who stated that the argument began because the suspect was singing too loudly. She reported that the suspect punched her on her right cheek and that he had blood on his hand. Officers spoke to the suspect who admitted that an argument had occurred but claimed that the victim had taken his phone and locked herself in a room. He stated that he kicked the door to gain entry and, once inside, asked for the phone again. When she refused, he said he pushed her against the wall. He further claimed that she punched him in the face, causing his nose to bleed, and that he then pulled her hair. Officers observed visible marks on the victim's face and noted that the suspect had marks and blood on his hand. Photographs of both parties' injuries were taken. The victim expressed concern for the suspect and asked officers what would happen to him. The suspect was arrested and taken to jail. A police report was written.

Non-domestic Case 21: A third-party caller contacted 911, reporting that a pregnant female (Black) had been hit by a male (unknown race) and may have sustained injuries. Prior to officers arriving on scene, they noted that the female residing at the address had a documented history of being a victim of domestic violence. According to dispatch, the victim also called 911, and voices were heard in the background before the call was disconnected. Attempts by dispatchers to call back were unsuccessful. Upon arrival, officers spoke with the victim, who stated that nothing had happened. She declined to provide any information about herself or the other party involved. The third-party caller had reportedly left the scene before officers arrived and was not located. The victim showed no visible injuries, though her shirt was torn around the neck area. Officers were unable to locate a suspect, no arrest was made, and no police report was written.

Domestic Case 22: A third-party caller contacted 911, reporting that a pregnant female (Black) had been hit by her boyfriend (Black male). The caller stated that the couple was in a romantic relationship, lived together, and had one child together and on the way. The caller also noted a history of prior violence between the parties. When officers arrived on scene, the suspect was present, but the victim was not. Officers learned that the suspect had prior police contact, he stated that he did not want to go to jail and denied doing anything to his girlfriend. He mentioned that he had recently been released from jail on another charge. After being contacted, the victim arrived on scene. She told officers that the situation was a misunderstanding and that no violence had occurred. She had no visible injuries. No arrest was made, and no police report was written.

Non-domestic Case 23: The victim (Black female) called 911 to report an incident at a grocery store. Upon arrival, officers spoke with the victim, who stated that while she was in line to pay for her groceries, two females (White) cut in front of her. The victim confronted them, telling them they needed to get in line. The younger suspect responded with a verbal altercation, and the older suspect attempted to separate them, making physical contact with the victim. The suspects left the store while the victim was on the phone with police. The victim, who noted that she was pregnant, expressed that she was very scared during the incident and felt it was inappropriate for the suspects to put their hands on her. She stated that she wanted to file a police report and mentioned that she had taken photos of the suspects. She also reported that the store had surveillance footage that likely captured the incident. After speaking with the victim, officers reviewed the store's surveillance footage. They then returned to the victim and informed her that a police report would be written. Officers noted that they could "see no intent of battery" in the recording. Officers did not locate the suspect and no arrest was made.

Domestic Case 24: The victim (Black female) called 911 reporting that she and her boyfriend were arguing and that he had pushed her during the dispute. After the call, the victim drove to the police station to file a sworn complaint. When speaking with officers, she stated that she and the suspect (Black male) lived together and had a history of prior violence. She expressed that she wanted help and believed the suspect should be arrested.

The victim reported that her lip was "busted" but declined to have officers photograph her injuries. The suspect was not present at the station but was later located by police. He acknowledged that an argument had occurred but claimed that the victim approached him and instigated a volatile interaction. He stated that he pushed her away to de-escalate the situation. He also mentioned that he had been battered by other women in the past and that this argument was a continuation of one from the previous day. No arrest was made however a police report was written.

Domestic Case 25: The victim (Hispanic female) called 911 and reported that her husband (Hispanic male) had hit her and attempted to attack her with a knife. Upon arrival, officers learned that the victim lived with the suspect and a child, and that there was a history of prior violence. Due to a language barrier, the information provided at the scene was limited. The suspect was not present when officers arrived. EMS responded and transported the victim to the hospital and at the hospital, an interpreter assisted in gathering further details. The victim stated that the incident began with an argument over loud music and the suspect wanting to leave the residence. She attempted to block the front door to prevent him from leaving. The suspect told her to move, and when she refused, he grabbed and pushed her before exiting the residence. Officers noted no visible injuries but photographed the victim. Attempts to locate the suspect were unsuccessful. No arrest was made, but a police report was written.

Non-domestic Case 26: The victim (White female) called 911 reporting that an unknown Black male (suspect) had grabbed her butt. When officers arrived on scene, the victim stated that she had been trying to help the suspect after he crashed his scooter outside her apartment. The suspect asked her for water, which she gave him. She reported that he then attempted to hug her and touched her butt. Following the incident, the victim followed the suspect to his apartment complex and showed officers the location and specific apartment unit. Officers knocked on the door and contacted the suspect, who initially denied involvement but later admitted to being at the scene. Officers observed an injury to the suspect's leg consistent with a scooter crash and noted parts of a vape in the suspect's apartment that matched one dropped outside the victim's residence. No arrest was made, and no police report was written.

Non-domestic Case 27: A third-party caller contacted 911 reporting a battery between two residents at the memory center of a live-in care facility. One resident pushed another, causing the victim (White female) to fall and hit her head. The victim sustained a bump on her head, and EMS responded to assess her injuries and transported her to the hospital. Due to the lowered cognitive capabilities of both the victim and the suspect (White female), officers did not speak directly with the suspect. Instead, they interviewed facility staff, who explained that the residents had gotten into a fight, resulting in one pushing the other. Staff noted that incidents like this occur occasionally and that neither resident had normal mental capacity. No arrest was made, and no police report was written.

Non-domestic Case 28: The victim (Black female), a care worker at a residential care home, called 911 reporting that she and several residents had been attacked by another resident. When officers arrived, multiple residents were present. Staff informed officers that the suspect (White female) had medical conditions affecting her behavior. The suspect was transported to the emergency room. One resident had visible marks, and the in-house nurse arrived to assess the resident medically. EMS also responded and transported another male resident to the hospital. The caregiver declined medical attention. Officers spoke with facility staff about the suspect and determined that, due to her medical condition, she lacked the mental capacity to form criminal intent. One officer noted that this was the first time he had encountered such a situation and consulted with other officers on scene. They collectively agreed that the suspect's mental status was a key factor in determining that no criminal intent was present. No arrest was made, and no police report was written.

Domestic Case 29: A child called 911 reporting that their mother had been hit by her boyfriend. Upon arrival, officers spoke with the victim (Black female), who stated that there was an active injunction against the suspect (Black male), prohibiting him from being at her residence. She reported that the suspect had broken into her apartment while she was away. When she returned home, she found him inside and they started arguing. The suspect was not present when officers arrived and the victim stated that she believed he may have fled to his mother's house. She also informed officers that the suspect had a history of drug use and prior criminal activity and expressed fear for that he might return to her residence. Officers interviewed the child who made the 911 call, and the child stated they saw the suspect touch their mother's face during the argument. Officers photographed the area where the victim said the suspect had broken in. A police report was written, and a warrant was issued for the suspect's arrest.

Domestic Case 30: The victim (Black male) called police reporting that he and his girlfriend (Black female) had been fighting, and that she refused to let him leave and hit him. Upon arrival, officers spoke with the victim, who stated that they shared a residence and had experienced many arguments in the past. He explained that during the current altercation, the suspect physically blocked him from leaving by positioning herself between him and the front door. At one point, she pushed him, nearly causing him to fall. Each time he attempted to leave, she pushed him back, and he stated that he did not feel free to leave. The victim expressed that he did not want to press charges and did not want the suspect to go to jail. When officers spoke to the suspect, she admitted to pushing the victim several times but claimed it was because he was "coming towards her." She did not allege that the victim had been physical with her but acknowledged that she had intentionally blocked the doorway to prevent him from leaving. As officers arrested her and escorted her to the police car, she loudly screamed at the victim. The victim repeatedly asked officers how he could get her out of jail. The suspect was arrested, taken to jail and a police report was written.

Domestic Case 31: The victim (Black female) called 911 reporting that the man she had been dating attempted to rip her clothes off. When officers arrived on scene, the victim stated that the suspect (Black male) had prior military training and knew how to inflict harm without leaving visible marks. She expressed fear of the suspect and noted that he had a prior injunction involving another female. Officers photographed the victim's clothing and provided her with resources from non-law enforcement agencies that could offer support. The suspect was not present at the scene, but officers later contacted him by phone. He claimed to be out of town and denied any knowledge of the incident. No arrest was made, but a police report was written.

Domestic Case 32: A third-party caller contacted 911 reporting that a woman had punched a man in the face and poured bleach into his eyes.

Upon arrival, officers spoke with the victim (Black male), who denied being victimized by the suspect (Black female). The responding officer had previously handled calls involving the same individuals and confirmed that there was an active injunction prohibiting the suspect from being at the victim's residence. The suspect was not present at the scene. When officers attempted to follow up with the 911 caller, the caller stated they did not have time to engage further and declined to speak with police. No arrest was made, and no police report was written.

Domestic Case 33: The victim (Black female) called 911 reporting that her boyfriend (Black male) had pinned her down and hit her. Upon arrival, officers noted that the suspect was not present at the scene but observed a broken window. When speaking with officers, the victim explained that she and the suspect had been arguing, prompting her to move her belongings into the hallway outside the apartment. As she stepped into the hallway, the suspect approached and slapped her on the left side of her face with an open hand. Several hours later, when the victim attempted to collect her belongings again to leave the residence, the suspect pushed her onto the bed, causing her leg to smash the window next to it. As she raised her hands to protect her face, the suspect struck her arm with his fist. The victim informed officers that the suspect had a history of violence with previous girlfriends and was currently under an injunction issued by another female. She expressed fear of the suspect and stated her intention to leave the relationship. Officers photographed both the victim and the broken window. The victim declined EMS assessment but completed a sworn complaint. She was provided with a referral to a women's shelter, which she indicated she would go to. Officers attempted to locate the suspect but were unsuccessful and no arrest was made. A police report was written.

Non-domestic Case 34: The victim (White female) called 911 reporting an incident with another female at a bar. Upon arrival, officers spoke with the victim, who stated that the suspect (Black female) had taken her phone and grabbed her by the hair during the encounter inside the bar. Several witnesses were present at the scene. Officers located the suspect, who was observed repeatedly looking over at the victim. The suspect was found to be in possession of the victim's phone, which officers returned to the victim. The suspect admitted to having the phone and acknowledged an encounter inside the bar. No arrest was made, and no police report was written.

Conclusion

In this this chapter I provided an overview of the 34 domestic battery cases that were followed during the six-month fieldwork period. General case characteristics were presented, including demographic information about the victims and suspects, the location of the victimization, whether witnesses were present, who placed the 911 call, whether children were involved, whether the victim sustained injuries, whether a report was generated, and whether the suspect was arrested. Information was also included about the police officers interviewed for each case, such as their gender, race, age, years of experience, and rank.

In addition to this, I shared case narratives for each of the 34 battery cases. These narratives offered more detailed context about the incidents, including the attitudes and perceptions of victims and suspects when available. They also described interactions between victims and officers, as well as investigative actions and decisions, when such information was accessible. All narrative content is based on information available through public records requests. However, identifying details were removed to protect the privacy of victims, witnesses, suspects, and officers.

The reason these narratives were included is to support data transparency (Esterberg, 2002) and to ensure that readers have access to contextual information that may not be repeated each time a case is referenced later in the book. This approach not only provides additional data and analytical depth but also allows readers to engage with the case material at their own pace as they move through the remaining chapters.

Reference

Esterberg, K. G. (2002). *Qualitative methods in social research*. McGraw-Hill.

6

Attitude, Cooperation, and Story

Introduction

I aim to provide a nuanced perspective of how victims' attitudes toward their victimization, their willingness to cooperate, and the narratives they provide are examined by officers as part of a broader assessment of credibility. Before delving deeper into the topic, it is essential to acknowledge the distinct nature of domestic versus non-domestic cases. Specifically, I want to emphasize the importance of contextualizing victim attitudes and cooperation within the framework of existing or nonexisting prior relationships between the victim and the suspect. Prior research highlights that the context, such as the presence or absence of a prior relationship, plays a crucial role in shaping victims' behaviors and attitudes. For example, prior relationships could influence both victims' willingness to disclose their victimization to police and the way officers assess credibility (Ambrozewicz et al., 2024; Mancini & Pickett, 2017). In domestic batteries, the presence of an intimate or familial relationship introduces layers of complexity, including emotional ties, potential fear of retaliation, and legal mandates that shape officer discretion. In contrast,

M. N. Eliasson, *Who Gets Believed?*, Palgrave's Critical Policing Studies,
https://doi.org/10.1007/978-3-032-22253-4_6

non-domestic cases often involve strangers or acquaintances, where officers may rely more heavily on behavioral cues and narrative clarity to assess credibility.

Although victims' attitudes toward their victimization could be an indicator of cooperation, it could also be a true reflection of that a victimization did not occur. In this book, attitude toward victimization was not interpreted as an indicator for cooperatio, instead, an indicator of cooperation was conceptualized as willingness to provide information and engage with law enforcement. Thus, independently of whether victimization had occurred or not, victims' willingness to give officers their information and make statements about what did or did not happen served as an indicator of cooperation. This interpretation aligns with previous research, which demonstrates that police officers often equate cooperation, such as providing detailed accounts, answering questions openly, and participating in evidence collection, with credibility and legitimacy (Ask, 2010; Bostaph et al., 2021; van Doorn & Koster, 2019). However, scholars also emphasize that reluctance or shifts in cooperation may be rooted in trauma, fear, or distrust, rather than intentional withholding of information (Overstreet and Quinn, 2016). The notion of victim cooperation is important in the context of the Ideal Victim Theory (Christie, 1986; Strobl, 2004). Victims who are forthcoming, emotionally expressive, and consistent in their accounts are often viewed as aligning with the Ideal Victim, while those who are reluctant or inconsistent may face skepticism, even when their behavior is shaped by trauma or fear.

In addition to cooperation I also discuss how officers assess the content and delivery of victims' stories, focusing on detail, consistency, and perceived truthfulness. These narrative features play a pivotal role in shaping perceptions of credibility, particularly in cases where officers have less evidence. As previous research has shown, officers' expectations for narrative clarity and emotional restraint are shaped by cultural norms which also informs the perception of an Ideal Victim, which may result in skepticism toward victims who do not conform to the expectations created by society (van Doorn & Koster, 2019; Mancini & Pickett, 2017).

Attitudes Toward Victimization

Researchers have highlighted that victims of violent crime face many barriers when seeking help from the police. For example, studies show that domestic violence victims and male victims of violent crime often face stigmatization (Ambrozewicz et al., 2024; Mancini & Pickett, 2017; Overstreet & Quinn, 2016), which may contribute to them not wanting to identify as a victim to the police. Mancini and Pickett (2017) specifically found that societal expectations often discourage men from self-identifying as victims reinforcing the idea that there is a gendered difference in victim acknowledgment. Men are often subjected to a set of normative expectations aligning with hegemonic masculinity stigmatizing behavior or experiences that can be viewed as a sign of weakness such as being a victim (Burcar, 2013), which also aligns with the concepts of the Ideal Victim (Christie, 1986) where the Ideal Victim often is seen as someone who is weak. These perceptions could be internalized by male victims and could make them reluctant to claim their victim label since they are not identifying with their own perception of what a victims is.

The literature also highlights that there is a wide range of variability in victim acknowledgment which can be influenced by the victim-offender relationship. Van Doorn and Koster (2019) found that the nature of the relationship between the victim and the offender plays a significant role in how victims construct and communicate their narratives to police. When victims know the offender, such as in domestic cases, they may feel pressure to protect the offender, fear retaliation, or experience emotional conflict, all of which can lead to more ambiguous, hesitant, or shifting accounts. In contrast, when the offender is a stranger or acquaintance, as is often the case in non-domestic incidents, victims may feel less constrained by these relational dynamics and thus are able to provide clear, direct, and consistent narratives. However, the authors also highlight that the absence of a prior relationship can introduce complexity. Victims may be unsure how to interpret the incident, may lack a clear understanding of the offender's motives, or may feel less confident in labeling the event as a crime. This can result in variability in acknowledgment, some victims may acknowledge their victimization, while others may offer mixed or tentative responses, reflecting uncertainty about how to present their experience to the police. Since women tend to be victimized at higher rates in domestic violence incidents and men at higher rates in cases of stranger violence (Tapp & Coen, 2025), this contrast offers compelling analytical layers for examining how attitudes toward victimization influence both domestic and non-domestic incidents and how these attitudes may shape officers' perceptions of victims.

In this book, although officers mentioned victims' attitudes toward their victimizations as impacting credibility in both domestic and non-domestic battery cases, it was more prevalent in non-domestic batteries. Among the domestic and non-domestic cases, three general patterns emerged: acknowledgment, denial, and mixed responses. These attitudes were not solely defined by a binary "yes" or "no" response to whether victimization occurred, but also by the degree and clarity of information provided. Victims who acknowledged the victimization either proactively stated that they had been subjected to violence or responded affirmatively when asked by officers. For example, in Non-Domestic Case 14, the victim called 911 and explicitly stated they had been victimized. On scene, I observed the victim actively and willingly communicate this to the officers, reinforcing their acknowledgment of the incident. In other cases, when victims denied that a victimization had occurred, I observed that the victims did not volunteer any information about the incident. This was often expressed through either a refusal to answer officers' questions or direct denials when asked if they had been subjected to violence. For example, in Non-Domestic Case 21, the victim responded to the officer's questions by stating: "Nothing happened, I'm fine." Additionally, she repeatedly answered "No" when asked whether she had been hit or victimized. When victims expressed mixed attitudes toward their victimization, as observed in Non-Domestic Cases 6, 7, and 15, they neither clearly affirmed nor denied that violence had occurred when asked by officers. However, they did volunteer information about their experiences. In Non-Domestic Case 6, for example, I observed a victim telling the officer that she had been in an argument with another person on the street and that a violent encounter had taken place. This type of response, while not a direct acknowledgment, still provided officers with relevant details. On the other hand, reluctance could manifest in shifting narratives. For example in Non-Domestic Case 7, I observed a victim initially stating that there had been an argument between him and another individual at a party, suggesting some level of conflict or victimization, however, this acknowledgment was later downplayed or denied, illustrating how victims' accounts can evolve during interactions with police.

One reason for the variation in victim attitudes may be that some victims changed their stance toward their victimization over the course of the case process. For instance, although victims in Non-Domestic Cases 6 and 7 initially acknowledged being subjected to victimization during their 911 calls, I observed that they expressed mixed attitudes when officers arrived on scene. These inconsistencies between the 911 call and on scene behavior were often mentioned by officers during the post-scene interviews, particularly in discussions about victim credibility. When comparing victims' initial statements during the 911 call with my on-scene observations, three out of the four victims who acknowledged their victimization during the call later displayed mixed attitudes at the scene. This shift in attitude was significant to officers, especially in non-domestic cases where they have greater discretion. Officers for example frequently emphasized that when victims do not acknowledge that a victimization occurred, it becomes more difficult to determine whether a crime took place and to proceed with an investigation. The officers statements alluded to the role extra-legal factors can play, such as victim acknowledgment, in certain cases, especially if there is a limited amount of evidence (Alderden & Ullman, 2012; Farrell et al., 2014).

Among the 20 domestic cases, 13 victims acknowledged during the 911 call that they had been victimized, either by stating it to the dispatcher or by having a third-party call to 911 and state that the victim reported being victimized. In 11 of these cases, the victims continued to acknowledge that they had been victimized once the officers got on scene, and in two cases the victim changed their mind and did not acknowledge their victimization. In the other seven domestic cases, a third party or witness called and reported that they had heard or witnessed the victim being victimized, thus the victim could not acknowledge to the 911 dispatcher whether or not they had been victimized. Of the seven cases, four victims denied being victimized when officers got on scene and three victims acknowledged that they had been victimized. Out of the total 20 domestic cases, 15 were report-yielding cases and five were non-report yielding. Among the 15 report-yielding cases, 14 cases mentioned that victims acknowledged being victimized; of those 14 cases, 10 cases had victims that acknowledged their victimization both in the 911 call and on scene with the officers. Hence, there was a high rate of victims acknowledging their victimization consistently at various points across the case development in the domestic batteries.

Across the 14 non-domestic battery cases, eight victims acknowledged that a violent incident had occurred, two denied being subjected to violence, and three displayed mixed responses. Among the non-domestic cases that resulted in police reports, it was more common for victims to have acknowledged their victimization. In contrast, non-domestic cases without reports more frequently involved victims who denied or were mixed in their responses, which was both true for domestic and non-domestic cases. Thus, when comparing victims' attitudes across multiple data points in non-domestic cases, including the 911 call, on-scene observations, officer interviews, and police reports, there was a high level of consistency in cases where victims acknowledged their victimization. For example, in the non-domestic battery case, in all but one of these cases, the acknowledgment was reflected across all data sources. In contrast, among cases that did not result in police reports, officers more frequently referenced victims' attitudes toward their victimization, and there was greater variation in how these attitudes were described and interpreted.

Compared to the domestic cases, non-domestic battery cases displayed a slightly greater variability in victim acknowledgment, suggesting that victims in non-domestic contexts may feel less compelled to affirm their experiences. In both domestic and non-domestic incidents, a little more than 50% of cases maintained throughout the case development that they had been victimized. These findings could be linked to the complex role and impact prior relationship could have on victims' likelihood of acknowledging their victimization (van Doorn & Koster, 2019).

Cooperation

Cooperation is another perimeter that is often used when assessing victim credibility according to previous research (Ask, 2010; Bostaph et al., 2021; van Doorn & Koster, 2019). During my observations, I noted a clear divide between victims who willingly shared details about their experiences and victims who chose not to engage with officers. In the domestic cases, 15 out of 20 victims were willing to provide information. Additionally, willingness to speak to officers was more common in report-yielding cases compared to non-report domestic yielding cases. In officer interviews, 13 victims were described as cooperative which had a positive influence on their credibility, while 6 were noted as unwilling to share information. Among the 15 report-yielding domestic cases, officers described 11 victims' cooperation through detailed accounts of their experiences. In contrast, in four cases the victims displayed reluctance, which officers often interpreted as a barrier for the investigation.

In 9 of the 14 non-domestic cases, officers stated during post-scene interviews that victims' willingness to provide information positively influenced their perceptions of the victims' credibility. Conversely, in four cases, officers noted that victims' refusal to share information negatively impacted their credibility assessments. This contrast was particularly evident when comparing non-domestic cases that resulted in police reports with those that did not. As a result, report-yielding cases were more likely to involve victims whose willingness to engage was viewed positively by officers. In contrast, non-report-yielding cases more frequently involved victims whose lack of cooperation was interpreted as a credibility concern. These findings suggest that victim cooperation may not only shape officers' immediate perceptions but can also play a role in determining whether a case was formally documented.

An example of how victims' willingness to provide information can be seen in Non-Domestic Case 14. The 911 call log noted, "adv male subj that his friend owes money to push him," indicating that the victim reported being pushed by the suspect due to a financial dispute. On scene, I observed the male victim actively engaging with Officer Clark, offering detailed information about what happened, where it occurred, why it occurred, and identifying witnesses. I also heard the victim express his desire to file a sworn complaint, which he spent several minutes writing at the scene. During the post-scene interview, Officer Clark described the victim's cooperation and commitment to acknowledging the victimization, stating:

> He was adamant that he was pushed. He was very willing to write us a statement, which does not always happen. It doesn't usually happen. Usually, people…they won't write anything. So, he was very willing to talk and let us know that the incident did occur.

In the subsequent police report, Officer Clark gave a lengthy explanation of the victims' statements which convey the detailed nature of the story that I earlier observed the victim telling Officer Clark on the scene. Thus, the victim's willingness to speak with officers on scene provided the officer with detailed information that supported the investigation. My observational notes, the post-scene interview, and the police report all emphasized the role of victims' active engagement. In Non-Domestic Case 14, the victim explained his relationship with the suspect, the reason he was present at the scene, what transpired during the incident, and identified both the suspect and potential witnesses. His decision to write a sworn complaint further reflected his commitment to acknowledging the victimization and cooperating with the police.

However, this level of cooperation was not consistent across all cases. As mentioned, victims' willingness to provide information sometimes shifted during the incident response, particularly in non-domestic incidents. In report-yielding non-domestic cases, victims generally demonstrated consistent cooperation and provided information during the 911 call and again on scene, except in Non-Domestic Case 21. In that case, the female victim did not initiate the 911 call and the report came from a third party. During my ride-alongs, I observed that several victims were unwilling to speak with officers, something that was later confirmed in the officers' post-scene interviews and reflected in the police reports. In contrast, among the non-report-yielding cases, victims' cooperation was generally consistent, with two notable exceptions. In Non-Domestic Cases 6 and 15, both victims provided information during the 911 call but were unwilling to engage with officers once on scene. These shifts in cooperation highlight that initial willingness to report does not always translate into continued cooperation. Although more prominent in the non-domestic cases, the shift in cooperation was noted in both domestic and non-domestic cases. In several cases, victims initially acknowledged their victimization and provided information to the 911 dispatcher, as seen in the CAD logs, but later withheld details when speaking with officers on scene. For instance, in Non-Domestic Case 6, the 911 transcript noted: "comp adv a drunk female hit her 1 min ago. adv subj has also been hitting her boyfriend," indicating that the victim reported being assaulted. Yet, when Officer Lee asked the female victim what had happened, she responded, "it was just an argument, an altercation." This shift in narrative illustrates how some victims may retract or minimize their earlier statements which potentially could complicate officers' ability to assess credibility and determine investigative actions.

In both domestic and non-domestic cases, officers highlighted the importance of victims' cooperation on the scene. For example, in Domestic Case 24, Officer Torres stated: "she was open on the scene, she wasn't hiding anything, very open. Like, if I asked her a question she would answer without any hesitation." When asked to describe the victim's demeanor, Officer Torres immediately referenced the female victim's openness and willingness to engage with police. He was one of several officers who described domestic battery victims' willingness to provide information as a key component of their demeanor during the encounter. These statements reinforce the broader idea that cooperation is not only a source of information but also a signal of credibility that can shape officers' perceptions and actions. This pattern aligns with previous research, which demonstrates that police officers often interpret cooperation as a marker of credibility (Ask, 2010; Bostaph et al., 2021; van Doorn & Koster, 2019). Ask (2010) and Bostaph et al. (2021) found that officers are more likely to trust and formally document cases where victims are forthcoming and engaged. However, these studies also caution that a lack of cooperation may not always indicate deception or evasiveness. Trauma, fear of retaliation, distrust of law enforcement, or emotional exhaustion can inhibit victims' willingness to cooperate (Overstreet & Quinn, 2016; Bostaph et al., 2021). In my data, reluctance or shifts in cooperation were sometimes interpreted by officers as barriers to investigation or as signs of reduced credibility. For instance, Officer Jackson noted that a victim's reluctance to provide information made it difficult to perceive her as entirely credible. This tendency to relate reluctance with evasiveness is echoed in van Doorn and Koster (2019), who argue that officers may misinterpret trauma responses or protective behaviors as dishonesty.

When discussing victims' willingness to provide information, many officers attributed it to the victim being "fed up" with their situation, which in turn influenced their perception of the victim's credibility. In Domestic Case 30, Officer Williams stated: "Yes, I do. Because he, once again, called law enforcement, because he was just fed up with her putting her hands on him." In this example, the officer interpreted the male victim's decision to call the police as both a sign of frustration and a marker of credibility. The act of reaching out to law enforcement was seen not only as a motivation rooted in emotional exhaustion but also as evidence that the victim was genuinely seeking help. This interpretation aligns with Ideal Victim Theory (Christie, 1986; Strobl, 2004), which suggests that victims perceived cooperative and actively seeking assistance are more likely to be viewed as legitimate. Officer Williams' framing of the victim as "just fed up" positioned him closer to the Ideal Victim, someone blameless, vulnerable, and motivated by a desire for justice.

Truthfulness or Lying: Consistency, Exaggeration, and Details

When examining willingness to provide officers with information, it became clear that officers valued not only the act of sharing but also the quality and consistency of the information provided. Officers described evaluating the consistency of the story, whether information was being withheld, and whether the details conflicted, in both domestic and non-domestic cases. These aspects served as informal credibility markers, helping officers determine if the victim was being truthful and if the story "made sense" from their perspective. These elements were referenced across many cases and contributed to the foundation of officers' credibility assessments, reinforcing the idea that narrative coherence plays a central role in shaping perceptions. This evaluative process highlights how officers rely not only on the presence of cooperation but also on the quality of the information shared. A story that was detailed, internally consistent, and aligned with officers' expectations could be viewed as contributing to the victim's credibility. In contrast, vague or conflicting accounts could lead officers to question the legitimacy of the victimization. These findings reinforce the idea that credibility can be constructed, in part, through both behavioral cues and narrative coherence (Ask, 2010; Bostaph et al., 2021).

In Non-Domestic Case 28, Officer Williams noted: "I did not get any signs of any of the victims lying to me on scene. And I don't believe that any of them had any reason to be anything but truthful." Similarly, in Non-Domestic Case 8, Officer Thompson described the victim as not lying, which he believed reinforced her credibility. Thus, these statements reflect how some officers relied on perceived honesty as a key indicator of credibility, when victims' narratives aligned with officers' expectations and appeared sincere, they were more likely to be viewed as credible.

> I found her credible. In terms of her response, she seemed like she was telling the truth…So when people lie, or they're being untruthful, I think there are just some cues. There are some physiological cues that if you're really paying attention you can pick up, like if they're being untruthful, sometimes like they're kind of looking left to right, it is just kind of like an indication of deception. If they're not making eye contact, that could be also a sign of untruthfulness. So basically, just her nonverbal language. She was open, she was basically in our faces, which is consistent with somebody that would be truthful.

Similarly, in Domestic Case 4, I observed a female victim giving Officer Lee a lengthy account of how she had been attacked with a knife by her husband who had Alzheimer's and who had previously attacked her, causing the police to respond to their house. When I later asked Officer Lee during the interview if she thought the victim in Domestic Case 4 was credible, she said:

> Yes, because her story made sense. She gave the same version of events again. Like she usually if people only hear generalized statements, but usually someone's telling you the truth about what happened, you can ask them the same question just in several different forms, and you're pretty much always gonna get the same answer, they can repeat the same details over and over again, people aren't being truthful, that's hard for them to do. Sometimes they will tell you something, and then forget later that they said something, or they'll contradict themselves, because they're, you know, trying to make something up and people can't often remember every inch that they make up. So, everything that she said was consistent evidence and her injury was consistent with what she said happened. And there didn't seem to be anything that I saw, as far as indicators that would give her a motivation to make something up. She wouldn't have benefited from that.

According to Officer Lee, she assessed the victim's truthfulness by noting that she was not exhibiting behaviors that, in her view, indicated deception. This behavioral evaluation, based on demeanor rather than evidence, was a recurring method some officers used to determine credibility. Although truthfulness was emphasized in most cases, the notion of lying was also explicitly mentioned by officers. In several interviews, officers described being alert to signs of dishonesty, such as conflicting details, evasiveness, or emotional disconnect. These assessments were often subjective, yet they played a central role in shaping how officers interpreted the credibility of the victim's account. For example, in Non-Domestic Case 5, Officer Moore explained:

> I think she was withholding a lot of information, though, that she was lying to me in the sense that she wasn't telling me the entire truth. She was withholding a lot of information… I think that was true with some of it. I don't think that she was truthful in the sense that it was just a verbal altercation. I think something physical did occur, and she was holding that back.

According to Officer Moore, she was not fully convinced that the female victim was being truthful or forthcoming, suggesting the victim may have had something to hide. Despite this suspicion, Officer Moore acknowledged that certain aspects of the victim's statements still could be true. However, the possibility that the victim was lying or withholding information influenced how she overall perceived the victim. Another officer, Officer Adams, who also was on scene during Domestic Case 4, further explained that body language and the consistency of the story were key factors in his credibility assessment. He noted that when a story is inconsistent, it could be a sign that the victim is lying. He stated:

> So sometimes when people either lie or whatever, their body movements become a little bit different. I mean, I'll only interview him one time, so I really can't say any…like, I really think about any inconsistencies in his story. But like what I say is, it's like…I really had to do too much digging on something like this because of that off the ground.

For Officer Adams, the inconsistencies in the victim's story were a critical tool in determining whether she was lying. To assess this, he looked for discrepancies in the events and details provided. In this specific case, he stated that the absence of inconsistencies contributed to the victim's credibility and served as an indicator that she was not lying. Officers in this study frequently relied on the consistency and detail of victims' accounts as informal markers of truthfulness. This approach is supported by Ask (2010) and Bostaph et al. (2021), who found that police officers often equate narrative coherence and the ability to repeat details with credibility. However, Officer Adams also acknowledged the difficulty of making such assessments based on a single interaction. He noted that because he only spoke to the domestic battery victim once, it was harder to determine whether her statements were consistent over time.

Two other aspects officers described considering when evaluating victims' credibility were potential exaggeration and the level of detail provided. When discussing exaggeration, officers noted during interviews, that their perception of a victim's credibility was positively influenced when they believed the victim did not exaggerate parts of the story or its details. The absence of embellishment was interpreted as a sign of honesty and emotional restraint, which officers associated with truthful reporting. For example, in Domestic Case 2, I observed a male victim who came to the police station to report being beaten with a stick by his former sexual partner. The victim gave an in-depth description of the nature of their relationship, stating that the suspect and he had "hooked up for three months several months ago" but that since then there had been nothing romantical between them. In the following interview Officer Willson told me that since the victim did not exaggerate the prior history between him and the suspect or their relationship as something that contributed to him perceiving the victim as credible:

> He could have exaggerated the relationship. He didn't exaggerate anything about their prior dealings. He mentioned the State Attorney's Office numerous times. So, he's hopeful that what he says is getting through to us and that we are going to start taking it seriously.

In another example, in Domestic Case 29, Officer Green highlighted the fact that the female victim did not exaggerate any of the injuries as something that influenced his perception of the victim's credibility:

> There was no…she didn't seem to make any outlandish claims. She didn't exaggerate. When we asked. At first, we thought he had choked recently. No, don't choke me. So, she didn't claim any injuries. A lot of times when people are exaggerating. It's fairly obvious. The claims are a bit outlandish.

In these two examples, victims' lack of exaggeration was something that, according to the officers, positively influenced their perception of the victims' credibility and indicated that the victims were not lying. Mancini and Pickett (2017) found that exaggeration is frequently interpreted by officers as a sign of dishonesty. However, their research also suggests that some victims may exaggerate details in an effort to be believed, especially if they anticipate skepticism or dismissal from law enforcement.

Details were similarly used by officers as a tool to assess the domestic battery victims' story as a potential indicator of not being truthful. For example, in Domestic Case 1, Officer Moore stated that victims who are not lying "can repeat the same details over and over again, people aren't being truthful, that's hard for them to do." According to her, the female victim's ability to repeat details contributed positively to her overall perception of the victim and her credibility. When discussing the positive influence of detail, several officers noted that when victims described elements such as where suspects lived or what they looked like added rigor to their account and enhanced credibility. For example, in Non-Domestic Case 26, when asked how he assessed the victim's credibility, Officer Williams stated: "...they were able to describe the apartment where the other true victim of this juvenile gang lives... So I do believe that she's very credible." This statement illustrates how the presence of concrete, verifiable details can serve as a marker of truthfulness in officers' assessments. It also suggests that specificity in storytelling may function as a form of evidence, reinforcing the credibility of the victim's account. Additionally, in Non-Domestic Case 8 Officer Thompson said:

> The story that she told me in the way that she explained it, she was very...to remember details, descriptions too were very strict to the point as to what happened. And then we had to coax much out over as far as the facts of the case or anything like that. So, she knew exactly where he stayed. I'd say she described him to a tee even to the color of his hair. So that made her very credible in my mind.

In both cases, Officers Williams and Thompson attributed significant value to the non-domestic battery victims' ability to provide details. They noted that it was not only the subject matter of the details that supported their investigation, but also that the presence of detail enhanced the victims' credibility. The specificity offered by the victims was interpreted as a sign of truthfulness and reliability, reinforcing the officers' confidence in their accounts.

However, while the ability to provide details had a positive influence in certain cases, there were also instances where the lack of detail negatively impacted officers' perceptions. In Non-Domestic Case 15, I observed that the female victim was not forthcoming with information about the incident, offering limited responses to the officer's questions. In the interview, Officer Clark described how this lack of detail contributed to shaping his view of the victim's credibility. The absence of specific information made it more difficult for him to assess the credibility of her account, suggesting that minimal disclosure may be interpreted as evasiveness or uncertainty.

> She was I guess distant she really wouldn't tell me much of what happened. The only thing that she said for sure she got hit in the head. She did not know by who, by what, or where she got hit in relation to where she was in the city. Yes, it's very hard to trust what she was telling me.

According to Officer Clark, the lack of details made him second guess the victim. Specifically, the lack of details made him suspect that the victim was not fully forthcoming, which made it more difficult for Officer Clark to trust what the victim said. Similarly, in Non-Domestic Case 6, I observed that the female victim did not give an extensive amount of detail in the answers she provided to Officer Lee about what she had experienced. In the interview Officer Lee noted that the lack of information influenced her way of assessing the victim's version of the story:

> I don't have enough information… Even talking to her like she didn't say anything about the incident at all, she seems more concerned that the girl (suspect) was talking to her for 10 seconds…knowing absolutely nothing else about that case. It makes me wonder if she and the girl just got into it. And then she decided to say something. I'm not saying what did happen or what didn't. But for her to call to report a battery or somebody in her…and then only give one line to describe the battery.

However, Overstreet and Quinn (2016) caution that trauma can disrupt memory and narrative clarity, meaning that victims who struggle to provide consistent or detailed accounts may be unfairly doubted. This was evident in several cases where officers interpreted vagueness or inconsistency as possible deception, even though such behaviors may reflect psychological distress rather than dishonesty.

Conclusion

Across both domestic and non-domestic cases, officers consistently assessed victim credibility through a combination of behavioral cues, narrative consistency, and the presence or absence of detail. Officer Thompson emphasized the absence of deceptive behavior, while Officer Moore expressed uncertainty about the victim's honesty, noting that even partial truth could coexist with perceived dishonesty. Officer Adams highlighted the importance of body language and consistency, stating that the lack of inconsistencies supported the victim's credibility, though he acknowledged the limitations of single interactions. Detail rich accounts, such as those described by Officers Williams and Thompson, were seen as enhancing credibility, whereas a lack of detail, as observed by Officer Clark, diminished it. Additionally, officers viewed the absence of exaggeration as a positive indicator of truthfulness, as illustrated in Domestic Case 2, where a male victim's specific account of his relationship with the suspect contributed to how officers viewed his credibility. Overall, the findings suggest that some officers rely on a nuanced mix of verbal and nonverbal indicators when evaluating victim accounts.

The reliance on consistency, detail, and the absence of exaggeration as markers of truthfulness in officers' assessments is well documented in previous research (Ask, 2010; Bostaph et al., 2021). However, Overstreet and Quinn (2016) and van Doorn and Koster (2019) note that trauma can disrupt memory and narrative coherence, meaning that victims who struggle to provide consistent or detailed accounts may be doubted by officers, even though they are being truthful. Officers' expectations for narrative clarity and emotional restraint could be argued to be shaped by cultural norms similar to ones listed by the Christie (1986) and Strobl (2004) about how victims should behave (van Doorn & Koster, 2019), which may result in skepticism toward victims who do not conform to these expectations. Victims who provided coherent and detailed accounts could more likely be perceived as credible. For example, Officer Adams emphasized consistency and body language, while Officers Williams and Thompson valued specific details that supported both investigative rigor and perceived truthfulness. The absence of exaggeration, as seen in Domestic Case 2, further reinforced credibility, suggesting that victims who avoid dramatization are viewed more favorably. These traits can potentially mirror the Ideal Victim as someone who is strong but not too strong in their claims of the victim label exaggerating or lying about their experiences.

Conversely, victims who failed to meet these expectations could be viewed with skepticism. Officer Clark, for instance, questioned the credibility of a female victim in Non-Domestic Case 15 due to her lack of detailed responses, while Officer Moore expressed doubt when a female victim appeared emotionally uncertain. These examples show how credibility assessments are not solely based on factual accuracy but are deeply influenced by whether victims conform to socially constructed norms of how a victim should behave according to officers. Those who deviate from the expected script, whether through emotional expression, limited disclosure, or perceived inconsistency, risk being viewed as not credible or less credible.

The findings in this chapter also show how officers' assessments of victim credibility are shaped not only by individual behaviors, such as consistency, detail, and emotional restraint, but also by the broader context in which the battery occurs. Domestic and non-domestic battery cases present distinct challenges, particularly due to the relational aspect inherent in domestic violence. In domestic cases, the presence of an ongoing or prior intimate relationship introduces emotional complexity, potential power imbalances, and heightened vulnerability. These dynamics can influence how victims present themselves and how officers interpret their credibility. For instance, in Domestic Case 2, the male victim's account of his past relationship with the suspect was seen as credible, suggesting that officers may expect a certain level of emotional control even in highly personal contexts. In contrast, non-domestic battery cases, such as those involving strangers or acquaintances, tend to be evaluated with a slightly different lens. Officers tended to place greater emphasis on the clarity and detail of the incident itself. In this study, the absence of a relational history made officers focus on the immediate facts, as seen in cases where victims' ability to provide specific details directly enhanced their perceived credibility. However, this also means that victims who fail to offer detailed accounts, like in Non-Domestic Case 15, may be viewed with greater skepticism. These differences can be further impacted by varying legal responses and departmental policies. Domestic violence cases often trigger mandatory arrest policies, specialized units, and victim advocacy protocols, which can shape officer expectations and investigative priorities. Non-domestic cases, lacking these structural supports, may rely more heavily on the officer's discretion and interpretation of credibility. Together, these findings highlight how relational context, legal frameworks, and institutional practices intersect to produce distinct patterns in how domestic and non-domestic battery victims are perceived and treated.

Overall, in this chapter I have highlighted the complex interplay between victim behavior and officer perception in both domestic and non-domestic battery cases. The findings reveal how officers interpret these elements not only as indicators of credibility but also in some cases as determinants of procedural action. Victims' acknowledgment, denial, or mixed responses to their victimization were shown to significantly influence officers' assessments, particularly in non-domestic cases where they have more discretion. Cooperation, especially the willingness to provide information, emerged as a central factor shaping officers' perceptions of credibility. Moreover, I discussed how officers evaluate the content and delivery of victims' stories, with detail, truthfulness, and narrative coherence serving as key markers of credibility.

References

Alderden, M. A., & Ullman, S. E. (2012). Creating a more complete and current picture: Examining police and prosecutor decision-making when processing sexual assault cases. *Violence Against Women, 18*, 525–551. https://doi.org/10.1177/1077801212453867

Ambrozewicz, P., Hammond, C., & Fido, D. (2024). Ending the stigma of male domestic violence and abuse victims: A mixed-methods study. *Journal of Criminal Justice, 93*, 102222. https://doi.org/10.1016/j.jcrimjus.2024.102222

Ask, K. (2010). A survey of police officers' and prosecutors' beliefs about crime victim behaviors. *Journal of Interpersonal Violence, 25*(6), 1132–1149. https://doi.org/10.1177/0886260509340535

Bostaph, L. G., King, L. L., & Brady, P. Q. (2021). How victim credibility and cooperation influence investigative decision-making: examining DOJ's gender bias principles for investigating domestic and sexual violence. *Policing: An International Journal, 44*(4), 612–627. https://doi.org/10.1108/PIJPSM-02-2021-0018

Burcar, V. (2013). Doing masculinity in narratives about reporting violent crime: Young male victims talk about contacting and encountering the police. *Journal of Youth Studies, 16*(2), 172–190. https://doi.org/10.1080/13676261.2012.704992

Christie, N. (1986). The ideal victim. In E. Fattah (Ed.), *From crime policy to victim policy* (pp. 17–30). Palgrave Macmillan. https://doi.org/10.1007/978-1-349-08305-3_2

Farrell, A., Owens, C., & McDevitt, J. (2014). New laws but few cases: Understanding the challenges to the investigation and prosecution of human trafficking cases. *Crime, Law and Social Change, 61*, 139–168. https://doi.org/10.1007/s10611-013-9442-1

Mancini, C., & Pickett, J. T. (2017). Reaping what they sow? Victim-offender overlap perceptions and victim blaming attitudes. *Victims & Offenders, 12*(3), 434–466. https://doi.org/10.1080/15564886.2015.1093051

Overstreet, N. M., & Quinn, D. M. (2016). The intimate partner violence stigmatization model and barriers to help seeking. In *Social psychological perspectives on Stigma* (pp. 109–122). Routledge.

Strobl, R. (2004). Constructing the victim: Theoretical reflections and empirical examples. *International Review of Victimology, 11*(2–3), 295–311. https://doi.org/10.1177/026975800401100206

Tapp, S. N., & Coen, E. J. (2025). *Criminal victimization, 2024.* Bureau of Justice Statistics. https://bjs.ojp.gov/document/cv24.pdf

van Doorn, J., & Koster, N. N. (2019). Emotional victims and the impact on credibility: A systematic review. *Aggression and Violent Behavior, 47*, 74–89. https://doi.org/10.1016/j.avb.2019.03.007

7

Corroboration

Introduction

In addition to speaking with the parties involved in the potential crime, officers attempt to gather evidence that supports the accounts given by victims or suspects. For example, this evidence may include photographs of injuries, physical evidence, injuries, witness interviews, or documentation of admissions made by the potential suspect (Ellison, 2002). Thus, corroboration is a central element in criminal investigations. It can shape how officers, prosecutors, and courts evaluate the credibility of victims and the reliability of their accounts (Maguire, 2012). In certain types of crime, especially domestic violence, corroboration often depends on the victim's statements, hence in cases where victims do not provide a statement and there is a lack of corroborating evidence, officers or prosecutors may have to "drop" the case and not pursue charges(Ellison, 2002; Phillips & de Roos, 2025). Previous research has shown that physical evidence, especially elements such as injuries or the use of weapons, influences the level of involvement police officers have in an incident, particularly in domestic violence cases. Jasinski (2003) found that the presence of injuries doubles the likelihood of police officers being called to the scene and increases the

M. N. Eliasson, *Who Gets Believed?*, Palgrave's Critical Policing Studies,
https://doi.org/10.1007/978-3-032-22253-4_7

chances of an arrest. The author also found that the history between the parties plays a role in officers' involvement with first time incidents being more likely to result in police intervention compared to cases of repeated violence.

Evidence is not only important for the decisions officers make or for case outcomes, but also a crucial part of how officers assess victim credibility, especially in cases of interpersonal violence (El Sayed et al., 2022). For example, photographs of injuries and the history between the parties can help strengthen the victim's credibility (El Sayed et al., 2022; Epstein & Goodman, 2019). However, scholars have also found variation in how different officers value evidence. For example, El Sayed et al. (2022) found that male officers consider physical evidence more important for assessing credibility than female officers. Male officers also view alcohol and drug use, involvement in illegal activities, and a previous criminal record as more influential on a victim's credibility compared to female officers.

Despite the importance of evidence, physical evidence is often limited in many cases, especially in cases involving domestic violence. Studies show that victims of domestic violence frequently lack access to items such as photographs or medical records often due to limited resources, the emotional difficulty of preserving such evidence, or the absence of legal guidance (Epstein & Goodman, 2019). These limitations make it more challenging for police to investigate cases where the victim is also not cooperating, as officers must then rely more heavily on physical evidence (Ellison, 2002).

In this book, the presence or absence of corroborating evidence such as physical traces, witness statements, or admissions by suspects influenced officers' perceptions of victim credibility. More specifically, when victims' accounts were supported by external evidence such as physical evidence or witness testimony, their perceived credibility increased. In contrast, the lack of corroborating evidence could, in some cases, negatively affect how credible victims appeared to officers. Officers also described differences in the types of corroborating factors they considered in domestic versus non-domestic cases. In non-domestic cases, corroboration often involved elements such as physical evidence or third-party witnesses. In contrast, domestic cases, which frequently occur in private settings, were less likely to produce such forms of evidence. As a result, officers sometimes relied on alternative indicators when evaluating credibility.

Below I examine the corroborating factors that officers identified as influencing their perceptions of victim credibility. I explore the types of evidence most frequently cited, the role of witnesses and suspect admissions, and the impact of prior history and injuries. By integrating insights from the Ideal Victim Theory (Christie, 1986; Strobl, 2004) with empirical findings, I highlight the complex relationship between evidence and police discretion in shaping how victim credibility is assessed.

Evidence

There are many different types of evidence, such as photos or videos obtained by victims or witnesses, surveillance footage , or weapons, that can be relevant for officers investigating batteries. During my time in the field, officers mentioned how evidence influenced victims' credibility in 6 of the 20 domestic cases. It was described as having a positive influence in four cases, a negative influence in one case, and both positive and negative influences by two different officers in one case. Evidence was also discussed in 10 of the non-domestic cases. In those, it was considered to positively influence victims' credibility in six cases, including three non-report cases and three report-yielding cases. It was described as having a negative influence in two report-yielding cases, and in one case, two officers each highlighted both a positive and a negative aspect.

In the four domestic cases where officers described evidence as a positive influence, they noted that its presence could strengthen the credibility of the victim by suggesting that a violent altercation had occurred and by confirming the victim's account. For instance, in Domestic Case 4, when asked whether he thought the victim was credible, the officer stated: "Yes, she did have some scarring, a little like a carpet burns just like she fell on the ground and in the house…there was a little bit of carpet in there." In this case, the environment where the victimization occurred showed signs of a struggle, as the carpet was out of place. The officer also noted that the carpet burns the female victim sustained matched the carpet found in the house. According to him, the presence of the carpet corroborated the injuries and supported the victim's version of events which positively influenced his perception of her credibility because they aligned with and reinforced her account of the incident.

In two other cases, the same officer described evidence as supporting victims' claims that no victimization had taken place, which influenced his perception of their credibility. In Domestic Case 16, I observed the two officersstanding outside the door of an apartment. They quietly leaned into the door and appeared to be listening. After approximately two to three minutes, Officer Willson, the primary officer, knocked on the door. A female opened the door and looked at Officer Willson, who asked whether she was alone in the apartment and if there had been a fight. The female stated that she was alone and explained that she had been crying because her grandmother had passed away. She also mentioned that she had been trying to hang a picture on the wall and had been hammering, which may have caused the noise. When she asked, "who called the cops?" the officers responded that it was someone in the building, to which she replied, "this is not the first time she has done that." In the follow-up interview, Officer Willson explained: "we listened to for a minute outside the door, didn't hear a single thing. The sound that the neighbor called for could have been her breaking something and learning of the news." In this case, the officer interpreted the absence of audible disturbance and the victim's explanation as consistent with a non-violent scenario. The environmental cues and timing of events were viewed as aligning with the victim's account, which, according to Officer Willson, contributed to his perception that her claim of no victimization was credible.

In another case, Domestic Case 32, I observed the same officer responding to a call from third-party stating that a man had been attacked by a Black female by pouring bleach in his eyes. When driving over to the victim's residence, the officer told me that he had been to the house several times before and that the victim had been in altercations with a female previously causing a no contact order between the two. When arriving on scene I observed the officer knocking on the door to the apartment, inside the apartment a male was sitting on the floor. Officer Willson asked the man how he was doing and what happened. The victim replied to the officers by stating "nothing has happened, I am fine" to which the officers stated that he had a call from a third-party stating the victim "got bleached poured in his eyes." The victim shook his head and again said that he was fine. In the interview Officer Willson then told me: "There was no evidence to what was described in the alleged assault, which would have been bleached to his eyes...and there was no aroma of bleach in the house." For Officer Willson the lack of evidence supporting the occurrence of victimization became a factor that contributed to his perception of the two alleged victims as credible. Specifically, Willson argued that the lack of evidence was something that strengthened the victims' credibility, because it corroborated their statements. Although victimizations still could have occurred despite victims' claims, the officer's statements in these two cases indicated that credibility can be assessed separately from the probable cause of a crime and that police perceptions of victims' credibility is relevant not only when aiming determining that a crime occurred, but also when concluding that a crime did not occur.

In Domestic Case 33, the two officers working the case had differing perceptions of both the victim and the presence of evidence, which ultimately influenced their assessments of her credibility. At the scene, I observed the female victim telling officers that she had been attacked by her boyfriend and that her foot had gone through the window. The window appeared to be broken, with visible cracks and broken pieces of glass scattered on the carpet below. In the interview, the primary officer, Officer Garcia, stated that he believed the victim was credible because of "the evidence that was presented inside the actual apartment where the incident allegedly took place." In contrast, Officer Mitchell, who was also present at the scene, expressed uncertainty about the victim's credibility, explaining that he "did not see any evidence." These differing interpretations of the physical environment suggest that officers can assess the same scene in different ways, which can lead to conflicting views of victim credibility. Officer Garcia's perception was shaped by the broken window, which he interpreted as corroborating the victim's account. Officer Mitchell, however, did not identify any evidence that supported her claims, leading to a more skeptical view. These differences not only influenced their individual assessments but also had implications for how the incident was documented. In this case, Officer Garcia wrote the police report and included a description of the broken window, stating: "The DEF shoved the VIC with such force that the VIC's leg kicked out from underneath her and ended up smashing the window in the bedroom." While the presence of physical evidence may be interpreted as corroborative by Officer Garcia who ultimately wrote the police report, its absence, or lack of recognition, by another, in this example, Officer Mitchell, can lead to contrasting conclusions. If Officer Mitchell had written the report, the explanation of the incident could have potentially excluded a description of the broken window since he did not acknowledge it as evidence of the incident. This omission could have impacted how the prosecutor evaluated the case when reviewing the police report, as the presence or absence of physical evidence in police report can inform prosecutorial decisions (Ellison, 2002; Phillips & de Roos, 2025). In three domestic cases, evidence was not brought up by officers as influencing their perception of victims' credibility during interviews, yet it was mentioned in the corresponding police reports. In those reports, officers focused on describing the presence of evidence primarily as supporting probable cause for the crime, rather than as a factor in assessing victim credibility. In the three reports, the officers wrote:

> Dispatch advised that a female attempted to give the address before the phone call was abruptly ended. Dispatch attempted to call (Name redacted) [VIC] back several times with no answer. This is consistent with (Name redacted) [VIC] `s account of (name redacted) [SUSP] taking her phone when she attempted to call for help. (Domestic Case 17, Officer Lewis)

> After searching the residence we observed the firearm inside a compartment built on the refrigerator inside the kitchen. The firearm located was also silver. (Domestic Case 19, Officer Robinson)

> (Name redacted) [SUSP] did have a napkin with blood on it and there was fresh blood on the inner rim of his right nostril. (Domestic Case 20, Officer Thompson)

Based on these findings, evidence could be argued to have a nuanced role and meaning in both the investigation and in shaping perceptions of victim credibility, as illustrated in Domestic Case 18. While on scene, I observed a female telling Officer Walker that she had gotten into a fight with her boyfriend, who had come home intoxicated. When I later asked whether he thought the victim was credible, Officer Walker responded: "I can say so…I mean, and also, there's no evidence that proves otherwise." However, in the corresponding police report, he noted: "No unbiased witness or additional evidence was found," and indicated an acknowledgment that there were no independent witnesses who could corroborate the victim's story. He also wrote that because of the absence of supporting evidence, he "did not develop probable cause for a crime." This case highlights how an officer may perceive a victim as credible yet still was not able to conclude if the victimization did occur due to the lack of corroborating evidence or witnesses. According to Officer Walker, the absence of evidence did not discredit the victim's narrative, but it did limit the procedural steps he could take in response to the incident.

In some of the non-domestic cases, evidence was discussed in relation to surveillance footage that could potentially corroborate the events of the incident or the story told by the victim. Surveillance footage was one of the more commonly referenced types of corroborating evidence in these cases. Notably, evidence gathered through surveillance or other forms was not mentioned by officers during interviews in any of the non-report-yielding cases. However, it was discussed in half of the report-yielding non-domestic cases. In those instances, officers described surveillance footage as having a positive effect on their perception of victim credibility in two cases, and a negative effect in one case. Moreover, the way evidence was described in the police reports for these three cases corresponded with how it was depicted in the interviews, suggesting some consistency between officers' verbal accounts and their written documentation. In Non-Domestic Case 12, a female victim reported being attacked by a customer at the restaurant where she worked. I observed the officer reviewing surveillance footage that had captured the incident. In the interview, Officer Thompson explained that the video confirmed the victim's account, which contributed to his perception of her credibility. He stated: "She explained her version of the incident in very detail…her place of employment had video surveillance because then the video surveillance confirmed her version of the incident." In this case, the officer interpreted the alignment between the victim's detailed narrative and the surveillance footage as reinforcing her credibility. The presence of video evidence served not only to document the incident but also to validate the victim's account in the eyes of the responding officer. In the subsequent police report, he described the impact of the surveillance:

> Surveillance footage from the establishment confirmed (Name redacted) [VIC]`s version of the incident. The surveillance footage showed (name redacted) [WIT 3] at the register asking for the refund. All parties (name redacted) [WIT 1, WIT 2, WIT 3.] then move to the front and exit the store. The video then showed (Name redacted) [VIC] standing at the front door and everyone entering back to (name redacted). Afterwards, it shows and (name redacted) [WIT 1] having a discussion when (name redacted) [WIT 1] "flicks" her finger at (Name redacted) [VIC] and exits the store. The video then showed (name redacted) [SUSP] entering from the (name redacted) side and engaging (Name redacted) [VIC]. The video shows (name redacted) [SUSP] closing the gap between her and while pointing her fingers in what appears to be a forceful motion. The video then shows (name redacted) [SUSP] "chest bumping" (Name redacted) [VIC] as she backs away due to the contact. The surveillance video did not have audio.

Thus, in Non-Domestic Case 12, the presence of surveillance footage confirming the incident was something that Officer Thompson explained impacted his perception of the victim's credibility because it validated and corroborated the statements she made. In the police report, Officer Thompson described the victim's version of the incident and was then able to detail how the incident appeared on the video. In another case, Non-Domestic Case 23, both officers explained that the video footage increased the female victim's credibility, even though the footage did not fully align with the victim's account. When asked whether he believed the victim was credible, the primary officer, Officer Clark, stated: "I do, mainly because we saw the video. On first interaction, the way that she described the physical aspect, I consider to be more than what actually happened on the video. But yes." Although Officer Clark noted that the incident may not have been as severe as the victim described, he still viewed the surveillance footage as lending credibility to her account. Hence, officers may interpret partial corroboration, where the evidence supports the occurrence of an incident but not necessarily its severity, as sufficient to positively influence their perception of victim credibility. In the following report he wrote:

> (Video) shows the verbal altercation between the two, with the older trying to get the younger to leave the area. At one point the older W/F got in between the two and put her arms out to separate the pair. I could see no intent of battery in the action. [Store name redacted] will retain the video if needed.

Thus, the video became a tool for the officer to evaluate the victim's credibility, even though it did not fully confirm the victim's account. In both examples, the presence of surveillance footage acted as a positive influence on the victims' credibility because it confirmed either the full story or key elements of it.

In the third case, Non-Domestic Case 10, there was no video footage available, which Officer Willson noted during the interview and in the police report, made the investigation more challenging. The absence of surveillance footage in this case was framed not as undermining the victim's credibility, but as a limitation in the ability to corroborate the account and establish probable cause. This contrasts with the previous cases, where the presence of video evidence served to reinforce officers' perceptions of credibility. Here, the lack of such evidence introduced uncertainty, highlighting how the availability, or absence, of surveillance can shape the investigative process and the framing of incidents in reports. In the police report Officer Willson wrote:

> I canvassed the (Store name) redacted for video surveillance footage. At this time I do not have any suspect information to proceed with criminal charges. I provided a GPD case report, report request form, and victims' rights brochure to (name redacted) [VIC] The store cameras only pick up views that involve the building. I do not have an exact location of the incident to begin a search for footage.

After meeting with the male victim, I observed Officer Willson drive to the store to locate potential witnesses and determine whether any video footage existed. Upon entering the store, he asked the clerk whether the store's camera faced the parking lot. The clerk responded "No" as we exited the store, Officer Willson told me that this meant there was no video footage of the incident. He explained that he felt his attempt to locate surveillance video demonstrated that he had "at least tried to investigate this, despite knowing that many officers probably would not follow up on a case with this little information." He went on to say that the reason he made the extra effort was because he enjoyed investigating and hoped to become a detective one day. As such, he wanted to ensure he practiced his investigative skills. Officer Willson's actions suggest that individual motivation and professional aspirations may influence the extent to which officers pursue corroborating evidence, even in cases with limited initial information.

Although the presence or absence of surveillance footage was discussed in the three non-domestic cases outlined above, it was not mentioned in most of the other cases. The majority of cases did not involve any surveillance footage, which may have influenced officers' likelihood of bringing it up during interviews. Specifically, officers did not discuss the importance of surveillance when it was not available. Despite this, the examples presented in this section highlight that when surveillance does exist, it can influence how officers perceive victim credibility, particularly when it corroborates all or part of a victim's account. These cases suggest that surveillance footage, when present, may serve as a conditional tool for validating victim narratives and shaping investigative outcomes.

Overall, the presence or absence of evidence held multiple meanings for officers, particularly in how it related to victim credibility which supports previous research (El Sayed et al., 2020; Epstein & Goodman, 2019). Evidence could strengthen victims' credibility by corroborating their accounts. However, it did not automatically lead to a determination of probable cause. As seen in Domestic Case 18, although there was no evidence that discredited the victim's statement, the officer noted in the report that there was not enough evidence to establish probable cause for a crime. This suggests that evidence may serve one function in shaping perceptions of credibility, and another in guiding decisions about whether a legal threshold, such as probable cause, has been met. The distinction highlights how officers may separate their belief in a victim's account from the procedural requirements necessary to move a case forward. However, as highlighted in previous scholarship, many cases in this study, especially domestic violence cases, did not have a lot of evidence such as photos to corroborate the stories which makes it more challenging for officers when investigating, and thus leave them to rely on other aspects of the case to prove whether or not a crime occurred (Ellison, 2002; Epstein & Goodman, 2019).

Witnesses

When discussing forms of corroboration, one of the central aspects brought up by officers was the presence and cooperation of witnesses. At every scene I observed all officers, per GPD policy, asking victims if there were any witnesses. I also discovered that while witnesses may be present during incidents, officers placed significant emphasis on whether those witnesses chose to cooperate. For example, even if a witness was physically present and may have observed the victimization, they could still opt not to participate in the investigation, either by expressing a desire to avoid involvement or by claiming they did not witness the incident. In some cases, this may have reflected genuine non-observation, meaning the witness was cooperating by honestly stating they had not seen the event.

During my time in the field, I observed that the witnesses who did not cooperate often were vocal about their refusal to participate. Among the cases that involved witnesses, cooperation emerged as a key factor in whether their accounts were used to corroborate the victim's story. This suggests that the mere presence of a witness does not automatically translate into usable evidence, rather, it is the willingness to engage with the investigative process that determines whether a witness can serve as a source of corroboration.

In half of the 14 non-domestic cases, officers mentioned that the absence or presence of witnesses was something that impacted victims' credibility. In four cases, it was discussed as positive and in three cases it was discussed as negative during the interviews. Among the seven cases that it was not brought up by officers, three cases had no witnesses, three cases had witnesses that were not cooperating and one case had a witness that was cooperating. Additionally, officers talked about it as a positive influence in three cases and as a negative influence in one case among the non-report cases and positive in one report-yielding case, and negative in one report-yielding case. Thus, when comparing the cases with reports to the cases with no reports, the impact witnesses had on the victims' credibility was brought up more as a positive more often among the non-report-yielding cases. When comparing how witnesses to non-domestic batteries were observed on the scene, depicted in the interviews and police reports, the findings show that witnesses were only brought up in two of the interviews, however, in the police reports it was mentioned in all cases except for one.

In the domestic cases, witnesses were not mentioned to the same extent as in the non-domestic cases. Specifically, in the domestic cases, the presence of witnesses was mentioned in a positive way in five of the 20 cases by officers during the interview and in only one for these cases was it also mentioned in the police report. Out of the 15 cases where it was not mentioned by officers in the interview, it was mentioned in three police reports which discussed as a positive aspect, a negative aspect and one was mentioned in a neutral manner.

Hence, overall, witnesses were mentioned more frequently in non-domestic cases compared to domestic cases. When they were mentioned, it was most often in reference to a positive influence on victim credibility. During the ride-alongs, most officers emphasized that witnesses contributed not only from an evidentiary standpoint but also served as a mechanism to validate and corroborate the victim's account. For instance, in Domestic Case, Officer Thompson stated: "A witness told me what had happened. Other than the victims, so I believe that the victim was credible because someone completely unrelated and uninvolved also told me what had happened." However, other officers clarified that it was not simply the presence or absence of witnesses that shaped their perceptions of credibility, but also the nature of the witness. Many officers highlighted the value of independent witnesses, those perceived as having no personal stake in the outcome, as particularly influential in enhancing victim credibility. For example, in Non-Domestic Case 8, Officer Thompson explained:

> "Her (victim) child is old enough to be able to have independent thought and not be caught by her. And his version of the incident, speaking separately from her, did match what she was saying."

Another officer similarly emphasized the importance of independent witnesses, noting that such individuals had no alternative motive and therefore nothing to gain or lose by telling the truth. Officer Moore described how the independent witness in Non-Domestic Case 5 had a positive influence on her views of the victim's credibility:

> Just based on the third party, you know, that she has no ulterior motive to call 911. It's not like they're not trying to get her in trouble. Not a sister-in-law, you know, it's not her cousin...there is no relation between these two, you know, and yet, she still called the police because she heard it was able to describe, you know, language sound, you know, things like that of a disturbance of somebody getting choked, smacked and pushed up against the wall. So nobody would just make that up and call us. The witness also seems disturbed by it and upset by what she heard and witnessed.

Both officers in these examples described the witnesses in their cases as independent. However, the officer in Non-Domestic Case 5 emphasized that her perception of the witness's independence stemmed from the fact that the witness had no relationship with any of the involved parties. In contrast, in the same case, the witness was the victim's son, yet officers still regarded him as independent. This contrast highlights a varied interpretation among officers regarding what constitutes an independent witness, and how that perception influences assessments of credibility. Officer Campbell further illustrated this distinction in Non-Domestic Case 34, where the victim's boyfriend was present as a witness but was not considered independent, and therefore not perceived as credible.

> The witness or quote on quote, witness, that she had was her boyfriend. So, it wasn't a credible witness. It wasn't independent. It was someone that she

knew. So, it wasn't an independent witness on the aspect of the fight happening.

Based on officers' statements throughout the interviews, it appeared that having a witness was generally perceived as preferable to having none. However, officers consistently emphasized that independent witnesses were more valuable than those with personal ties to the victim or suspect. Notably, the definition of "independent" varied among officers. Some considered individuals with any form of relationship to the victim, such as family members or close acquaintances, as still capable of being independent witnesses, while others viewed any personal connection as compromising the witness's objectivity and credibility. This variation in interpretation highlights the subjective nature of how officers assess witnesses and their influence on their evaluation of victim credibility. These findings inform previous research which has highlighted the important role witnesses play when assessing victim credibility (El Sayed et al., 2022).

Suspect Admission

Suspects admitting to victimizing the victim was also discussed by officers during interviews as a factor that influenced their assessment of victims' credibility. These admissions were seen as corroborating the victim's account or aligning with the events officers believed had occurred. Suspects' admissions were not discussed in the non-domestic battery cases, but were brought up in several domestic cases. While on scene, I observed four suspects who admitted guilt and four who did not. In 12 domestic cases, it was unknown how the suspects responded to the accusations, as they were not located during the officers' initial response. Suspects' admissions were mentioned in four police reports, each corresponding to cases where officers also discussed the admissions as having a positive impact on victim credibility.

Although suspects admitted guilt in only four cases, all of which were report-yielding, officers consistently noted that these admissions were central to their credibility assessments. Specifically, officers explained that when suspects acknowledged the victimization, it served to corroborate the victim's account and strengthen their perception of the victim's credibility. For example, in Domestic Case 11, the victim called 911 stating that "his girl going mad, breaking stuff and throwing stuff at comp." On scene, I observed the suspect admit to "throwing an ashtray" at the victim. In the corresponding police report, the primary officer, Officer Sanchez, documented: "Post Miranda, (name redacted) [SUSP] admitted to throwing an ash tray at (Name redacted) [VIC] two times, striking him once with it." When asked about if they perceived the victim as credible both officers said:

> I mean, he called and said what happened…And then when we spoke to the suspect, she confirmed…. Ultimately, with this investigation, she admitted to throwing an ashtray at his headfirst. That's the main aggressor, unquote. And that's what we have to go by. So that's why she was arrested. (Officer Harris)

> Honestly, yes for like this type of situation because she basically admitted so yeah. So honestly, even talking like she would wear were where she was literally like, a week or two before I ever heard where that she was seen by a by passer kicking her boyfriend, who was always outside of the house, and like it like he liked he was the victim and I'm talking to him. He's like, No, that never happened. She didn't hit me. It was only verbal, this, this and that. So literally, he was like, he was literally saying like, No, nothing happened. But she said, Yes, I went through his home, I found out he was cheating. So yes, I pushed him out the house and then he failed, and I started kicking them all around. So, at that point, it doesn't matter. Honestly, what the victim says if the offenders admitting to what the alleged crime, then honestly, whatever the victim says, I'm going to say it doesn't really matter. But, I mean, you have to have the person who's probably will go to jail, stating that they did something to send them to jail. (Officer Sanchez)

For these officers, the suspect's admission played a significant role in shaping their perception of the victim's credibility. By admitting to throwing the ashtray, the suspect corroborated the account the victim had provided both to the 911 operator and to responding officers, thereby reinforcing the victim's credibility.

In Domestic Case 30, I observed the victim telling officers that his girlfriend had pushed him and refused to let him leave their shared apartment during an argument, an incident he stated had occurred multiple times before. As officers escorted the girlfriend out in handcuffs, I heard her say, “Yes, I did push him, but he did stuff to me too.” In the subsequent interview, Officer Nelson explained that this admission influenced their perception of the victim's credibility: “I mean, based off of his statements, his demeanor on first him being and then actually having the credibility of the offender back him up and say, Well, I mean, I did push.”

In Domestic Case 24, the suspect's admission appeared to have a different impact on officers compared to Domestic Cases 11 and 30. According to the CAD, the victim contacted police and reported that she and her husband had been arguing, and that he had pushed her while buckling their daughter into a car seat. Officers later located the suspect at his workplace, where he admitted to pushing the victim “to get her away from him and his child.” Unlike the previous examples, this admission seemed to be framed more as a defensive action, potentially complicating the officers' interpretation of victim credibility. In the corresponding police report the primary officer, Officer Torres stated:

> [SUSP] explained that she came to his car and “yanked” the rear car door to the point where he heard it cracking. (name redacted) [SUSP] stated he pushed to protect his property…I did not charge (name redacted) [SUSP] with battery due to the physical contact that was used to prevent from damaging his vehicle and him trying to leave the residence. I did not have probable cause to make an arrest based on my investigation…Ofc. (name redacted) provided with a Victim's Rights brochure, a Domestic Violence brochure and a case report request card.

When describing the victim's credibility in the interview Officer Torres said:

> I asked questions and let suspected talk… those questions…when I asked him, they all lined up. What he was saying was making sense. He's just trying to protect his kids. He's trying to leave the situation. He did say they got into an argument…the way she started…her credibility…she kind of

> lost where she didn't want to allow us to take pictures to show us the mark the alleged mark on her face.

According to Officer Torres, despite the suspect admitting to pushing the victim, this did not enhance the officers' perception of the victim's credibility. Officer Torres explained that the suspect's account "made sense" and was perceived as justified under the circumstances. Additionally, other factors had already diminished the victim's credibility in the eyes of the officers, most notably, her reluctance to show her injuries. Thus, as demonstrated in Domestic Case 24, a suspect's admission does not automatically result in the victim being viewed as credible. The statements suggest that even with a suspect's admittance, officers may still determine that probable cause for a crime is lacking.

Conversely, in Domestic Case 20, the suspect's admission played a central role in the officer's determination of probable cause and facilitated the investigative process. Officer Thompson explained: "It was fairly easy just because the suspect has basically provided all the information we needed to find the probable cause for the arrest." In the corresponding police report, he stated: "Due to the statements from both parties I determined that (name redacted) [SUSP] was the primary aggressor and as such took him into custody." In this case, the suspect's admission, combined with the victim's statement and other contextual factors, contributed significantly to the establishment of probable cause and ultimately led to the suspect's arrest. This stands in contrast to Domestic Case 24, where the suspect also admitted to pushing the victim, but the officers did not view the victim as more credible, nor did they find probable cause for an arrest. Officer Torres explained that the suspect's story "made sense" and was perceived as justified, and that other factors, such as the victim's reluctance to show injuries, had already diminished her credibility. These two cases illustrate that suspect admissions are not interpreted uniformly; their impact depends on how officers assess the context, justification, and corroborating evidence.

Altogether, although suspects admitted to victimizing victims in only four domestic cases, officers discussed these admissions in each of those cases. The suspect's admission did not only influence officers' perceptions of victim credibility but also played a central role in determining probable cause, as reflected in both interview statements and corresponding police reports. These findings highlight the discretionary nature of officers' assessments and the multifaceted role that suspect admissions play in shaping investigative outcomes.

History of Violence

Another aspect that officers identified as influencing their perceptions of victim credibility was the history between the victim and the suspect, particularly the presence, or absence, of prior violence, which is supporting previous findings (El Sayed et al., 2022). In non-domestic cases, the lack of a prior relationship was mentioned only sparingly, primarily as a procedural step to determine whether the case met the criteria for classification as a domestic incident. Since most parties in non-domestic cases had no prior relationship, history was largely irrelevant to credibility assessments in those contexts. In contrast, in the domestic cases, prior violence between the parties was a recurring theme. In all but three domestic cases, either the victim or the suspect claimed that previous violent incidents had occurred.

The presence of a documented or alleged history of violence appeared to shape how officers interpreted the current incident, often reinforcing or undermining their assessment of the victim's credibility depending on how consistent the narrative was with past behavior. In the vast majority of cases, the occurrence of previous violence was brought up by either the person calling 911 or the 911 dispatcher. In 11 domestic cases previous violence was reported in the 911 call, in two cases no previous violence and in six cases previous violence was not mentioned during the 911 call.

During my tine in the field I observed victims or witnesses referencing prior violence in 16 domestic cases, while the absence of previous violence was noted in two cases, and no mention of prior violence was observed in another two cases. During the interviews, officers brought up the presence of previous violence in seven cases, all of which were report-yielding. In contrast, prior violence was not mentioned in 13 domestic cases during interviews. Additionally, the occurrence of previous violence was documented in seven out of the 15 report-yielding domestic cases, and in these cases, it was also discussed during officer interviews. The absence of previous violence was mentioned in two cases, while no mention was made in eight cases. These patterns suggest that previous violence was a recurring theme, often emerging early in the case formation process and discussed throughout the investigation. Officers frequently used this history to contextualize the current incident or to explain the victim's motivation for contacting law enforcement. For example, officers in Domestic Cases 11 and 29 acknowledged prior incidents of domestic violence and described them as contributing factors in how they interpreted the present situation.

> I wouldn't say it was a typical domestic because all domestic situations are different, but a misdemeanor wasn't bad. Like he wasn't like he didn't seem like he obviously didn't seem angry, didn't seem mad about anything. And honestly, it seemed like he was just on…actually just fed up with I believe the previous domestic stuff that they have going on and they haven't called the cops for that because that's normally how it is people it normally they normally don't call it is the first time something happens…but then it normally balls up and balls up and then boom, someone's like, alright, yeah, not have all this like, you know. (Interview Domestic Case 11, Officer White)

> Domestic battery, a long-term relationship. He has several prior domestic batteries. Seems like he's doing a bit more than just the battery…and trying to control her everyday activities including breaking into her apartment. (Interview Domestic Case 29, Officer Green)

In police reports officers tended to be more specific when documenting prior violence. They often noted whether law enforcement had previously responded to incidents involving the same individuals and, when applicable, included case numbers to substantiate the history. In Domestic Cases 11 and 29, the reports explicitly referenced prior police involvement offering a documented pattern of behavior that they could use to frame the current incident as part of a broader cycle of violence.

> (Name redacted) [SUSP] and (Name redacted) [VIC] do not have any documented history of domestic violence/battery in our database with each other. There are no active no contact order/injunctions. (name redacted) [SUSP] said that she called LEO in the past in reference to (Name redacted) [VIC] striking her and when the police responded, he was not taken to jail. (Police Report Domestic Case 11, Officer White)

> The Vic stated that she has and active Domestic Violence Injunction on the DEF in which she is the protected party. The DEF and Vic have an extensive History of DV, dating back to at least 2015. (Police Report Domestic Case 29, Officer Green)

In Domestic Case 11, the officer noted that the suspect claimed there had been previous violence between the parties and that police had been called, however, upon investigation, the officer found no record of prior police response. This discrepancy highlights how claims of past violence may be acknowledged but not always substantiated through official records, which could influence how officers interpret credibility and context. In contrast, Domestic Case 29 displayed a different scenario. The officer emphasized an extensive history of domestic violence between the parties and noted that there was an active injunction against the suspect. This formal documentation of prior incidents appeared to strengthen the officer's framing of the current event as part of a continuing pattern of abuse, likely reinforcing both the victim's credibility and the seriousness of the offense.

Other police reports referenced prior violence more generally, without providing specific case numbers or commenting on the validity of the information. For instance, the report in Domestic Case 17 states: "During the course of their relationship stated that (name redacted) [SUSP] had been physically and emotionally abusive to her." Similarly, in Domestic Case 25, the report notes: "However, (Name redacted) [VIC] told Officer (Name redacted) that (name redacted) [SUSP] has a history of domestic violence from when he was living in Puerto Rico." Hence, while prior violence was often mentioned, the level of detail and corroboration varied across cases.

When discussing victims' credibility, officers mentioned a history of prior violence as a factor that positively influenced their assessments in five cases, all of which were report-yielding. In these interviews, officers described prior incidents as lending credibility to the victim's statements, suggesting that a documented or alleged pattern of abuse made the current claims more believable. There were no cases in which officers described the absence of prior violence as negatively impacting their perception of the victim's credibility. Instead, the presence of a history was framed as a validating element that appeared to help officers contextualize the incident and interpret the victim's motivations for contacting law enforcement. For example, in Domestic Case 4 Officer Thomas noted:

> She gave me some information about how the police had responded out there before. So, I was able to look up the call history at that address and confirm that we have been out there for disturbances between the two of them before.

Similarly, in Domestic Case 2, Officer Willson highlighted the importance of the previous history between the victim and the suspect, which he, in the police report, describes as:

> (name redacted) [SUSP] has displayed on-going behavior of stalking and violations of the injunction. Since then, (Name redacted) [VIC] has suffered multiple batteries at the hands at (name redacted) [SUSP] and a few violations of the outstanding injunction between the two.

Officers described the history between the parties, particularly the victim's prior efforts to contact police and report incidents, as contributing positively to their perception of the victim's credibility. In the interview, Officer Willson explained that he believed the victim was credible, "Because even though he's filed before, and we've not been able to locate the suspect, he still tries." Thus, Officer Willson interpreted the victim's continued engagement with law enforcement as a sign of sincerity and persistence. The combination of a documented or alleged history of violence and the victim's repeated attempts to seek help was a theme echoed by other officers, who similarly viewed these efforts as reinforcing the credibility of the victim's account. In Domestic Case 22, Officer King noted:

> I want to say it's more…I think, it not being the first time that this has occurred. For her to finally had call 911. On this incident of violence with already a history of violence. I think puts good notes or a good solid, you know, credibility to her.

It was not only the history between the victim and the suspect that shaped officers' perceptions of victim credibility. In some cases, officers considered the suspect's broader history of violence with others as a relevant factor. For example, in Domestic Case 31, Officer Clark noted that one reason he viewed the victim as credible was because the suspect had a documented history of violence involving other women, including one who had an active injunction against him. This broader behavioral pattern contributed to the officer's belief that the suspect was capable of the violence described, thereby reinforcing the credibility of the victim's account.

> Although she said she was slapped, I did not see any marks on her face. That is that happens all the time. She said before that she has busted her eardrum She said that she's caved in and just done whatever he wants either sexually…or whatever it was. She's done that before. I have no reason not to believe her. He has a history, career history of doing things like this. He had domestic battery in the past with I believe his ex-wife. So, I have no reason not to believe.

Specifically, Officer Clark emphasized that although he did not observe any visible injuries on the victim in Domestic Case 31, he still believed her to be credible. He explained that the suspect had a "career history" of committing similar offenses and had previously been violent toward his ex-wife. In this instance, the suspect's history of violence involving other women, particularly a former partner, was a factor that contributed to Officer Clark's perception of the victim's credibility. Similarly, in

Domestic Case 19, the suspect's criminal background played a prominent role in shaping officers' views at the scene, as the suspect was a convicted felon, and this status was mentioned multiple times by officers during the incident. The female victim reported that the suspect had hit the mother (another victim on the scene) of his child and threatened their children. This information was also reflected in the corresponding police report, where Officer Robinson listed several of the suspect's prior offenses: "The DEF has three prior felony convictions (cocaine possess, Battery on LEO, Possess Controlled Substances)." In this case, Officer Robinson did not limit his documentation to previous violent crimes but also included non-violent offenses, suggesting that the suspect's overall criminal history was relevant to the officer's framing of the current incident and the victim's credibility.

The history of violence was often discussed alongside the prior relationship between the parties. Although no officers explicitly described relationship status as a factor influencing their perception of victim credibility, it was mentioned in every case. One plausible explanation for relationships being mentioned was due to the due to the legal and organizational procedural requirements that instruct officers to manage domestic and non-domestic cases differently. Under GPD policies, officers follow different investigative guidelines depending on whether the incident qualifies as domestic violence, dating violence, or non-domestic violence. Therefore, while relationship status may not directly shape credibility assessments, it remained a consistent element in case documentation and classification reenforcing its procedural importance.

When examining the role that history between parties plays in assessing victim credibility in relation to the Ideal Victim Theory (Christie, 1986; Strobl, 2004), a complex picture emerges. On one hand, a documented history of violence between the victim and the suspect supports the narrative of ongoing victimization. This reinforces the victim's status as "ideal," especially when the victim is consistently targeted and not responsible for the violence. If the victim has never perpetrated violence against the suspect, their suffering appears more plausible and aligns with the concept that Ideal Victims are repeatedly or systematically harmed. In contrast, victims with no history, or whose history is ambiguous or contested, may not be seen as "ideal," and their credibility may be undermined. According to this perspective, previous violence between parties should positively influence the credibility of domestic violence victims, particularly in cases involving repeated abuse. However, Christie argues that victims of domestic violence, especially women, face greater challenges in being recognized as legitimate victims. This challenge stems from the perception that they do not fit the Ideal Victim profile. For example, a woman who remains with her partner after prior incidents may be viewed as complicit, or if she is perceived as "too strong," her culpability may be questioned. This tension reveals a duality within the Ideal Victim framework which highlights the complexity of relational history when assessing victim credibility. In contrast, victims of non-domestic battery who do not know their assailant may more easily attain Ideal Victim status. Because they lack a prior relationship with the perpetrator, they are less likely to be viewed as responsible for the violence, depending on the context in which the victimization occurs. The environment becomes a key point of discussion in this context, as victims who are harmed while performing tasks that they "could not be blamed for" are more likely to be viewed as Ideal Victims according to Christie's theory. For example, if a domestic battery victim is assaulted in their own home while cleaning, and a non-domestic battery victim is assaulted outside a bar during a fight, the domestic violence victim may be considered more ideal than the non-domestic victim. Hence, the both the environment and the nature of the activity during which the victimization occurs can create a complex dynamic when assessing and assigning credibility to a victim.

Injuries and Marks

One of the most frequently mentioned corroborating factors influencing officers' perceptions of victim credibility, across both domestic and non-domestic cases, was the presence or absence of injuries or marks on victims or suspects. The importance on visible evidence aligns with findings from previous research. For instance, Jasinski (2003) highlighted that the presence of injuries can significantly influence whether police become involved in non-domestic battery cases. Similarly, Buzawa and Austin (1993) found that the nature of the injury was a key determinant in the likelihood of arrest in domestic battery cases. Their study showed that cases involving no injuries were less likely to result in arrest compared to those with minor injuries, while cases involving severe injuries were the most likely to lead to arrest. These findings underscore how physical evidence not only can shape officers' decisions about arrest but also informs their assessments of victim credibility. In the cases I observed, officers often referenced injuries as tangible proof that supported the victim's account, and the presence, or absence of injuries, was frequently discussed during both scene observations and interviews.

Out of the 14 non-domestic cases, I observed that victims in four cases had injuries and marks, two of which led to police reports and two cases did not lead to police reports. In half of the cases, the injury status was reported in the 911 call by either the victim or a third-party, in five cases I observed that officers asked victims about it or that victims mentioned their injuries on scene, and in two cases it was not brought up in the 911 call or on scene by the victims or officers. The absence or presence of injuries and marks on officers' perceptions of victim credibility was discussed by officers during the interviews in six of the 14 non-domestic cases, specifically, it was discussed as a negative in three cases, neutral in one, and positive in one case. In one of the six cases, two officers discussed it differently, with one as a positive and one as a negative. Furthermore, injuries and marks were discussed in three non-report-yielding cases and three report-yielding cases, and in all these cases injuries were also observed on scene. In the three report-yielding cases, it was brought up in both the interviews and the police reports. In one of the cases, the lack of injury and marks was brought up in the interview, but not in the police report. In one case, the lack of injury was brought up in the police report but not in the officer's interview.

In the domestic cases I observed that per GPD polices, officers frequently asked about injuries and documented the injuries and marks on scene. When looking at all domestic cases, I observed that victims in eight domestic cases had injuries and 12 had no injuries, which I determined through a combination of victims telling officers they had injuries or marks and or me observing visible marks on the victims. Injuries or marks were mentioned by officers during the interviews in eight cases as impacting the officers' perceptions of credibility. Of these eight cases, six were report-yielding cases and two were non-report-yielding cases. In the interviews officers specifically described the presence of injuries or marks as contributing positively to victims' credibility in four cases, and the lack of presence of injuries as negative in two cases, and in two cases the two officers interviewed had different opinions. In both cases, the one officer described it as positive and the other one as a negative influence. Injuries and marks tended to be more often discussed during the interviews in relation to credibility in report-yielding cases compared to non-report-yielding cases. Furthermore, the presence, absence, and nature of injuries and marks were mentioned in 11 of the 15 police domestic reports and were thus the topic most frequently mentioned in police reports out of the credibility factors discussed by officers during the interviews. When mentioned in police reports, officers tended to describe whether victims said they had injuries and if they observed any injuries.

Injuries shaped perceptions of credibility in different ways, with injuries and marks playing two critical roles in officers' perceptions and decision making. First, they could corroborate victims' statements and second, serve as evidence of probable cause that a victimization had occurred. During interviews, officers consistently noted that the presence of injuries strengthened their perception of credibility because it provided physical confirmation of the victim's account. This dynamic was evident in Domestic Case 20, where I observed the victim telling officers that her boyfriend of six months had hit her and pulled her hair. She informed Officer Thompson that the suspect had also sustained an injury to his hand and that there was blood on the wall inside the apartment. Furthermore, she showed officers red marks on her face, which visibly supported her narrative. In this case, the injuries not only corroborated her story but also contributed to the officers' ability to establish probable cause, reinforcing the seriousness of the incident and justifying further investigative action. When I asked if he thought the victim was credible, Officer Thompson explained:

> Yes. Found her credible based on just the injuries that she did have. And she also mentioned that the suspect had some kind of wound or some kind of abrasions on his hand from the incident which he did have. And then of

> course, the male suspect, just excited utterance of what happened and he just confirmed the credibility of the victim.

In another case, Non-Domestic Case 28, Officer Williams highlighted that injuries and marks became a way to validate the victim's story. When describing victim credibility he noted:

> Typically, if somebody's not being truthful, it's pretty obvious because visible injuries would not be consistent with the statements that are made by certain victims. But in this case, all the visible injuries on the victims were consistent with the statements that were made.

Officer Williams described injuries and marks as a tool for assessing whether the victim was being truthful. When the injuries aligned with the account provided by the victim, he interpreted it as consistency which became an indicator of credibility. In his view, physical evidence served not only as corroboration but also as a filter for detecting deception.

The presence of injuries was not a factor that guaranteed that officers would find victims more credible. For example, Non-Domestic Case 10, I observed that the victim had multiple injuries and marks, which he stated came from the victimization. Despite this, Officer Willson questioned the injuries and marks the victim had. When asked if he found the victim credible, he stated:

> Yes and no. I believe something happened but I'm not quite sure it happened the way he remembers it happening. Just the evidence. He says he was hit hard enough that he lost a tooth. There was no swelling on his face. The lip injury appeared to be a couple days old and already healing. There was no bruising on his ribcage. So, I believe that he is missing items that he says he's missing but I don't know how that happened.

Officer Willson questioned the concurrence between the victim's account and the injuries he observed. Although the victim in Non-Domestic Case 10 claimed that the visible marks were sustained during the incident, Officer Willson noted that the injuries appeared to stem from older wounds, which led him to doubt the credibility of the victim's story. Hence, in certain cases officers may not only assess the presence of injuries but also interpret their age and consistency with the reported timeline of events. When injuries are perceived as inconsistent with the victim's narrative, they may be used to undermine rather than support credibility. In the subsequent police report, he elaborated further:

> (Name redacted) [VIC] had a small laceration on the inside of his lip and stated that a tooth in the back of the left side of his mouth was missing. He complained that the left side rib area was tender to touch... I did not observe any physical injury other than the lip, which appeared to be healing for a couple days.

Thus, in Non-Domestic Case 10, it became evident that when Officer Willson perceived the injuries as inconsistent with the victim's account, the presence of marks did not enhance credibility; instead, it prompted skepticism. Hence, physical evidence was not inherently validating and its interpretive value may depend on whether it is seen as corroborative of the victim's narrative.

Although the presence of injuries generally had a positive influence on officers' perceptions of victims, the absence of injuries did not always lead officers to view victims as less credible. This was evident in Domestic Case 17, where I observed the victim telling Officer Lewis that her boyfriend, who had military training, had attacked her, causing her to pass out. Despite the lack of visible injuries, Officer Lewis later stated during the interview: "Yes, I think that she definitely has dealt with abuse. And I think that he definitely is verbally abusive. As far as the battery aspect of it, there were no visible injuries." Officer Lewis explained that although the victim did not have any marks or injuries from the battery in this instance, he still believed she had been victimized. Hence, officers sometimes relied on contextual factors, such as the victim's demeanor, narrative consistency, and the suspect's background, to assess credibility, even in the absence of physical evidence.

In Non-Domestic Case 21, Officer Young emphasized that injuries and marks were key components of the physical evidence that shaped his perception of the victim's credibility. At the scene, I observed that the victim denied being victimized. When I later asked Officer Young about his assessment of her credibility, he explained that her denial combined with the lack of visible injuries made the incident more difficult to investigate. He stated: "In terms of physical evidence, I didn't see anything other than what I pointed out with a torn strap. She did have a very quick response to that. I did not observe any bruising or anything." Another officer, Officer Willson, who was also present and authored the police report, similarly noted the absence of injuries: "(Name redacted) [VIC] had a torn strap to her top, but no other visible injuries." Hence, the absence of physical evidence, particularly injuries, can complicate officers' ability to assess credibility and proceed with enforcement actions especially when the victim denies the occurrence of violence. Lack of injuries was not only acknowledged during interviews with officers but also documented in police reports. For example, when describing the lack of injuries or marks in reports, officers wrote:

> I did not observe any lacerations, swelling, or bruising on her person. Officer (Name redacted) then asked her where on her head she was injured and told her that she forgot. (Domestic Case 25, Officer Torres)

> While on scene I did not observe any physical injury to the VIC. (Domestic Case 29, Officer Green)

> I asked if he sustained any injuries from the incident and was unable to see any bruising or make anywhere on his body. (Domestic Case 30, Officer Williams)

Lack of injuries was more frequently mentioned in domestic case reports than in non-domestic case reports. This difference between domestic and non-domestic cases could suggest that in domestic cases, injuries may carry more procedural weight, possibly due to the structured guidelines under GPD policies that govern domestic violence investigations. The formal inclusion of injury details in reports may reflect both the seriousness with which these cases are treated and the evidentiary expectations tied to them. However, it could potentially also signal that non-domestic cases that do not have visible injuries or marks have a lower likelihood of being formally documented.

In two other cases, the lack of injuries actually served to strengthen the victims' credibility in the eyes of the officers, as it corroborated the victims' statements that no violent incident had occurred. In Domestic Case 32, Officer Willson stated: "He clearly didn't have any injuries to his face," which aligned with the victim's claim that there had been no physical altercation. Similarly, in Domestic Case 22, Officer King noted the absence of injuries as consistent with the victim's account, reinforcing his perception that no battery had taken place.

> Just her story and the fact that like, she didn't have any injuries really separated. So, she did have, she had plenty opportunity. Like he didn't even know she was here. Yeah, she had plenty of opportunity to like, if something did happen, she could have easily told me.

Officers in these examples interpreted the lack of marks or injuries as consistent with the victim's account, thereby reinforcing its plausibility. As seen in cases like Domestic Case 17, officers could still find victims credible despite the absence of physical evidence, relying instead on contextual cues such as demeanor, narrative coherence, and the suspect's background.

Although officers most often agreed in their interpretation of the presence or absence of injuries or marks, there were example of officers not agreeing. For example, in Non-Domestic Case 34, the victim reported that she had been involved in a fight with another female in the downtown area during the early morning hours. While one officer appeared to accept her account and viewed the injuries as consistent with her story, the other officer expressed skepticism, suggesting that the marks did not fully support the narrative. This difference illustrates how the interpretation of physical evidence is not always uniform and can vary depending on the officer's perspective, experience, or expectations. Officer Wright who was the primary officer, noted that he did not think the victim was credible because of the lack of injuries and marks by stating:

> There were no indicators of a fight between the two…in these situations here, it is hard because, you know, unless you have, like indicators of abuse… any fighting scuffle marks or anything like that, like a ripped shirt, I can't say it is credible.

However, another officer, Officer Campbell stated that she believed the victim partially because of the injuries and marks:

> Like I said, based on what she'd already previously reported, saying she got punched in the face and had an injury to her lip suggests that she was punched in the face, saying the girl had her phone and then the girl did have her phone. That's why I believe her.

While both officers interacted with the same victim, they formed different opinions regarding the presence of injuries and the victim's credibility. One officer believed the injuries were consistent with the victim's account, while the other questioned whether any injuries were present at all. Despite this difference, both officers' statements suggest that injuries played a central role in shaping their perceptions of credibility. In Domestic Case 33, I observed another example of differing interpretations. The victim told officers that her boyfriend had punched her; however, the officers on scene interpreted the presence and absence of injuries were perceived differently. While one officer may have viewed the lack of visible injuries as a reason to question the account, another may have considered the context or other signs of distress. When I asked if they perceived the victims as credible, the two officers stated:

> Yes. So, I mean, her story and her account of the incident was fairly consistent with how injuries were portrayed. (Officer Garcia)
>
> I don't know…Well, unfortunately, a lot of times in these cases for me, I look for evidence of what's the victim said happened with the understanding that somebody can hit somebody and not leave a bruise. But based on what she said she said her leg was it pushed through the window. I didn't see any cuts on her leg. She said her lip was busted. She got punched in the face. I didn't see it. So, I mean, just based on what she said. I like that's how I determine credibility. (Officer Mitchell)

In Domestic Case 33, Officer Garcia, the primary officer, described observing injuries that corroborated the victim's account of the incident. He emphasized this in the subsequent police report, stating: "The VIC sustained a minor laceration on the inside portion of their upper lip which I observed on scene." This observation served to validate the victim's narrative and was formally documented. However, the second officer on scene offered a contrasting perspective, arguing that he had not observed any injuries or marks, which led him to question the victim's claims. Specifically, he expressed skepticism about the absence of bruises, given the victim's description of a violent encounter. This difference in perception highlights how injuries functioned as a credibility filter, but also how subjective interpretation could lead to conflicting assessments, even within the same case. Although the two officers had different viewpoints on the presence and significance of injuries, both statements underscore that injuries played a central role in shaping their perceptions of the victim's credibility.

While disagreements between officers were rare in this study, it is crucial to highlight these instances due to their potential consequences for victims. In Non-Domestic Case 34, no report was written, but had one been filed like in Domestic Case 33, it would have been authored by the primary officer, whose interpretation of the injuries would have been the one officially recorded. This means that in Non-Domestic Case 34, the female officer's observation of injuries and marks might have been excluded from the formal documentation. Although this detail may seem minor, it could significantly influence how a prosecutor or judge evaluates the case, particularly in decisions about whether to file charges or pursue further legal action. Similarly in Domestic Case 33, because Officer Garcia was the primary officer, his observations were the ones formally recorded in the police report, thus the injuries and marks were mentioned. These examples stress the subjectivity involved in interpreting physical evidence and how report authorship can influence the official narrative, potentially affecting prosecutorial decisions and the trajectory of the case. It also raises important questions about how officer hierarchy and report authorship can affect the preservation, or omission, of potentially critical observations.

Another example of officers disagreeing was in Domestic Case 3, the three officers involved had differing perceptions of the victim's injuries, which directly impacted how they assessed her credibility. I observed the female victim crying behind a bar, and according to witnesses, she had been attacked by her boyfriend at that location. The victim had visible marks on her face, which were described in the police report by the primary officer, Officer Thomas, as: "a red swollen area on her left cheekbone underneath her eye which is consistent with getting punched in the face." When the officers later discussed factors influencing their credibility assessments, Officer Thomas did not mention the injuries, despite having documented them. In contrast, the two other officers on scene did reference the injuries as part of their evaluation. Officer Jackson stated: "Yes, because her physical interest in her statements was consistent with her injuries," suggesting that the alignment between the victim's account and her physical condition reinforced her credibility. However, Officer Brown offered a contrasting view: "No, because no outstanding or excessive injuries. It was minor bruising to her face. She wasn't unconscious. She was breathing normally. It was a simple battery. She didn't get stabbed or anything." For Officer Brown, the lack of severity in the injuries diminished the victim's credibility. His statement implies that more severe injuries can validate claims of victimization, a perspective not echoed by any other officers in the sample. However, they are important to highlight for two key reasons. Firstly, this case reinforces the idea that officers working the same incident can hold differing views about the injuries a victim did or did not sustain, which in turn shapes their credibility assessments. In Domestic Case 3, while Officer Jackson viewed the victim's injuries as consistent with her account and therefore credible, Officer Brown dismissed the victim's credibility based on the perceived lack of severity, stating that "It was minor bruising to her face… She didn't get stabbed or anything." Secondly, Officer Brown's comments suggest that for some officers, the severity of injury may be a threshold factor in determining whether a victim is believable. This introduces a dynamic where less severe injuries, even if consistent with the victim's account, may be undervalued or dismissed. It also reinforces the findings of Buzawa and Austin (1993), who noted that the severity of injury plays a significant role in shaping arrest outcomes in battery cases. For example, leading to that injuries that does not leave visible marks are not considered as severe as in injuries that leave marks.

When describing the presence of injuries, officers did more than simply note whether victims claimed to be injured or whether they themselves observed injuries. They often provided specific details about the nature and location of the injuries, which added nuance to their assessments of credibility. For example, officers would distinguish between bruises, scratches, or swelling, and specify whether these were located on the face, arms, or torso. In doing so, officers demonstrated that injuries were not just binary indicators of harm, but interpretable evidence that could either support or challenge the victim's narrative depending on how well the physical signs aligned with the reported events.

> He had a cut above his left elbow and bruising on his right forearm. (Name redacted) [VIC] had multiple scrapes, cuts and bruises on his person. (Domestic Case 2, Officer Willson)

> I observed a red bruise on (Name redacted) [VIC] 's left arm approximately three inches in size. (Domestic Case 4, Officer Martin)

Injuries and marks played a significant role not only in officers' credibility assessments but also in the initial response decisions made by 911 dispatchers. The presence and severity of injuries helped dispatchers determine which services to send to the scene, for example, whether to dispatch police alone, or include EMS or the fire department. This was evident in the 911 call logs, where dispatchers frequently noted injury-related information reported by victims. For example:

> "Y inj bruises adv she has pictures. Adv poss needs ems" (Domestic Case 9)

> "Adv head hurts requesting ems. Comp adv she may pass out from being hit in the head" (Domestic Case 25)

"Lip busted, no ems needed" (Domestic Case 33).

Injuries were a key factor in case formation, shaping how dispatchers triaged the situation and allocated resources. Once on scene, officers continued this process by observing and asking about injuries, reinforcing the central role that physical evidence played from the initial call through to on-scene investigation.

Overall, officers consistently referenced the presence and absence of injuries and marks both in interviews and police reports, highlighting their central role in shaping perceptions of victim credibility. During interviews, officers described injuries as having the potential to positively influence credibility when they aligned with the victim's account. However, my time in the field also revealed that injuries, even when present, can be perceived negatively if officers believe they do not align with the victim's narrative. For example, discrepancies between the severity or location of injuries and the described incident could lead officers to question the victim's truthfulness. These findings align with El Sayed et al. (2020) who found that the presence and severity of injuries are key factors in police decisions to arrest and in their assessments of victim credibility. I also found that officers working the same case can interpret the presence or absence of injuries differently, leading to divergent assessments of credibility. This was particularly evident in Domestic Case 3, where one officer viewed the injuries as consistent and corroborative, while another dismissed them as insufficiently severe to support the victim's claims. These variations highlight that injury interpretation is not uniform and can be shaped by individual officer thresholds, biases, and expectations. Taken together, these findings suggest that while injuries often serve as important corroborative evidence, their influence on credibility is context-dependent and subject to officer discretion, which can introduce inconsistency in how victimization is assessed and documented.

The presence or absence of victim injuries and marks is closely connected to Ideal Victim Theory (Christie, 1986; Strobl, 2004). According to Christie, society and authorities are more likely to recognize and support victims whose suffering is visible and aligns with expected stereotypes. When a victim presents clear injuries that corroborate their suffering, their vulnerability and harm become more apparent. This visibility can enhance the victim's credibility and serve as evidence of their suffering. Such physical evidence reinforces the perception that the victim is blameless and has genuinely endured harm, which are key characteristics of the Ideal Victim. In contrast, when injuries or marks are absent, the victim's account may appear less convincing. Without physical signs, officers may question whether the incident occurred as described or doubt the seriousness of the harm which can lead to skepticism and reduced support for the victim, even when their account is truthful, especially if no other evidence is available to corroborate the victim's statement.

Conclusion

In this chapter I have discussed how different types of corroborating factors informed officers' perceptions of victim credibility. Specifically, officers emphasized the importance of corroborating factors, such as physical evidence, injuries and marks, and suspect admissions, in positively shaping their perceptions of victim credibility. Conversely, the absence of injuries or marks could negatively impact those perceptions, particularly when officers expected physical evidence to align with the victim's narrative. These findings align with prior research that stress the evidentiary weight of injuries, especially in domestic violence cases (El Sayed et al., 2022; Waaland & Keeley, 1985). Together, these findings reinforce the complex and layered nature of credibility assessments in battery investigations. They highlight how officers draw on a combination of injury interpretation, prior history, and suspect admission in domestic battery cases, while in non-domestic batteries emphasizing the role of witnesses and evidence such as surveillance in addition to injuries in marks.

Extensive research has also emphasized the importance of the relationship between the victim and the offender in shaping officers' perceptions of victims in domestic violence cases (Clark, 2021; DeJong et al., 2008; Felson et al., 1999; Horwitz et al., 2011; Kang & Lynch, 2014; Rollwagen & Jacob, 2018). During my fieldwork officers did not explicitly mention the nature of the victim–suspect relationship as a factor that directly influenced their credibility assessments. In contrast, and in line with previous research on domestic battery (El Sayed et al., 2022; Holloway & Wiener, 2018), this study found that criminal history between the victim and the suspect was a factor that in some cases positively influenced officers' perceptions of victim credibility. Officers noted that a previous history of violence between the two parties served to strengthen the victim's claims, however, officers did not suggest that the absence of prior violence diminished credibility.

References

Buzawa, E. S., & Austin, T. (1993). Determining police response to domestic violence victims: The role of victim preference. *American Behavioral Scientist, 36*(5), 610–623. https://doi.org/10.1177/0002764293036005006

Christie, N. (1986). The ideal victim. In E. Fattah (Ed.), *From crime policy to victim policy* (pp. 17–30). Palgrave Macmillan. https://doi.org/10.1007/978-1-349-08305-3_2

Clark, V. E. (2021). Victim-blaming discourse underpinning police responses to domestic violence: A critical social work perspective. *Social Work & Policy Studies: Social Justice, Practice and Theory, 4*(1), 1–15. https://openjournals.library.sydney.edu.au/SWPS/article/view/14959

DeJong, C., Burgess-Proctor, A., & Elis, L. (2008). Police officer perceptions of intimate partner violence: An analysis of observational data. *Violence and Victims, 23*(6), 683–696. https://doi.org/10.1891/0886-6708.23.6.683

El Sayed, S. A., DeShay, R. A., Davis, J. B., Knox, K. N., & Kerley, K. R. (2022). A blue step forward: An exploratory study of law enforcement perceptions of intimate partner violence in the southern United States. *Journal of Interpersonal Violence, 37*(9–10), 6514–6534. https://doi.org/10.1177/0886260520966675

Ellison, L. (2002). Prosecuting domestic violence without victim participation. *The Modern Law Review, 65*(6), 834–858. https://doi.org/10.1111/1468-2230.00412

Epstein, D., & Goodman, L. A. (2019). Discounting women: Doubting domestic violence survivors' credibility and dismissing their experiences. *University of Pennsylvania Law Review, 167*(2), 399–462. https://scholarship.law.georgetown.edu/facpub/2037

Felson, R. B., Messner, S. F., & Hoskin, A. (1999). The victim-offender relationship and calling the police in assaults. *Criminology, 37*(4), 931–948. https://doi.org/10.1111/j.1745-9125.1999.tb00510.x

Holloway, C. P., & Wiener, R. L. (2018). Abuse history and culpability judgments: Implications for battered spouse syndrome. *Psychology, Public Policy, and Law, 24*(3), 279–291. https://doi.org/10.1037/law0000167

Horwitz, S. H., Mitchell, D., LaRussa-Trott, M., Santiago, L., Pearson, J., Skiff, D. M., & Cerulli, C. (2011). An inside view of police officers' experience with domestic violence. *Journal of Family Violence, 26*(8), 617–625. https://doi.org/10.1007/s10896-011-9396-y

Jasinski, J. L. (2003). Police involvement in incidents of physical assault: Analysis of the redesigned National Crime Victimization Survey. *Journal of Family Violence, 18*, 143–150. https://doi.org/10.1023/A:1023512420703

Kang, J. H., & Lynch, J. P. (2014). Calling the police in instances of family violence: Effects of victim–offender relationship and life stages. *Crime & Delinquency, 60*(1), 34–59. https://doi.org/10.1177/0011128709359655

Maguire, M. (2012). Criminal investigation and crime control. In *Handbook of policing* (pp. 430–464). Willan.

Phillips, A., & de Roos, M. S. (2025). Gender stereotypes and perceptions of stranger violence: Attributions of blame and motivation. *International Journal of Offender Therapy and Comparative Criminology, 69*(1), 43–61. https://doi.org/10.1177/0306624X221124849

Rollwagen, H., & Jacob, J. C. (2018). The victim–offender relationship and police charging decisions for juvenile delinquents: How does social distance moderate the impact of legal and extralegal factors? *Youth Violence and Juvenile Justice, 16*(4), 378–394. https://doi.org/10.1177/1541204017710315

Strobl, R. (2004). Constructing the victim: Theoretical reflections and empirical examples. *International Review of Victimology, 11*(2–3), 295–311. https://doi.org/10.1177/026975800401100206

Waaland, P., & Keeley, S. (1985). Police decision making in wife abuse: The impact of legal and extralegal factors. *Law and Human Behavior, 9*(4), 355–366. https://doi.org/10.1007/BF01044476

8

Help-Seeking and Emotional Display

Introduction

In this chapter I explore two themes that emerged during my time in the field, the motivations behind help-seeking among non-domestic victims, and the role of emotional display in shaping officers' perceptions of credibility. In both domestic and non-domestic cases, officers discussed how victims' demeanor impacted perceptions of credibility during on-scene interactions. However, when reviewing the cases I discovered some differences between the aspects brought up by officers in the domestic cases and the non-domestic cases.

Officers discussed motivation and help-seeking as impacting their perception of credibility in non-domestic cases but not in the domestic cases. Scholars have found that officers' perceptions of victim motivation are shaped by context, gender, and the perceived legitimacy of the request. For example, victims who do not want help are often viewed with suspicion or as less credible, but officers also recognize that reluctance may stem from fear, dependence, or social factors (DeJong et al.,

M. N. Eliasson, *Who Gets Believed?*, Palgrave's Critical Policing Studies,
https://doi.org/10.1007/978-3-032-22253-4_8

2008; El Sayed et al., 2022). Furthermore, there is a gap between what officers observe and what is formally documented. Hence, even though emotionality and motivation can influence officers' decisions in the field and perceptions, they are inconsistently recorded by officers in reports (Ask, 2010), which can have an impact on how other criminal justice professionals perceive the victim and the case when reading the police report.

Officers also described how emotional displays by victims in both domestic and non-domestic cases influenced their perceptions of credibility. Victims' emotions and motivation for seeking help are two aspects that previous literature has emphasized as influencing perceptions of victim credibility. Studies show that emotional display increases perceived credibility among police (Ask, 2010). Research also demonstrates that gender stereotypes shape expectations of emotionality among victims. Specifically, female victims are expected to show more emotion than male victims, and this emotionality tends to be more accepted among female victims compared to male victims (Phillips & de Roos, 2022). Studies also indicate that the credibility of female victims is often discounted due to stereotypes about how "real" victims should behave. If female victims react with no emotion or show little emotion to officers, these responses can be misinterpreted as signs of deception or lack of credibility (Epstein & Goodman, 2019). This chapter I build on this literature by contrasting how emotional expressions, such as crying, fear, or frustration, are perceived in both domestic and non-domestic contexts. While some officers acknowledged that emotional cues positively influenced their assessments of credibility, these interpretations were not consistently documented in police reports. The chapter's findings on emotional display and perceived vulnerability directly intersect with Christie's (1986) Ideal Victim Theory, which posits that victims who are weak, visibly distressed, and engaged in respectable activities are most likely to be granted victim status by police and society. Strobl (2004) extends this framework, showing that victims who present themselves as helpless, avoid provocative behavior, and cooperate with authorities are more readily recognized as legitimate victims. In practice, officers' assessments of credibility often mirror these Ideal Victim attributes, privileging those who conform to expected emotional and behavioral scripts while discounting those who do not (Van Wijk, 2013).

Help-Seeking

Victims' needs and motivations for seeking help, can vary significantly depending on the individual and may shift as the case progresses. When reviewing cases, it became evident that officers started assessing victims' needs and motivations for seeking help early in the case formation, which was discussed more frequently in the non-domestic cases compared to the domestic cases. When the victim initiates the call, officers often interpreted it as a conscious decision made at some point before, during, or after the victimization and the calls seemed to be frequently understood as indicators that the victim either required assistance or lacked the capacity to manage the conflict or situation independently. In some of the cases a third-party caller, such as a bystander or witness, contacted 911. In these cases, the victim's motivation for engaging with police became more complex, as they were not the ones who initiated the interaction with the police or the criminal justice system. Hence, while some victims may not have wanted police involvement at all but were drawn into the process due to someone else's intervention, others may have initially resisted police presence but changed their minds once officers arrived and decided they did want help. Conversely, even victims who made the initial call could later revise their stance on the need for police assistance between the time of the 911 call and the officers' arrival on scene.

The review of cases suggest that victims' motivations, both prior to contacting the police and during the interaction, can shape how officers assess credibility. Officers in this study described two primary frameworks for interpreting victim motivation, first, the victim's need for help, and second, the victim's preferred outcome. These interpretations were not fixed but instead evolved in response to the victim's behavior, statements, and the broader context of the case. Out of the 14 non-domestic victims, I observed that nine expressed a desire for help once officers arrived on the scene. Notably, eight of these victims were the 911 callers. These victims were vocal and explicit in communicating what they wanted from the police. For instance, in Non-Domestic Case 23, I observed the victim assertively stating that she wanted the suspect to understand that she could not "put her hands on other people." Similarly, in Non-Domestic Case 26, the victim expressed that the suspect needed to know "he could just not walk around and touch people like that." In both cases, the victims articulated clear expectations, using the interaction with officers to signal to the suspects that their behavior was unacceptable.

Among the non-domestic cases, I observed three cases where victims did not want help. Among these, only one was the 911 caller, while in the other two, a third party had contacted emergency services. For example, in Non-Domestic Case 21, a third party called 911 reporting that her friend had been victimized by a man. However, when officers arrived, I observed the alleged victim denying being victimized and explicitly stated that she did not want any assistance from the police. This case shows how the motivations and needs of victims can diverge from those of third-party callers, and how officer engagement may be shaped by conflicting signals regarding the desire for help. Finally, in one case, the victim, who was also the 911 caller, was observed to be neutral about receiving help. Specifically, in Non-Domestic Case 6, I observed a female who stated that she had been slapped by another female in the downtown area, and that the suspect had also slapped the suspect's boyfriend. I observed the victim as she responded to the officer's questions about the incident. She described the situation as an argument and an incident that had occurred but did not express any need for assistance.

When comparing across groups, five out of the six report-yielding non-domestic cases involved victims who expressed a desire for help from police, with only one victim who did not want help. Conversely, among the eight cases that did not result in a police report, four victims wanted help, two did not want help, and one was neutral. Thus, it was more common for victims in report-yielding cases to express a need for help, whereas victims in non-report-yielding cases more frequently displayed neutrality or a lack of desire for assistance. This finding suggests that victims' expressed motivation, particularly their desire for help, may play a role in whether a case results in a formal police report. The presence or absence of expressed need appears to influence how officers interpret the situation and whether they proceed with documentation which aligns with earlier observations of that officers assess credibility not only through the facts of the case but also through the victim's engagement and clarity of purpose during the interaction.

Motivation for Help-Seeking

Based on the statements officers made during the interviews, it became clear that the reasons why victims either needed or did not need help influenced officers' perceptions of credibility. Officers appeared to assess the underlying motivations behind victims' requests, or refusals, for assistance, and judged whether those reasons were legitimate. This evaluative process shaped how officers interpreted the victim's overall credibility. Officers' assessments of victim motivation show that police can rely on culturally shaped expectations about "real" victims when interpreting help-seeking behavior, which also aligns with the normative expectations of victim behavior illustrated by the Ideal Victim Theory (Christie, 1986; Strobl, 2004). Officers' scrutiny of victims' motivations for help-seeking reflects the Ideal Victim Theory's emphasis on blamelessness and engagement in respectable projects. Van Wijk (2013) notes that victims who are perceived as having contributed to their own victimization, or who are involved in ambiguous or "unrespectable" activities, are less likely to be granted victim status. Strobl (2004) further demonstrates that social recognition of victimhood depends not only on the facts of the case but also on the victim's ability to communicate suffering in a way that aligns with societal expectations. This dynamic is evident in officers' interviews, where victims who clearly articulate their needs and present themselves as law-abiding and not engaging in confrontational behavior are more likely to receive support.

Additionally, previous empirical research found that Swedish police and prosecutors expected domestic assault victims to display expressive self-presentation and self-blame, and tended to view emotionality as a sign of truthfulness, even though research shows this is not a reliable indicator of accuracy (Ask, 2010). Similarly, DeJong et al. (2008) observed that officers sometimes interpreted reluctance to seek help as a sign of manipulation or lack of credibility, but also recognized that social and economic factors, such as fear of retaliation or financial dependence, could explain victims' hesitation. This duality highlights the risk of double discounting, where victims who do not seek help or who seek help for reasons deemed less legitimate can be viewed as less credible. For example, in Non-Domestic Case 14, I observed a victim who told police that he had been pushed by a person who owed him money. He explained that he called the police because he "did not want [the] fight to escalate." In this instance, the victim's rationale for seeking help was framed as preventative rather than reactive. His motivation was not solely about the harm already experienced, but about avoiding further conflict which can be perceived by officers as pragmatic and intentional, potentially enhancing the victim's credibility in their eyes. During the post-scene interviews when discussing credibility Officer Clark described the victim's motivation:

> I mean, because most people don't call the police over something like a push. So, if he did call this either because he'd like you to say he didn't wanna take his own hands or he was worried that it would escalate, escalate, he did not want that to happen.

In Non-Domestic Case 8, I observed the victim telling police officers that she was worried the harassment from the suspect would escalate and that more people would get hurt. Her motivation for seeking help extended beyond her own immediate safety; it reflected a broader concern for potential harm to others. Similar to what was observed in Non-Domestic Case 14, these observations suggests that victims may frame their need for police assistance in terms of prevention and protection, not only for themselves but for the wider community. Officers appeared to interpret such motivations as legitimate and thoughtful, which may positively influence their perception of the victim's credibility. During the interview Officer Thompson stated:

> I think she truly cares. Yeah, she truly cares about what's going on. And she's, she's trying to, like, you know, prevent something further from escalating to happening to one of her kids, or all the other kids in the complex.

When the victims expressed that they wanted help for reasons that officers deemed as legitimate, as in Non-Domestic Cases 14 and 8, it served as a positive influence on officers' perceptions of the victim's credibility. Hence, officers do not merely respond to whether a victim wants help but also evaluate why the victim wants help. When the rationale is perceived as grounded in safety, escalation prevention, or communal concern, it may align more closely with officers' expectations of a "legitimate" victim, thereby reinforcing credibility assessments.

In cases where the victim did not want help, officers stated that this could negatively affect the case by creating challenges for the investigation. However, they also acknowledged that there could be various reasons why a victim might choose not to engage. Officers did not elaborate extensively on these reasons, but their comments suggested an awareness that a victim's reluctance to receive help did not necessarily mean the incident lacked credibility. Instead, they appeared to consider the victim's stance as one factor among many in assessing the situation. For example, in Non-Domestic Case 21, I observed a victim telling two officers that she had not been victimized and that she did not want any help. In the post-scene interview Officer Young stated:

> Unfortunately, is the norm in this area or this, this type of residential environment, if you will. A lot of these women feel like they put their breadwinners in jail, then they're stuck. And so, the women continue letting this behavior go on. And a lot of times they use this just to get them just to get the offender to stop doing what they're doing.

Despite the victim denying that a victimization occurred, the officer linked her refusal to accept help in relation to the geographical area where the incident took place. During the observation, I noted that the victim lived in a residential area locally known to be low-income, with Section 8 housing, which officers also brought up during the interview. Officers had previously told me that the area had a high population of non-Whites and a high number of domestic battery calls. Officer Young also stated that the female victim had a prior history of being the victim of domestic violence. According to the officer, her denial stemmed from financial dependence on the suspect, and the police were used as a tool to stop or threaten the suspect. During the interview, the officer also explained that this case was not classified as a domestic violence incident because they lacked information about the identity of the perpetrator. Despite the presence of a history of domestic violence at the scene, the officer could not determine whether the potential suspect was someone the victim had been or was romantically involved with.

In another example, in Non-Domestic Case 15, while I was in the police car, I read the CAD which stated that a victim had called 911 reporting that she had been hit in the head. She told the dispatcher that she only wanted EMS assistance and not police involvement. However, due to local policy, police were also dispatched. When officers arrived on scene, I observed that the victim provided very limited information about the victimization when questioned by the officers. When describing if he thought the female victim was credible Officer Clark stated:

> I do not. Just based on, like, from a normal person's perspective, if something happened to them, and they were injured, she would have given

> more about what occurred, why it occurred. But as soon as we showed up, she didn't. Either she changed her story, or she didn't know what to say because she didn't expect law enforcement to show up. She fully expected his EMS to show up. And even later on in the call after she I looked at my EMS. She wanted to know if the rescue team came. And I explained to her, yes, that's who was coming. So, she definitely wanted…She did not want any involvement with law enforcement. And that just leads me to believe that something else occurred and she did not want to tell me what occurred.

Officer Clark explained that he believed the reason the victim did not want help from the police was because she was hiding something. This interpretation influenced his perception of the victim's overall credibility. The fact that the victim expressed that she had been victimized and appeared to be in pain, yet still declined police assistance, were factors the officer considered when forming his assessment. Her reluctance to engage with the police was not viewed in isolation but was interpreted as potentially indicative of withheld information or conflicting motives.

It was not only motivations for not wanting help that impacted officers' perceptions. Some officers viewed the reasons behind why a victim wanted help as more or less legitimate depending on the context. For example, in Non-Domestic Case 7, I observed the victim stating that he had been victimized by a female friend after asking her to leave his party. I also observed tears coming down his face while telling officers that he wanted the suspect prosecuted. However, a few minutes later, I heard him speaking loudly, appearing agitated, and telling officers that he no longer wanted to be part of the investigation as he walked away. In the post-scene interview, Officer Martin described his perception of the victim's credibility: "I think he was crying and wanting some help… I think he just wanted more revenge, you know, he got mad at the suspect and wanted her to go to jail." Martin further explained: "You know, to me, it seemed like he wanted some to get back…to intentionally get under their skin to get a reaction out of them you know, obviously, he was mad." In this case, Martin interpreted the victim's motivation for wanting help as driven by revenge, which contrasted with the motivations observed in Non-Domestic Cases 8 and 14, where victims expressed concern about escalation or harm to others. Thus, as exemplified in Non-Domestic Case 7, although some victims expressed a desire for police assistance, which officers often viewed positively, the reason behind that desire was also a factor in how officers perceived the victim's credibility. Motivations seen as emotionally reactive or retaliatory could be viewed as less legitimate than those framed around safety or prevention.

Even though victims' desire or non-desire for police assistance was frequently mentioned by officers when discussing credibility, the findings in this study suggest that it was not merely the presence or absence of that desire that influenced officers. Rather, I found that officers assessed the reason behind why victims wanted or did not want help, and this reasoning informed their perception of the victim. For example, when a victim's motivation was viewed as legitimate, such as wanting to prevent escalation or protect others, it shaped officers' views differently than in cases where the motivation was perceived as less legitimate, such as revenge or manipulation.

Filing Charges

The second component of victims' motivation, as described by the officers, was related to victims' attitudes toward filing charges against suspects and was mostly observed in non-domestic cases. During their interactions with the police, the victims in this study were observed to have three attitudes toward filing charges. The first type of attitude I observed were victims who expressed that they wanted charges to be filed against the suspect, the second, were victims who said they did not want charges to be filed. The third and final were victims that were neutral, meaning that they did not express any specific desire toward filing or not filing charges against the suspect. In 4 out of the 14 non-domestic cases, I observed victims expressing that they wanted to file charges, additionally I observed six victims who did not want charges to be filed and three victims who appeared to be neutral toward filing charges. Thus, overall, it was more common during my observations that victims expressed not wanting to press charges compared to being neutral or wanting charges to be filed.

Among the cases that did not lead to a police report, only one victim was observed to want charges to be filed, while five victims expressed that they did not want charges filed, and one appeared neutral. In contrast, among the cases that yielded police reports, I observed that three victims expressed a desire to file charges, two were neutral, and one did not want charges filed. Thus, it was more common in the non-report cases for victims to express that they did not want charges filed, whereas in the report-yielding cases, victims were more likely to either want charges filed or be neutral.

The victim's preference regarding filing charges was discussed in five of the non-domestic cases during officers' interviews, thus in the majority of cases, officers did not mention charges as a major factor contributing to credibility. In the five cases where it was discussed, the victim's desire to file charges was mentioned in three, and the desire not to file charges was mentioned in two. When officers did refer to this issue in post-scene interviews, it was not framed as something that strictly improved or undermined the victim's credibility. Instead, it was discussed alongside other factors, such as the victim not wanting help, as something that made the officers' job either more difficult or more straightforward.

In most non-domestic cases, I observed officers on scene either asked the victim if they wanted to file charges, or the victim independently told the officers without being prompted. However, in two cases, Non-Domestic Cases 27 and 28, the notion of filing charges was handled differently by officers. Both incidents occurred in residential settings, one in a care facility for individuals with memory issues, and the other in a group home for individuals with disabilities. In one case, the violence occurred between residents; in the other, it was between a resident and a staff member. In Non-Domestic Case 28, I observed officers interacting with both the suspect and the victim. While on scene, I heard Officer Williams, the primary officer, tell another officer that due to the suspect's mental capabilities, he did not believe there was criminal intent behind the battery. I also observed a staff member telling Officer Williams that she did not want charges to be filed but instead hoped the resident would receive help. Additionally, Officer Williams asked an onsite care worker about the suspect's disability. The staff member explained that the suspect had behavioral issues related to her disability, which they believed had caused the incident. In Non-Domestic Case 27, which was also handled by Officer Williams, I observed that there no conversation occurred between Officer Williams and either the victim or the suspect. While observing the care staff speaking with Officer Williams, I heard the staff state that there was no point in speaking to either individual due to "their lack of capability to remember." Since the officers had to rely solely on the staff member's information, I asked the officers during the post-scene interview what he would have done if there was no staff member present to discuss the incident, and he replied:

> If the staff wasn't telling me, yeah, best verifying that, yeah, we were not needed, then we would still more than likely have one unit, go to the hospital with the victim, and have one unit pushed a little further, a little harder to talk to the other party involved. (Officer Williams)

Officer Williams had only six months of experience at the time of the incidents and noted that he had never handled cases like these before. On both scenes, Non-Domestic Cases 27 and 28, he was accompanied by senior officers, whom I observed him consulting with about how to manage the cases and how to navigate the issue of filing charges. In both cases, I observed that he was advised there was no criminal intent in the suspects' actions due to their mental capacity, and therefore charges should not be filed. Although this occurred in only 2 of the 14 non-domestic cases, both are important because they highlight how officers' discretion and actions can be shaped by laws and policies, specifically those related to criminal intent and the mental state of suspects.

Compared to victims' desire for help, attitudes toward filing charges were less commonly discussed by officers during post-scene interviews. Victims' attitudes toward filing charges were mentioned in only five cases, whereas their desire or non-desire for help was discussed in 11 non-domestic cases. These findings suggest that when officers talk about victim credibility, they tend to focus more on victims' motivations for seeking help than on their stance toward filing charges. Although the findings indicate that officers less frequently discussed victims' desire to file charges compared to their desire or non-desire for help, in certain cases both components were discussed together as part of the victim's overall motivation for engaging with police. In these instances, officers did not treat the desire to file charges and the desire for help as separate considerations, but rather as interconnected elements that shaped their perception of the victim's credibility and willingness to cooperate. This suggests that, while filing charges may not have been a dominant theme across all cases, it became relevant when aligned with broader motivations for seeking police involvement. For example, when discussing victims' desire for charges in two cases, two male officers explained:

> The victim, who was also a caretaker, or staff member at the group home, was not concerned with pressing charges for the battery nature or battery aspect of the incident but just wanted the subject to get help. Possibly, adjusting medication, or just talking to somebody, whatever, whatever workout. (Non-domestic Case 28, Officer Williams)

> But I believe that the victim understood that people suffered different mental issues, and she did not want to press charges on the alleged suspects. He just wanted him to know that that was not okay. (Non-domestic Case 26, Officer Torres)

In both cases, the victims' decision not to file charges was not discussed by officers as something that negatively impacted their perception of the victims. Instead, officers expressed that they believed the victims were more interested in helping the suspects than in pursuing punitive outcomes. As a result, even though the victims did not want to press charges, officers still found ways to assist them, primarily by identifying support options for the suspects to help prevent future victimization.

Overall, the officers' statements, observational data, and review of police reports suggest that motivation is a factor officers consider when forming an overall image of victims' credibility. Officers tended to discuss victims' need and desire for help more frequently than their preferences regarding filing charges. These two components desire for help and attitude toward filing charges were discussed both separately and, in some cases, simultaneously, depending on how officers interpreted the victim's overall motivation for engaging with police.

There are several factors that could influence why officers did not mention help-seeking and motivations for help-seeking in domestic cases. For example, domestic battery cases often involve ongoing relationships between victims and suspects, such as romantic partners, family members, or cohabitants, which can complicate the victim's willingness to seek help or press charges. Officers may anticipate ambivalence or emotional complexity in these cases and therefore may not explicitly discuss the victim's motivation unless it stands out as unusual or contradictory. In contrast, non-domestic cases often involve one-time or situational conflicts between acquaintances or strangers, where motivations for seeking help or filing charges may be more straightforward and thus more likely to be discussed. Additionally, officers may rely more heavily on departmental protocols and legal mandates in domestic battery cases, such as mandatory reporting or arrest policies, which can reduce the perceived relevance of the victim's preferences. In these cases, officers are obligated to proceed with certain actions regardless of the victim's stated desires, which could explain why motivation and charge preferences are less frequently mentioned in post-scene interviews. I observed several instance where officers told domestic battery victims that if they found that a crime had occurred and there was probable cause for an arrest, officers had no choice but to arrest the suspect. What the victim wanted or not wanted did not matter for the procedure as the petitioner was not the victim, but rather the state according to the law. Thus, even though the victim was the individual who experienced the victimizations, officers had to press charges because they had no discretion. Officers' reliance on departmental protocols and legal mandates in domestic battery cases is reflected in empirical findings that police are more proactive in offering assistance to domestic violence victims, even though actual arrest rates remain low (Sun, 2006). Although the legal guidelines are directing officers decisions in domestic cases to a higher degree than in non-domestic cases, Sun's also found that while officers are more likely to provide information and support to domestic violence victims, their responses to direct requests for help, such as filing charges or making arrests, are shaped by victim characteristics such as wealth, willingness to cooperate, and context. This could suggest that systemic patterns of proactivity may coexist with selective responsiveness, reinforcing the importance of understanding both formal policy and informal discretion in shaping victim outcomes.

Emotional Display

Contrary to the role of help-seeking and motivations for help-seeking, emotional display was something that was mentioned by officers and observed in both domestic and non-domestic cases. However, it was brought up in slightly different ways depending on the context.

Due to the emphasis that previous scholarship place on the importance of victims' behavior and emotions (Ask, 2010), I paid close attention to the demeanor victims displayed at the scene and asked officers to describe the victims' demeanor following their encounters. Across both types of cases, I observed that victims displayed a wide range of behaviors, which aligns with previous research exploring the variations in trauma responses (Figley, 2013). Additionally, many victims shifted their demeanor during the encounter with police.

I specifically noticed some variations between the behaviors I observed on scene and how officers later described the victims, which may be attributed to several factors. Although I observed four non-domestic battery victims crying during their interaction with police, only in two of those cases did officers mention that the victim had cried during the interviews. This omission could be due to differences in perception, officers may not have interpreted the behavior in the same way I did, or it may reflect selective recall or a decision not to discuss that aspect during the interview. When describing victim demeanor, officers frequently used emotional labels such as "upset," "angry," or "calm." In contrast, my observation notes focused on describing specific behaviors and physical cues. For example, I recorded statements such as "victim has a loud voice and is using animated body language," or "the victim is speaking with a quiet and calm voice and is sitting down while speaking to the officer."

Emotional Distress and Behavioral Cues

While speaking about victims' demeanor in domestic cases officers brought up the display of emotional distress, such as victims being upset, sad, crying, or distraught. While on scene, I observed 11 domestic victims crying during their interaction with officers, and 4 victims speaking with a loud voice. When asked to describe the victims they encountered, officers used terms such as upset, sad, crying, or distraught in 11 out of the 20 domestic cases. These emotional descriptors were mentioned in three of the corresponding police reports. However, when officers specifically discussed credibility, they only noted in three cases that these negative emotions directly impacted their perception of the victim's credibility.

When describing victims' demeanor officers' statements suggested that they considered a range of behavioral cues which they then assigned emotional meaning. These cues included crying, tone of voice, facial expressions, and body language. Yet, the emotional labels assigned, such as "upset" or "distraught," did not always translate into credibility, for example, in Domestic Case 20, Officer Thompson stated:

> When we contacted the female, she did have some redness to her right cheek. And her eyes were watery, red, and puffy as if she'd been crying. And as she was trying to explain the incident, she was upset and her voice was breaking. They were able to communicate well in English, considering they are of Asian descent. So, we did not have to use a translator their English was good enough to conduct the investigation, but you can still tell he was very visibly upset.

Thompson emphasized that, although there was at times a language barrier, he could still understand the behavioral cues and emotions the victim was displaying during the encounter. He explained that these cues impacted how he perceived the victim during their interaction, however he did not say that the victim's emotional display increased her perceived credibility. Thus, in this example, although not impacting the credibility emotional and behavioral indicators transcended the verbal communication and still influence officers' assessment of victims.

In addition to being mentioned during interviews, behavioral cues and emotional displays were also noted in a few police reports. For example, in the report for Domestic Case 2, Officer Willson wrote: "Multiple times during the interview, he began to cry and was shaken about the incident. He truly believes that she might try to kill him one day." In Domestic Case 17, another male officer wrote: "I made contact with (Name redacted) [VIC] who was upset and appeared to be crying." These examples show that emotionality was sometimes documented, but not consistently across cases. When comparing the cases where emotional cues were mentioned in both the interview and the report as influencing officers' perception of victim credibility, I found no overlap. In none of the cases where officers described emotions as positively influencing their perception of credibility was it mentioned in the corresponding police report. Because officers did mention emotions such as sadness, crying, or being distraught, while describing victims, the findings indicate that emotions are something officers observe and remember, even if they are not formally recorded or directly tied to credibility assessments in documentation.

Throughout the interviews officers pointed out that victims react differently to victimization and therefore may behave in different ways when they encounter police, which confirms previous research that shows that emotional diversity is a hallmark of trauma response (Figley, 2013). However, as highlighted in Epstein and Goodman (2019), this emotional diversity is often not fully appreciated in practice, and victims who do not display expected emotions may be subject to credibility discounting. Furthermore, empirical studies show that gender and intersectional stereotypes continue to shape both expectations and interpretations of victim behavior. For example, Phillips and de Roos (2022) found that emotionality is more expected and accepted in female victims, while male victims' emotional displays are often interpreted differently or even penalized and Epstein and Goodman (2019) demonstrate that women's credibility is more easily discounted, especially for those who are poor, non-White, or otherwise marginalized.

Although the gendered and racial differences could not be further explored in this study due to the limited sample and uneven gender and racial distribution of the sample, the recognition of emotional diversity was evident in several cases. For example, when describing the demeanor of the victim in Domestic Case 4, Officer Lee noted: "she was upset I guess, to a certain extent, I mean, not as upset as some people that you know, different people handle things differently." The officers statement reflects an awareness that emotional reactions are not standardized and that officers may interpret victim demeanor within a broader context of individual variability. Some victims were not described as sad or crying, but rather as frustrated or upset. The fact that officers acknowledged this range of emotional responses could suggests that they may observe and interpret victim demeanor through a flexible lens and that they recognize that emotional expression is shaped by personality, context, and the nature of the incident.

Another example was in Domestic Case 33 where the two officers described the victim:

> She seemed very animated when we first got there and seemed to be quite emotional about the events that took place and were still, you know, kind of yelling while explaining the whole situation. And going back to the drawing, it's always there different for each victim, on how they respond to law enforcement or just reenacting or remembering the incident that they went through. (Officer Garcia)

> She appeared to be frustrated. I think she really was frustrated with the situation. (Officer Mitchell)

Despite the awareness of that demeanor can vary between victims, some of the officers' statements suggested that certain normative assessments were still made based on behavioral cues, particularly those that aligned with emotional distress, which they then linked to victims' credibility. For example, in Domestic Case 4, I observed the victim crying while speaking to officers and expressing worry about her husband. In the interview, the Officer Willson noted that the victim became more credible because of her voice and facial expression, and described the victim as "emotional and upset." When asked whether he found her credible, he said: "Yes. Once again, like just that sound of her voice. That and the facial expressions. You know, you can tell there's something that had happened." In this example, the officer interpreted the victim's emotional display, specifically her voice and facial expression, as evidence that something had occurred, which positively impacted his perception of her credibility. Another example was in Domestic Case 30, where Officer Williams stated that the victim seemed credible:

> Yes. Because he just seemed genuine genuinely stressed out with ongoing issues. And I could tell that he almost regretted calling law enforcement once he realized what the results may be. I could tell that he was genuine genuinely upset about ongoing issues, and I could tell that he was being

> sincere when he was venting to me. Because typically people who are being sincere about venting, have based on my experience, a hard time focusing on my direct questions, because they're just so upset about what's been going on.

In both cases, officers indicated that the emotions victims displayed during the encounter positively impacted their perception of the victims' credibility. These examples show how emotional expression, particularly when it aligns with officers' expectations of distress, can serve as a validating factor in assessing the authenticity of victim narratives. Whether through crying, vocal tone, or facial expressions, the emotional demeanor of victims was not only observed but actively interpreted as evidence of truthfulness. This may suggest that while officers are trained to recognize a wide range of victim responses, emotional display remains a powerful heuristic in field assessments, and it also highlights the dual role of emotional display as a behavioral cue that can act as a credibility marker. However, it is essential to again emphasize that the display of emotions, such as crying or being sad, to inform credibility assessment was only seen in a few domestic battery cases.

An important finding from observing non-domestic battery victims and interviewing officers is that officers in this study did not consistently mention emotions as a major contributor to their perceptions of victim credibility. Victim demeanor was brought up in 8 of the 14 non-domestic cases, four non-report-yielding cases and four report-yielding cases. Among the four non-domestic cases that yielded reports, victims' demeanor was not mentioned in any of the corresponding police reports. In interviews, officers described demeanor as influencing their perception of credibility in eight cases, three negatively, three positively, and two neutrally. However, instead of noting that the emotional display was impacting credibility officers discussed victims' demeanor as an indication of their willingness to cooperate. For example, in Non-Domestic Case 23, both male officers described the victim as "standoffish" and linked this to her unwillingness to cooperate, stating: "She was uncooperative." Similarly, in Non-Domestic Case 14, Officer Clark explained, "She had a hard time communicating with me verbally, but I could tell that she was very angry based on her body language and noises that she was making." In both cases, officers interpreted emotional cues, such as anger or withdrawal, as signs of non-cooperation or difficulty in communication. Thus, emotional displays in non-domestic cases were less frequently linked to credibility assessments., instead, while officers still observed and described victims as upset or distraught, these emotions were not consistently interpreted as validating the victim's account but rather linked to cooperation.

Although officers did not mention that victims' emotions impacted their perception credibility in non-domestic cases, they recognized and mentioned emotional display. I noticed that officers tended to discuss the victims' demeanor by describing what they thought caused the victim to behave or feel in a certain way. For example, in Non-Domestic Case 8, Officer Thompson stated:

> I think she was a little, she was a little affected. I mean, I think at some point, you could physically see her frustration. I think her voice fluctuation would change slightly as she was describing the incident or the event. With her interaction with the potential suspects. You could hear her voice raise up and her speech will get accelerated. At some points. I think she was so frustrated that her eyes would water. So, I think you could say that she was very alarmed and very, very emotional about the incident.

In this example, Officer Thompson ascribed the victim's behavior and emotional display as a direct result of the victimization. He drew parallels between the victim's demeanor and the behaviors that are socially expected of victims, applying these normative expectations to interpret the victim's emotional state which resulted in a perceived relationship between the victim's demeanor and the experience of victimization itself.

Officers did not seem to exclusively describe victims' demeanor because of the incident. In several cases, they also attributed emotional responses to the victims' interactions with police. This dual framing, where demeanor is seen both as a reaction to trauma and as a response to law enforcement, suggests that officers may view emotional display as fluid and context dependent. It also highlights how officers' interpretations may not only be shaped only by the event itself but by the relational dynamics that unfold during the encounter. For example, Officer Campbell explained the demeanor of the victim in Non-Domestic Case 34:

> She was obviously agitated, upset by the situation, her body language was. Like her arms were crossed off not wanting to be bothered, especially in sight of the girl who did it to her. She seemed agitated, initially that I guess she thought the police weren't going to do anything or that they didn't believe her. So definitely frustrated.

Rather than assuming that the victimization caused the victim's demeanor, Officer Campbell alluded to the victim's interaction with police and her preset expectations of potentially not being believed, influenced her conduct during the encounter. Similarly, another officer described the victim's demeanor by suggesting that there were factors beyond the victimization that influenced how she behaved during the interaction. This framing implies that officers sometimes recognize that victims' emotional displays may be shaped by broader psychological, social, or situational factors, including prior experiences with law enforcement, fear of disbelief, or internalized expectations about how a "credible" victim should behave. Officer Moore, described the victim of Non-Domestic Case 5:

> She was nervous. Upon my arrival, she immediately shut the door behind her to the hotel and wanted to go to the hotel room and kind of wanted to get away from it. There's probably something inside of the hotel room she was concerned about, might have been like, you know, something illegal, maybe narcotics, I'm not sure. But, you know, she was smoking a cigarette, which a lot of people do to kind of calm their nerves down. But she was totally okay with being near the suspect. She went out and borrowed a lighter from him and said everything was fine. But in terms of her demeanor, other than just being nervous, with law enforcement presence, it appears like she was nervous because I was ask-

ing her about battery, but she was nervous about something else for some reason.

Officer Moore alluded to potential illegal activities as a cause of the victim's behavior and emotional display. She based this interpretation on several observational clues, including the victim's reluctance to show officers the place she was staying at, visible nervousness, and smoking a cigarette. These cues were not described as emotional responses to victimization, but as indicators of possible concealment or guilt, suggesting that officers may sometimes interpret demeanor through a lens of suspicion rather than trauma.

Fear and Worry

During my observation and interviews I also found that officers brought up the victims' level of fear or worry, however this was almost exclusively in domestic cases. Among the domestic cases fear and worry was the most frequently mentioned emotional theme, appearing in nine of the report-yielding cases and in one non-report-yielding case. It was also documented in four police reports, two of which aligned with what officers mentioned during interviews, and two where fear was noted in the report but not discussed in the interview.

Fear and worry were described as having a positive influence on credibility in four report-yielding domestic cases and in one non-report-yielding case. In these report-yielding cases, fear and worry were consistently mentioned across the case progression, at the scene by the victim, during the interview by the officer, and in the corresponding police report. In two additional cases, fear and worry were mentioned only at the scene and in the interview. In the one non-report-yielding domestic case where fear and worry were described as positively influencing credibility, these emotions were mentioned both at the scene and by the officer during the interview.

When officers discussed victims' fear and worry as influencing their perceptions of credibility, they did so in two distinct ways. First, they described perceiving that the domestic battery victim felt fear during their interaction with police. Second, they noted that victims explicitly told them they had experienced fear during the incident. In both instances, officers interpreted the presence of fear and worry as indicators of credibility, even in instances where officers ultimately determined that no crime had been committed. During interviews, some officers specifically mentioned that victims had expressed fear during the incident. For example, in Domestic Case 9, Officer White stated: "Part of me feels she knew what she was doing, trying to get out of town. But I feel she had a genuine fear of this gentleman that she was accusing of battering her." Similarly, in Domestic Case 33, Officer Garcia noted: "She said she was scared of her boyfriend." In both cases, the officers emphasized the victims' fear of their abusers, and this emotional response was the first aspect of demeanor they mentioned when asked to describe the victim.

While not all officers led with fear in their descriptions, many highlighted it as a central emotional cue. Hence to many officers it seem like fear, whether observed or disclosed, was often interpreted as a sign of authenticity and emotional display with the victimization narrative. It also reinforces the idea that emotional display, particularly fear and worry, can serve as a credibility-enhancing factor in officers' assessments, even when the legal outcome does not result in a report. In Domestic Case 2, Officer Willson stated:

> The victim was shaken. He had bruises, cuts and scrapes all over his person. He had tears in his eyes at one point and generally fears for his safety… He is…You can tell he's frightful. He's frustrated that nothing seems to get done on his…this case or his prior cases. He's very worried that it's escalating and that he's gonna get seriously hurt. He's fearful for one that he comes and even talks about it because most men would not report a demotes domestic or dating violence. The fact that he cries and gets emotional when he's talking about what happened to him, and that he's willing to provide statements and the fact that he's willing to take photos. All of that leads to that.

Willson did not only discuss the domestic battery victim's fear when describing his demeanor during the interview, but also documented it in the subsequent police report. Officer Willson depicted the victim's emotional state by stating: "This behavior has caused emotional distress to the point that he is in fear for his safety." In his report, Willson noted that the victimization had caused the victim to fear for his life, an emotion the victim also expressed during the interaction. After the interview concluded, Officer Willson reflected that the victim's fear made him feel strongly about wanting to arrest the suspect. This suggests that the victim's emotional display, particularly fear, may have influenced the officer's motivation and sense of urgency, possibly in combination with other factors.

It was not only the domestic battery victims' own fear or worry that contributed to their perceived credibility. In Domestic Case 19, where the victim was threatened with a firearm and her children were present, the officer explained that the children's fear also impacted his perception of the victim's credibility. Officer Robinson noted: "We talked to the kid before even speaking to them [the victim]. Their stories of fear for life… the kids definitely were in fear because they ran outside." For this officer, the fear described by the children reinforced the credibility of the victim's account. In the corresponding police report, Officer Robinson also documented the victim's fear: "The VIC stated that when she saw the firearm she became in fear for her life." Thus, in Domestic Case 19, both the victim's and the children's emotional responses were acknowledged by the officer and formally recorded, further illustrating how fear, whether expressed by the victim or observed in others, can serve as a credibility-enhancing factor.

Another way that victims' fear and worry were discussed was in relation to how officers perceived victims' demeanor during their interactions. In these instances, officers did not refer to fear as something victims explicitly expressed but rather used it to describe how victims appeared to feel or behave during the encounter. For example, in Domestic Case 25, Officer Torres described the victim as "Frantic, Scared and looking… Just kind of like a nervous state." Here, Officer Torres combined the label "scared" with other descriptors such as "frantic" and "nervous," suggesting that fear was inferred from the victim's physical and emotional presentation rather than directly stated. In another example, in Domestic Case 4, the victim had been attacked by her husband of ten years, who was suffering from Alzheimer's disease. When describing the domestic battery victim's demeanor on the scene both officers highlighted the victim's fear:

> Victim was pretty emotional. Which that's, you know, standard from someone being in a, almost potentially being stabbed. But, you know, she was you know, she was just in a heightened sense of fear. She wanted, she wanted help, she needed help. She was looking for us to give it to him. (Officer Martin)

> She seemed afraid of him. She didn't want to go back across the house. She kept asking if he was there. She wanted to show us the knives. I don't know if she was worried that we wouldn't believe her or not. That's not abnormal, though. But she didn't want to go back over there. She's asking if he was there if we were going to take him anywhere, which we did, ultimately. (Officer Lee)

Officer Martin, the primary officer on the case, explained the impact the victim's fear had on his perception of her credibility:

> Just the level of fear and emotion that she had. You could tell that that wasn't something that was just this, she wasn't pretending…like just that sound of her voice. That's the facial expressions. You know, you can tell there's something that had happened.

In this case, the primary officer noted that the victim's voice and facial expression showed that she was scared of her husband. He explained that the victim's fear indicated she was not pretending to have been victimized, and that her emotional display gave credibility to her account of the incident. In Domestic Case 29, the victim's son called 911, reporting that his mother's boyfriend had hit her. When I arrived on scene, the suspect was no longer present, and the victim was at her apartment with her two minor children. The victim explained to officers that she had a long history of domestic violence with her ex-boyfriend, whom she had been with on and off for ten years and who was the father of her youngest child. She stated that they were no longer together and that she had an injunction against him. Despite this, she reported that he had broken into her home while she was away overnight, and when she returned and asked him to leave, he grabbed her by the neck. During her interaction with police, I observed the victim cry several times and heard her say that she was really scared of him coming back and hurting her. One of the officers on scene, Officer Green, described the victim as "she's very scared. And she was concerned that we would not be able to do anything for a short period of time and that he would come back… She was scared. Absolutely upset. Hoping we arrest him soon." This officer's description highlights how fear was not only observed but also interpreted as a legitimate emotional response to the threat, reinforcing the victim's credibility and urgency of the situation. Furthermore, when I asked Officer Green whether he thought the victim was credible and why, he responded "yes," noting that it was because "she seemed genuinely scared." The victim's fear was also documented in the corresponding police report, where an officer wrote: "The Vic advised that she is extremely scared that the DEF will return and hurt her. The VIC stated that the DEF said that if she called the police 'he will have something for me.'" In Domestic Case 29, the victim's fear was thus mentioned in both the interview and the report, and was explicitly noted as a factor that impacted Officer Green's perception of her credibility. The officer's statements and the documentation in the report reflected the fear I observed on scene, where I heard the victim state several times that she was scared of the suspect coming back to hurt her. Domestic Cases 4 and 29 both highlight that domestic battery victims' fear of the suspect, and their display of this fear during interactions with officers, are taken into consideration when assessing credibility. In some cases, fear and worry were mentioned in both interviews and reports, and in others, they were directly linked to officers' assessments of credibility.

Overall, fear and worry were notions that indicated credibility for some officers. However, these emotions did not solely lend credibility to the occurrence of a violent altercation, they also assigned credibility to the victims themselves. For example, in Domestic Case 13, a victim visited a doctor who then called the police due to the statements the victim was making. After arriving at the scene and speaking with the victim, the officer told me that he had established the victim had not experienced battery. Instead, she was worried that the arguments and fight she had with her former partner were going to escalate into a physical altercation. When discussing the credibility of the domestic battery victim, Officer Clark noted: "Her doctor that call it in because the statements that she made to him that she was scared that it would get to something physical with this subject that was at her house." Although the officer determined that no physical altercation had occurred and that she was not a victim of battery, he still believed the victim was credible due to her fear of escalation.

Conclusion

In this chapter I discussed the impact help-seeking and its motivations as well as victims' emotions have have on credibility. In non-domestic cases officers highlighted that victims' motivations, both prior to contacting the police and during the interaction, can shape how officers assess their credibility. Officers noted that the victim's need for help, and the victim's preferred outcome can impact their level of credibility. However, the findings indicate that some officers make a normative assessment on the reasons for why victims seek help and can deem certain reasons as aligning more with reasons of why victims should want to seek help. For example, when victims frame their need for police assistance as prevention and protection, officers may interpret the motivations as legitimate which can positively influence their perception of the victim's credibility.

Previous research has found that victims' behavior and emotional expressions can significantly influence officers' perceptions of credibility in domestic violence cases (Ask, 2010; Ask & Landström, 2010; Coulter et al., 1999; Stewart & Maddren, 1997). However, the findings in this study provide only partial support for these conclusions. While some officers did highlight that victims' demeanor, particularly expressions of fear and worry, positively impacted their perception of credibility, such observations were limited to a small subset of cases. Specifically, these officers noted that when victims expressed being scared or worried during the incident, or were observed to display fear during the encounter, these emotional cues contributed to a more favorable assessment of credibility. Similarly, emotions such as crying or appearing upset were occasionally linked to credibility, but again, only by a few officers.

The findings also point to inconsistencies between what is observed and discussed in interviews and what is formally documented in police reports. Emotional displays were rarely recorded in reports, even in cases where officers acknowledged their influence on credibility. This may suggest that while emotionality may shape officers' perceptions in the moment, it is not systematically captured in official documentation, potentially limiting its procedural impact. The gap between officers' field observations and what is formally documented in police reports is a recurring theme in the literature. Ask (2010) and DeJong et al. (2008) both note that while emotionality and motivation may influence officers' field decisions, these factors are inconsistently recorded in official documentation.

References

Ask, K. (2010). A survey of police officers' and prosecutors' beliefs about crime victim behaviors. *Journal of Interpersonal Violence, 25*(6), 1132–1149. https://doi.org/10.1177/0886260509340535

Ask, K., & Landström, S. (2010). Why emotions matter: Expectancy violation and affective response mediate the emotional victim effect. *Law and Human Behavior, 34*(5), 392–401. https://doi.org/10.1007/s10979-009-9208-6

Christie, N. (1986). The ideal victim. In E. Fattah (Ed.), *From crime policy to victim policy* (pp. 17–30). Palgrave Macmillan. https://doi.org/10.1007/978-1-349-08305-3_2

Coulter, M. L., Kuehnle, K., Byers, R., & Alfonso, M. (1999). Police-reporting behavior and victim-police interactions as described by women in a domestic violence shelter. *Journal of Interpersonal Violence, 14*(12), 1290–1298. https://doi.org/10.1177/088626099014012004

DeJong, C., Burgess-Proctor, A., & Elis, L. (2008). Police officer perceptions of intimate partner violence: An analysis of observational data. *Violence and Victims, 23*(6), 683–696. https://doi.org/10.1891/0886-6708.23.6.683

El Sayed, S. A., DeShay, R. A., Davis, J. B., Knox, K. N., & Kerley, K. R. (2022). A blue step forward: An exploratory study of law enforcement perceptions of intimate partner violence in the Southern United States. *Journal of Interpersonal Violence, 37*(9–10), 6514–6534. https://doi.org/10.1177/0886260520966675

Epstein, D., & Goodman, L. A. (2019). Discounting women: Doubting domestic violence survivors' credibility and dismissing their experiences. *University of Pennsylvania Law Review, 167*(2), 399–462. https://scholarship.law.georgetown.edu/facpub/2037

Figley, C. R. (2013). *Trauma and its wake*. Routledge.

Phillips, A., & de Roos, M. S. (2022). Gender stereotypes and perceptions of stranger violence: Attributions of blame and motivation. *International Journal of Offender Therapy and Comparative Criminology*, Online first. https://doi.org/10.1177/0306624X221124849

Stewart, A., & Maddren, K. (1997). Police officers' judgements of blame in family violence: The impact of gender and alcohol. *Sex Roles, 37*, 921–933. https://doi.org/10.1007/BF02936347

Strobl, R. (2004). Constructing the victim: Theoretical reflections and empirical examples. *International Review of Victimology, 11*(2–3), 295–311. https://doi.org/10.1177/026975800401100206

Sun, I. Y. (2006). Police response to victims of domestic and non-domestic violence. *Journal of Health and Human Services Administration, 29*(2), 145–172. http://www.jstor.org/stable/25790685

Van Wijk, J. (2013). Who is the 'little old lady 'of international crimes? Nils Christie's concept of the Ideal Victim reinterpreted. *International Review of Victimology, 19*(2), 159–179. https://doi.org/10.1177/0143034312472770

9

Perceptions and Depictions of Victim Credibility and the Ideal Victims

Introduction

In this final chapter, I return to the three central research questions that guided this book: a) How do police officers perceive victim credibility among battery victims?, b) How do police officers describe and depict victim credibility in police reports?, and c) What are the similarities and differences between officers' descriptions of victim credibility in reports and their reflections after encounters with victims? Drawing on data collected through ride-alongs, interviews, and police reports, this chapter offers a deeper analysis of how officers construct and communicate credibility assessments. I examine the interplay between observed behavior, emotional display, institutional documentation, and post-incident reflection. These findings are then situated within the framework of the Ideal Victim Theory developed by Christie (1986) and expanded by Strobl (2004), allowing for an examination of how normative expectations shape officers' interpretations of victimhood.

Before addressing each research question in turn, it is important to acknowledge the dynamic and multifaceted nature of credibility assessments. Officers' perceptions are influenced by a combination of factors,

M. N. Eliasson, *Who Gets Believed?*, Palgrave's Critical Policing Studies,
https://doi.org/10.1007/978-3-032-22253-4_9

including emotional expression, injury, cooperation, and contextual cues, that do not operate in isolation. These elements interact in complex ways, often shaped by both formal training and informal norms. As such, my aims are not only to answer the research questions but also to reflect on the broader implications of how victim credibility is constructed, documented, and understood within the policing context.

In previous chapters, various aspects of victim credibility, such as emotional display, injury, and cooperation, have been discussed in detail. However, it is important to acknowledge that these factors were often presented as distinct and dichotomous, which may suggest that they operate independently. This is not true. Officers consistently described their credibility assessments as being shaped by multiple, interrelated factors rather than isolated cues. In nearly every case, officers referenced more than one element, such as the victim's emotional state, physical injuries, demeanor, and willingness to cooperate, as contributing to their overall perception. This emphasizes the dynamic and layered nature of credibility construction, where factors interact and reinforce one another in complex ways. Rather than functioning as discrete indicators, these elements form a combination of cues that officers interpret in context, shaped by both institutional expectations and individual judgment. During our discussion of a victim, one of the officers, Officer Lee explained the many factors that impacted her perception of the female victim.

> She gave me some information about how the police had responded out there before. So I was able to look up the call history at that address and confirm that we have been out there for disturbances between the two of them before. She also, as I said had injuries that were clearly fresh because the one on her arm was red, it was a fresh abrasion, the one on her left eyelid was, you know, clearly just occurred those, you know what she was saying happen was backed up by injuries that I saw to her. Later on, after her husband was taken away from the house, I went inside with her. There were things knocked over here and there. The knives that she described were a small one, and a big one, they were on the kitchen counter next to each other. There was like an area rug that was kind of crooked a little bit. And then it was kind of scrunched up like the edge had been pushed

> towards the middle. So, there were different things that were placed in the house that were consistent with kind of them moving throughout different locations in the house, a struggle occurred.

The statements provided by officers such as Officer Lee illustrate the multifactorial nature of credibility assessments. Officer Lee's account demonstrates how emotional display was not interpreted in isolation but was considered alongside the victim's injuries, the history with the suspect, and the coherence of her narrative. Similarly, Officer Green's reflection in Domestic Case 29, "Everything was pretty straightforward, nothing outlandish claims of injuries, and she seemed genuinely scared," shows that his perception of credibility was shaped by a combination of the victim's emotional state, the plausibility of her account, and the presence of physical evidence. These examples are not isolated, nearly all officers in the sample described their credibility assessments as being informed by multiple, overlapping factors. Only two cases deviated from this pattern, further emphasizing that officers rarely rely on a single indicator when evaluating victims. Therefore, the various factors discussed throughout this book should not be viewed as independent or hierarchically ordered. Specifically, the findings do not suggest that one factor consistently outweighs another in officers' assessments., rather they reveal that officers interpret credibility through a holistic lens, where elements related to the victim, the suspect, and the incident itself are interwoven.

The interconnectedness of credibility factors during my time in the field challenges the notion that officers rely on isolated cues when assessing victims. Instead, officers appear to engage in a form of situational assessment, where emotional display, injury, cooperation, and narrative coherence are interpreted collectively, while also using organizational policies and laws and professional experiences. The process reflects a dynamic construction of credibility, where no single factor is determinative but rather contributes to a broader impression shaped by context. For example, emotional expressions such as fear or crying were often interpreted more favorably when accompanied by visible injuries or a coherent account of events. Conversely, the absence of one factor, such as physical evidence, did not necessarily undermine credibility if other elements aligned with officers' expectations, suggesting that officers are not applying rigid criteria but are instead navigating a fluid evaluative process informed by multiple, overlapping cues.

The complex relationship and combination of factors impacting victim credibility aligns with and simultaneously complicates the framework of Ideal Victim Theory. Christie (1986) posits that the Ideal Victim is weak, blameless, and emotionally affected, traits that officers in this study did recognize and respond to. However, the findings also reveal that officers do not apply these characteristics uniformly. Strobl's (2004) expansion of the theory emphasizes the role of the audience in constructing victim legitimacy, and in this context, officers act as that audience, selectively interpreting which traits matter and when. The presence of injuries may signal weakness, and emotional distress may suggest authenticity, but these traits only gain credibility when they are perceived as congruent with the broader narrative and context. Thus, one can argue that the Ideal Victim is perhaps not a fixed template but a flexible construct shaped by officers' interpretations of multiple, interrelated factors. Hence, to understand victim credibility we may need to view credibility not as a checklist of traits but as a negotiated outcome influenced by institutional norms, personal judgment, and situational dynamics.

How Do Police Officers Perceive Victim Credibility Among Battery Victims?

The findings presented in this book indicate that for most of the 34 cases included in this sample, officers perceive victims to be credible, a perception that persists across both non-domestic and domestic cases. This consistency suggests that skepticism toward victim accounts tends to be uncommon regardless of the relational context of the violence. However, while the overarching perception of credibility remains stable, the factors officers mention as influencing these perceptions reveal both similarities and differences between the two case types. Officers in both domestic and non-domestic batteries emphasize the importance of victims' willingness to provide information to the police. A cooperative stance is interpreted as enhancing credibility, whereas reluctance is viewed as diminishing it.

Similarly, officers in both domestic and non-domestic cases stress the significance of narrative detail and consistency. When victims are able to provide a coherent and detailed account, their credibility is heightened and when they cannot, it tends to impact credibility negatively. This finding aligns with previous scholarship exploring domestic and interpersonal violence (Ask, 2010; Bostaph et al., 2021), reinforcing the notion that narrative coherence functions as a key credibility marker. The presence or absence of physical injuries also plays a central role in shaping officers' assessments. Injuries and visible marks are often interpreted as corroborative evidence, enhancing credibility, while their absence tends to have the opposite effect. This pattern confirms earlier empirical studies on officers' perceptions of credibility among victims of domestic violence (El Sayed et al., 2022; Waaland & Keeley, 1985).

In addition to the shared factors influencing officers' perceptions of victim credibility, this study also reveals distinct differences between domestic and non-domestic cases. In non-domestic cases, officers described how victims' need for help and their motivation for seeking assistance influenced their perceptions of credibility. This dimension, where the urgency or clarity of the victim's help-seeking behavior serves as a credibility marker, was notably absent in officers' accounts of domestic cases. Moreover, officers handling non-domestic incidents more frequently emphasized the role of external corroboration, such as witnesses and surveillance footage, in shaping their assessments. The presence of such evidence was seen as positively reinforcing the victim's account, whereas its absence could weaken credibility. This reliance on third-party validation was not mentioned in the context of domestic cases, suggesting a divergence in the types of evidence officers prioritize depending on the relational context of the violence. Officers also highlighted the prior history of violence between the victim and the offender as a factor that shaped their credibility assessments in domestic cases. This finding supports earlier research on domestic violence (Bostaph et al., 2021), yet it stands in contrast to non-domestic cases, where prior criminal history was not mentioned as influencing officers' perceptions.

How Do Police Officers Describe and Depict Victim Credibility Among Battery Victims in Police Reports?

GPD general investigation guidelines do not present specific rules on how officers should write reports, but I observed that most officers, seem to rely on templates from previous reports they had written. Every report they submitted had to be approved by a sergeant or corporal, which added a layer of oversight but did not standardize the content or structure. I noticed that officers appeared to have more discretion in deciding whether or not to write a report in non-domestic cases compared to domestic cases. This discrepancy may be attributed to the pro-arrest policy in place for domestic batteries and the fact that investigation guidelines were more specific for domestic batteries than for non-domestic ones. In non-domestic batteries, officers noted that staffing and workload, along with the victim's willingness to participate in the investigation, influenced their decision to document the incident formally. These practical constraints often shaped whether a report was written at all.

Among the 34 cases in this study, 21 resulted in a police report. Of the 20 domestic cases, 15 had reports, while only 6 of the 14 non-domestic cases were documented. This disparity highlights how procedural expectations and policy frameworks, such as the pro-arrest stance in domestic violence, can lead to more consistent documentation in domestic cases. However, it also suggests that non-domestic victims may be less likely to have their experiences formally recorded, potentially limiting their access to justice and support services.

Officers' depictions of victims and their credibility in the reports were notably limited. When discussing victims, officers typically included the victims' version of events, and in some cases noted if the victims were reluctant to provide information. They also recorded the presence or absence of injuries, and when injuries were present, officers often described their location. These injury descriptions appeared more frequently in domestic case reports. In several instances, officers indicated whether victims were willing to have photographs taken of their injuries, which added a layer of documentation but also reflected the victim's level of cooperation.

Other forms of corroborating evidence, such as video footage and witness statements, were more commonly mentioned in non-domestic cases. This discrepancy may be attributed to the fact that most domestic cases lacked witnesses present during the victimization, limiting the availability of third-party accounts. In contrast, non-domestic incidents often occurred in public or semi-public settings, increasing the likelihood of external evidence. Officers also documented the relationship between the involved parties. In domestic cases, this was typically described through the nature of the romantic relationship, such as marriage or dating, and the length of that relationship. Officers noted whether there had been prior violence between the parties or between the suspect and other individuals. In non-domestic cases, officers usually explained the context in which the victim and suspect encountered each other, which often involved no prior relationship. The limited inclusion of emotional cues, reluctance, and relational history in reports may obscure the full context of domestic victimization, while non-domestic victims benefit from clearer narrative structures and more readily available third-party evidence. Although GPD guidelines do not prescribe specific standards for report writing, the discretion afforded to officers may inadvertently reinforce disparities in how different types of victims are represented and validated within the investigative process.

Overall, the depiction of victim credibility in police reports was very limited compared to how it was discussed during interviews and observed on scene. This limitation may stem not only from the relatively small number of cases that resulted in written reports, particularly among the non-domestic cases, but also from the content of the reports that were generated. Several factors may explain this constrained representation. First, officers exercised discretion in deciding whether or not to write a report, which directly contributed to the limited number of documented cases. Second, when reports were written, officers followed certain procedural norms and organizational practices, such as using basic templates or aligning their content with the preferences of supervising sergeants or corporals. This oversight may have influenced how officers framed their narratives, potentially prioritizing information that supported probable cause for arrest over more nuanced depictions of victim credibility.

These findings confirm previous scholarship that highlights how both organizational structures and individual-level discretion shape the content of police reports (Hess & Wrobleski, 1996; Redwine, 2003). The institutional emphasis on formatting, evidentiary thresholds, and supervisory approval may constrain officers' ability or willingness to include subjective assessments of victim demeanor, emotional state, or credibility. As a result, the richness of officers' on-scene observations and interview reflections often fails to translate into the formal documentation process.

What Are the Similarities and Differences Between Police Officers Describing Victim Credibility in Reports and After Encounters with Victims?

Overall, the results indicate that while some of the aspects officers emphasized in interviews as influencing their perception of victim credibility could be found in the police reports, these elements were only briefly mentioned when they appeared. The limited number of reports, particularly among the non-domestic cases, further constrained the ability to draw meaningful comparisons between the interviews and the written documentation. Nevertheless, despite the small sample of non-domestic reports, some similarities and differences emerged in how victims and their credibility were depicted across the two formats.

One recurring topic in both interviews and reports was the presence of injuries and marks. In interviews, officers discussed injuries and marks as indicators that lent credibility to the victim's account by corroborating that a victimization had occurred. In the reports, the presence or absence of injuries, along with their location and nature, was mentioned in most cases. However, while injuries may signal corroboration and contribute to credibility assessments, their inclusion in reports may also reflect procedural priorities. Specifically, injuries are a tangible form of evidence that can support probable cause for arrest, which may explain their consistent documentation. This dual function, serving both as a credibility marker and as a legal justification, illustrates how organizational practices shape the content of reports, sometimes at the expense of more nuanced or subjective observations discussed during interviews.

One of the differences uncovered in the depiction of credibility between domestic and non-domestic cases was the role of victims' emotions. Among the non-domestic cases, officers did not mention victims' emotions as influencing their perception of credibility, either in interviews or in reports. In contrast, in domestic cases, officers did note that victims' emotional expressions impacted their credibility assessments, and in some reports, victims' demeanor and emotional state were explicitly mentioned.

It is important to recognize that the narrative provided in a police report primarily serves to convey what happened during the incident. However, reports also function as legal documents that justify probable cause for arrest or charges. While victim credibility is a meaningful component of the case process and contributes to officers' overall perception of the incident, its representation in reports may be constrained by procedural norms. The rules, practices, and organizational expectations that govern report writing often prioritize factual and evidentiary components over subjective assessments. As a result, the depiction of victim credibility in reports is limited, even when officers discuss it more openly and in greater detail during interviews.

These findings confirm that organizational-level practices shape the formal documentation of victim credibility, while case-specific characteristics guide can officers' verbal assessments. The dual influence appears to apply across both domestic and non-domestic cases, despite the limited number of reports available in the non-domestic sample.

Credibility and the Ideal Victim

In their pursuit to describe the Ideal Victim, Christie (1986) and Strobl (2004) developed eight characteristics that describe the victims perceived as most legitimate in their claims to the victim label in the eyes of society. These characteristics are: (1) the victim is weak, (2) the victim is carrying out a respectable activity, (3) the victim could not be blamed for the location they are in, (4) the offender is "big and bad," (5) there is no prior personal relationship between the victim and the offender, (6) the victim is powerful enough to make his/her case known without threatening strong countervailing vested interests, (7) the victim should not have behaved provocatively toward the offender, and (8) the victim should cooperate perfectly with the criminal justice system. In previous studies the conceptualization and application of the Ideal Victim characteristics have not been conducted in a uniform and systematic way. In this book I adopted a broad conceptualization of the various Ideal Victim characteristicsas an attempt to apply an open-minded approach to how the characteristics could be understood several decades after they were developed. When considering the characteristics developed by Christie (1986) and Strobl (2004) in relation to how officers perceive victims' credibility, it can be argued that some characteristics can be linked to officers perception of credibility.

Previous studies have conceptualized "weakness" through markers such as age, gender, and race (Wilson & O'Brien, 2016). Törnqvist (2022), however, expanded this definition to include being emotionally or physically broken down due to prior domestic violence. Although this study did not find specific indications that officers explicitly referenced age, gender, or race as influencing their perceptions of victim credibility, other factors mentioned by officers may relate to the broader conceptualization of weakness. Many officers described injuries and marks as influencing their perceptions of credibility. Specifically, the absence of injury was in many cases seen as diminishing credibility, while the presence of injuries and marks tended to enhance it. Officers explained that injuries and marks were important not only because they corroborated the victim's account or the occurrence of victimization, but also because they served as evidence and contributed to the probable cause assessment. Injuries were one of the few topics consistently mentioned across both domestic and non-domestic case interviews, and they appeared frequently in many of the domestic case reports. I argue that marks and injuries can also be conceptualized as exemplifying the power dynamic between the parties involved in the victimization, where suspects often occupy a superior power position by inflicting pain and victims being subjected to the pain can be viewed as being in a weaker power position, especially if there are injuries as a result of the victimization. When marks and injuries are present on victims, the unequal power positions become more visible compared to when absent and the visibility can make the victim appear weak, aligning with one of the Ideal Victim characteristics and impacting victim credibility.

The discussion of weakness is important because it is one of the major characteristics of the Ideal Victim according to Christie (1986) and because it alludes to a position of subordination or power disadvantage. When reviewing several of Christie's (1986) and Strobl's (2004) characteristics, it becomes evident that multiple traits refer, either directly or indirectly, to that in order to be viewed as an Ideal Victim, the individual must be perceived as being in a disadvantageous power position, either in society or in relation to the suspect. Specifically, characteristics 1, 4, 6, and 7 all reflect this imbalance. For example, Christie's Ideal Victim illustrates societal and relational vulnerability. The "old lady" lacks the physical and social capacity to defend herself and is easily taken advantage of, both by other members of society and by a specific offender. One way this power disadvantage can be made visible is through the harm suffered during the victimization, which may be symbolized by injuries or marks. If these physical indicators are interpreted as signs of weakness, because they highlight the victim's inability to resist or prevent harm, they can be seen as reinforcing the victim's subordinate position before, during, and after the victimization. In this way, the findings of this study partially support Christie's characteristics, particularly the notion that visible harm contributes to the perception of victim legitimacy through the lens of power imbalance.

However, weakness is not only applicable to the victim's position in society but must also be considered in relation to the dynamic between the victim and the suspect. This emphasizes the importance of the relationship and the power imbalance it introduces into the interaction. This claim appears to be supported by what I learned during my time in the field, particularly through the emphasis placed on previous violence and the presence of injuries and marks. Both elements can be interpreted as indicators of the victim's power disadvantage relative to the suspect, where the suspect is perceived as "big and bad" and the victim as weak, thus enabling the suspect to inflict harm either in the past or during the current incident. Hence, characteristics 1 and 4 of the Ideal Victim framework are reinforced, if the victim is viewed as being at a power disadvantage compared to the suspect, they can attain Ideal Victim status. However, this also challenges Christie's (1986) assertion that the Ideal Victim should not have a prior relationship with the offender as the findings suggest that even when a prior relationship exists, such as in domestic cases, the victim may still be perceived as legitimate if the power imbalance is evident and harm has occurred.

Finally, it is important to emphasize that when discussing the victim's position, there are multiple dimensions that must be considered. It is necessary to look not only at the interaction between the victim and the suspect but also at the dynamic between police officers and victims. One essential factor, particularly relevant given this study's focus on understanding officers' perceptions, is for example race. Although Christie (1986) and Strobl (2004) did not include race as a component of the Ideal Victim Theory, other scholars have stressed the importance of incorporating racial dynamics into discussions of victim status (Long, 2021). Additionally, some researchers have used race as a measure of weakness in relation to the first Ideal Victim characteristic (Wilson & O'Brien, 2016), suggesting that racialized perceptions may influence how victim credibility is assessed. Although I did not explore the impact of race and ethnicity on officers perceptions, it is crucial to recognize the potential impact it can have on individuals interactions with professionals within the criminal justice system.

In this study, officers also noted that victims' level of cooperation impacted their perceptions of credibility in both domestic and non-domestic battery cases. Strobl (2004) argued that victims who "perfectly cooperate" with the criminal justice system are viewed as more legitimate by society and are therefore more likely to attain Ideal Victim status, which is supported by some of the findings presented in this book. Officers noted that when victims demonstrated a willingness to provide information or participate in the investigation, their credibility was perceived more positively. Conversely, when victims were reluctant or refused to cooperate, officers reported that this negatively influenced their perception of the victim's credibility.

Although the findings indicated that cooperation was influential in both domestic and non-domestic battery, it was especially emphasized by officers in the non-domestic cases. In these cases, officers stated that factors such as the victim's motivation for seeking help and being vocal about their victimization heavily influenced not only their perception of the victim's credibility but also their decisions regarding report writing. Since officers have more discretion in non-domestic cases, this study found that victims' level of cooperation influenced officers' actions and decisions, particularly in relation to whether a report was written, to a greater extent than in domestic cases. Thus, while cooperation impacted officers' perceptions of credibility across both case types, it was also seemed to be one of the factors that shaped officers' decisions to document the incident in non-domestic cases. When discussing victims' cooperation it is also essential to recognize that some victims in this sample may have been perceived as uncooperative due to the underlying power dynamics between officers and victims. The gender and race of both parties must be acknowledged as potentially influencing their behavior toward one another. Although no officer explicitly stated that race or gender influenced their perceptions, the structurally embedded gender and racial norms present within organizations and society are likely to exert influence, whether overtly or covertly. These norms may subtly inform how officers interpret victims' behavior and credibility, reinforcing the importance of critically examining the institutional context in which these interactions occur. There is a deep history of racial and ethnic tensions between officers and certain communities creating a power imbalance which could impact levels of trust in the police and the likelihood of victims cooperating with police.

Comparing domestic and non-domestic battery cases through the lens of Ideal Victim Theory presents both analytical challenges and theoretical opportunities. While the framework developed by Christie (1986) and expanded by Strobl (2004) offers a set of characteristics that help explain societal and institutional perceptions of victim credibility, its application across different types of violence must be approached with nuance. Domestic battery cases often involve prior relationships, emotional entanglements, and repeated victimization, whereas non-domestic cases typically involve strangers or acquaintances and are more likely to align with the traditional image of a one-time, clear-cut victimization. These contextual differences complicate the direct application of Ideal Victim characteristics, particularly those related to the absence of a prior relationship and the clarity of the victim's weakness.

One of the central tensions in applying Ideal Victim Theory to domestic battery cases lies in the contradiction between the theory's emphasis on the victim having no prior relationship with the offender and the reality that domestic violence inherently involves such relationships. Christie's (1986) assertion that the Ideal Victim should be attacked by a "big and bad" offender with whom they have no prior connection is more easily fulfilled in non-domestic cases. Yet, as the findings in this study suggest, officers still perceive domestic victims as credible when other characteristics, such as visible injuries, emotional distress, and cooperation, are present. This indicates that some Ideal Victim traits may override others in practice, and that the framework may need to be adapted to account for the relational complexities of domestic violence.

The comparison between domestic and non-domestic battery cases is further complicated by the differing legal and policy frameworks that shape officer discretion and response. In domestic cases, mandatory arrest policies and structured reporting procedures often constrain officers' autonomy, requiring action regardless of their subjective assessment of victim credibility. In contrast, non-domestic cases typically afford officers greater discretion, allowing them to decide whether to pursue charges or document the incident based on their interpretation of the victim's behavior. The legal distinction means that Ideal Victim characteristics, particularly cooperation and perceived weakness, may carry more weight in non-domestic contexts, where procedural mandates are less rigid and officers' perceptions play a more decisive role. As noted in the findings, officers reported that victims' willingness to engage with the investigation significantly influenced their decisions to write reports in non-domestic cases. Cooperation, attitudes towards victimization, and perceived motivation for seeking help were all mentioned as factors that shaped officers' assessments of credibility. These discretionary judgments reflect how Ideal Victim traits can be operationalized in practice, especially in contexts where officers are not bound by automatic procedures. While domestic cases may reduce the influence of subjective perceptions on whether a report is filed, those same perceptions still shape how officers interpret victim credibility.

Domestic battery cases also involve complex relational dynamics that can influence how officers interpret victim behavior. Victims in domestic situations may display ambivalence, fear, or reluctance to cooperate, behaviors that can be misread by officers as signs of dishonesty or lack of credibility. These reactions are often rooted in trauma, dependency, or ongoing coercive control, yet may be perceived as inconsistent with the Ideal Victim image, which assumes clarity, passivity, and cooperation. Organizational factors, such as time constraints, case volume, and departmental culture, further influence how officers engage with these cases. Officers may rely on situational facts or past experiences to assess credibility, which can inadvertently reinforce biases tied to race, gender, and perceived victim behavior.

Despite the challenges with comparing domestic and non-domestic battery cases it is essential to pursue in order to advance and deepen our understanding of how Ideal Victim Theory operates within varied legal, organizational, and relational contexts. It allows for a more comprehensive examination of how institutional actors, particularly police officers, apply victim legitimacy frameworks in practice, and how they navigate credibility assessments under different constraints. Domestic cases, shaped by mandatory policies and complex interpersonal dynamics, contrast sharply with the discretionary nature of non-domestic cases, where officers' subjective evaluations play a more prominent role. These differences reveal how power dynamics, between victims and suspects, and between victims and officers, can shape perceptions of credibility. By exploring these distinctions, this book contributes to a more nuanced application of Ideal Victim Theory, one that moves beyond its original criteria to account for structural and institutional influences on victim perception. It highlights the limitations of idealized victim narratives, especially when applied to relational forms of violence, and underscores the need for theoretical expansion that reflects the realities of police officers assessments and decision-making

Contribution and Implications

My goal with book was to deepen our understanding of how officers perceive the credibility of battery victims. By examining both organizational-level and individual-level factors, the findings contribute to the current body of policing scholarship by demonstrating that the influences on officers' perceptions are multifaceted and dynamic. While much of the existing research has traditionally focused on either individual-level factors, such as officer demographics or case characteristics, or organizational factors like formal policies and informal practices, my book aimed to bridge these domains byshowing that organizational rules and norms, alongside individual discretion, jointly shape how officers perceive and depict victim credibility. The findings reveal that officers consider a wide range of elements related to the victim, the suspect, and the broader context of the case when assessing credibility after the encounter. However, these nuanced perceptions are rarely reflected in the official documentation. The gap between internal assessment and external reporting stresses the complexity of credibility evaluation and suggests that police reports may not fully capture the factors influencing officers' judgments. These insights reinforce the need to revisit how Ideal Victim Theory is applied in policing contexts, as officers' assessments often extend beyond the theory's rigid criteria and are shaped by institutional pressures, discretionary space, and broader social dynamics.

The findings presented in this book are important because they suggest a disconnect between how officers depict victims' credibility in written reports and how they describe those same victims in person. As a result, key details about the victim's demeanor, emotional state, and interaction with the officer may not be passed on to detectives or prosecutors, which can have significant implications. For example, criminal justice professionals who encounter the victim later in the case process may lack insight into the dynamic on-scene interaction, potentially leading them to question the victim's credibility based on the limited information available in the report or during brief follow-up meetings. One potential solution is for officers to include more well-developed narratives about their interactions with victims, either within the police report itself or in supplemental memos that can be shared with other criminal justice professionals. These narratives would not necessarily increase officers' influence over case progression but could serve as a tool to provide richer contextual information beyond what is captured in body camera footage or standard documentation. As previous scholarship has shown, both police officers and other criminal justice professionals consider extra-legal factors when assessing victims and cases. By offering more detailed accounts, officers can increase transparency around what occurred on scene and ensure that subsequent assessments are based on a fuller understanding of the victim's experience.

Other key findings reveal that while officers generally perceived most battery victims as credible, the criteria they used to assess credibility varied. These factors differed not only across individual cases but also between domestic and non-domestic contexts. This study contributes to existing scholarship on police officers' perceptions of victim credibility by expanding the scope of victimizations examined in victimological research. In particular, it brings attention to non-domestic battery, a form of violence that has often been overlooked in academic literature.

Moreover, the findings suggest that certain elements commonly discussed in domestic and interpersonal violence literature, such as the presence or absence of injuries, emotional expression, the availability of witnesses, and victims' willingness to provide information are also relevant in officers' assessments of non-domestic battery victims. This supports previous research on domestic violence while extending its applicability to non-domestic contexts. In doing so, the study argues for a broader understanding of how credibility is constructed across different forms of violence, and demonstrates that some of the evaluative criteria used in domestic cases may be transferable to non-domestic ones. This not only reinforces the importance of contextualizing victim credibility but also underscores the need for future research to include a wider range of victimization types when examining police decision-making. Additionally, this study offers contributions to existing research by directly contrasting and comparing officers' perceptions of victim credibility in both domestic and non-domestic battery cases. By expanding the scope of victimological literature, this book shares new knowledge about the similarities and differences in how officers assess credibility across these two contexts. These findings open up important discussions about the need to further examine the distinctions between domestic and non-domestic batteries, particularly in relation to how officers interpret victim behavior, cooperation, and emotional expression. Understanding these nuanced views is essential for developing more accurate, equitable, and context-sensitive approaches to evaluating victims of violent crime.

In addition to the varying perceptions officers hold of victims in domestic and non-domestic battery cases, this book reveals that officers also manage these cases differently. For example, fewer reports and arrests are made in non-domestic batteries, which can be attributed to the distinct legal and policy guidelines governing officer discretion. According to Florida State Law and GPD's policy guidelines, officers have significantly less discretion in arrest decisions for domestic batteries compared to non-domestic ones. However, the findings also highlight instances where officers do not adhere to these guidelines in both types of cases, particularly in report writing. This is especially evident in domestic cases, where statutory requirements mandate documentation regardless of arrest. According to Florida Statute 741.29 "Whether or not an arrest is made, the officer shall make a written police report that is complete and clearly indicates the alleged offense was an incident of domestic violence. Such report shall be given to the officer's supervisor and filed with the law enforcement agency in a manner that will permit data on domestic violence cases to be compiled." Despite this clear directive, the study found examples where officers failed to document domestic incidents as required, suggesting gaps between policy and practice.

If officers consistently followed statutory provisions, all domestic battery cases would result in a written police report. However, this study found that 25% of domestic cases lacked documentation, despite the clear requirement outlined in Florida Statute 741.29. This not only reveals potential noncompliance with policy but also highlights the number of victimizations that may go unrecorded in official statistics. The issue is even more pronounced in non-domestic battery cases, where 57% lacked a report. While guidelines for non-domestic cases are less strickt and allow for greater officer discretion, the potential implication of this discretionary power is that fewer incidents are formally documented, increasing the number of crimes excluded from official data. Traditional statistical outlets and scholarly research often rely on cases that result in police reports, meaning a substantial portion of battery incidents, especially non-domestic ones, are omitted from datasets such as UCR and NIBRS. Although this study includes a limited sample, it contributes to empirical research by offering insight into cases that are typically excluded from these data sources. It sheds light on officers' perceptions of victims in cases that do not lead to a report, revealing how discretion influences not only documentation practices but also credibility assessments.

One of the things that can be derived from this book is that greater efforts are needed to collect and capture more accurate data on batteries that do not result in a formal police report. While there will always be a "dark number" of batteries this book highlights another gap, which are cases that are reported to police but not documented. Developing policies that encourage officers to anonymously log basic information about cases that do not lead to a formal report could help police agencies build a more accurate picture of the true occurrence and nature of battery incidents. Such practices would enhance transparency, allow for better identification of geographical patterns of violence, and support more strategic resource allocation. Additionally, they could help agencies detect individuals who have both experienced and perpetrated violence, offering a more holistic understanding of local victimization dynamics.

Finally, the findings in this book contribute to the theoretical development of the Ideal Victim Theory. Several characteristics outlined by Christie (1986) and Strobl (2004), such as victim vulnerability and cooperation with police, were reflected in officers' credibility assessments across both domestic and non-domestic cases. By examining these perceptions in relation to both types of battery, this book expands the conceptualization of the Ideal Victim and engages with Christie's argument that female victims of domestic violence often face greater challenges in attaining legitimate victim status. The comparative approach taken here stresses how institutional and relational contexts shape credibility assessments, and how Ideal Victim Theory must evolve to account for these complexities.

Limitations and Future Research

As with any research, this study has several limitations. Below, I discuss four central limitations, how I navigated them, and how future research could address these issues to build on the knowledge generated here. It is important to note that these are not the only limitations of the study, but they represent key areas that warrant further discussion. Additional methodological limitations are addressed in the methodology appendix.

First, while the findings contribute to existing research by confirming, challenging, or expanding prior empirical work, they are limited in scope. Specifically, although the study identifies factors that officers perceive as influencing their assessments of victim credibility, it does not measure the degree to which each factor impacts those perceptions. In other words, the book offers insight into what officers say matters, but not how much each factor matters in shaping their judgments. Despite this limitation, the book still contributes with important knowledge by mapping out a range of factors officers consider and describing the nuanced ways in which these are interpreted. To address this limitation, future research could employ quantitative or experimental designs to isolate and measure the influence of specific factors. For example, researchers could use vignette-based methods to present officers with hypothetical scenarios in which variables such as victim cooperation, injury presence, or emotional expression are systematically manipulated. This type of experiment would allow for a more precise understanding of which factors carry the most weight in officers' credibility assessments and how these may vary across different types of battery cases.

Additionally, the findings in this book cannot establish whether the factors informing officers' perceptions of victim credibility serve as causal mechanisms for differential treatment. This is a key limitation, as the inability to determine causality restricts the practical implications of the findings. While it may be tempting to interpret the data through a causal lens, especially when seeking justification for policy or procedural changes, it is important to emphasize that this book was not designed to examine causal relationships. Rather, its aim was to identify and explore the factors that officers perceive as influencing credibility, and to examine whether these perceptions vary between domestic and non-domestic cases and across different stages of case formation. To address this limitation, future research could investigate the causal relationship between officers' perceptions of victim credibility and differential treatment or case outcomes. Such studies would benefit from longitudinal designs that follow cases from initial police contact through their progression in the criminal justice system. Additionally, surveys or interviews with criminal justice professionals involved in each case could provide insight into how credibility assessments influence decision-making at various stages. These professionals could be asked to identify which factors shaped their perceptions and to reflect on how those perceptions affected their actions, such as charging decisions, resource allocation, or victim support.

A third limitation of this study is its inability to clearly distinguish how organizational-level and individual-level factors influence officers' perceptions of victim credibility. These influences are often deeply intertwined, making it difficult to isolate whether officers' assessments are shaped more by institutional norms, policies, and training, or by personal experiences, case-specific characteristics, and individual discretion. Although this is an important limitation to acknowledge, the findings shared still offers insight by examining both levels simultaneously, providing a more holistic understanding of the dynamic nature of policing and credibility assessments. Rather than focusing exclusively on one dimension, this book attempts to integrate organizational and individual factors to reflect the complexity of real-world decision-making. Future research could build on these findings by designing studies that more explicitly examine the relationship between these two levels, for example, by comparing departments with different policy environments or conducting interviews that probe officers' interpretations of institutional expectations versus personal judgment.

Another limitation is the lack of in-depth insight into how group dynamics and hierarchical power structures influence officers' perceptions. Specifically, this study could not determine whether officers' credibility assessments were shaped by interactions with peers or superiors. Although I observed officers interacting with one another and with supervisors before, during, and after responding to scenes, the influence of these interactions on their perceptions was beyond the scope of this study. This is an important area for future exploration, as informal norms, peer influence, and supervisory expectations may play a significant role in shaping how officers interpret victim behavior and credibility. Future studies could address this gap by using focus groups or structured interviews with officers across different ranks, asking targeted questions about how group dynamics and hierarchy influence their views on victim credibility. By examining interactions among officers with varying levels of experience and rank, future research could better understand how norms surrounding victim credibility are shared, reinforced, and learned within police culture.

Conclusion

In this chapter I bring together the central findings of the study, offering a nuanced analysis of how police officers perceive, describe, and document victim credibility in both domestic and non-domestic battery cases. Officers' assessments of credibility rarely hinge on a single factor; rather, they emerge from a constellation of interrelated elements such as emotional display, physical injuries, cooperation, narrative detail, and contextual cues. These factors interact dynamically, shaped by formal training, informal norms, and the broader institutional and social context in which officers operate.

Across both domestic and non-domestic cases, willingness to cooperate, narrative coherence, and visible injuries consistently serve as credibility markers. However, differences arise in how contextual elements are interpreted. In non-domestic cases, officers place greater emphasis on external corroboration such as witness statements and surveillance footage and victims' motivations for engaging with the investigation. In domestic cases, emotional presentation and the history of violence between the parties play a more prominent role.

A gap exists between how officers discuss credibility in interviews and how they document it in reports. Interviews reveal an array of factors influencing credibility, yet police reports tend to prioritize procedural and evidentiary details, often omitting nuanced observations about victim demeanor or emotional state. This selective documentation may inadvertently privilege victims who present physical evidence or clear narratives while obscuring the experiences of others, particularly in domestic violence cases where external corroboration is less accessible. In some cases, credibility appears to be implicitly considered but not explicitly recorded, raising questions about transparency and consistency.

The findings also stress the role of structural and legal frameworks in shaping officers' discretion. Florida Law and GPD policy mandate reduced discretion in cases involving aggravating factors such as strangulation, pregnancy, or documented histories of violence, especially when incidents are domestic in nature. These conditions can elevate a simple battery to a felony, triggering mandatory reporting and arrest protocols. Conversely, in misdemeanor cases that are non-domestic and lack aggravating circumstances, officers have greater latitude, and credibility assessments may weigh more heavily in decisions about arrests or report writing.

Viewed through the lens of Ideal Victim Theory (Christie, 1986; Strobl, 2004), the book suggests that while traits associated with the "Ideal Victim" such as weakness, cooperation, and blamelessness surface in officers' assessments, they are not applied uniformly. Instead, officers engage in situational context, interpreting multiple cues in context and adapting evaluations to case complexities. Power dynamics, particularly those shaped by gender and race, further influence victim behavior and officer interpretation, reinforcing the need for a flexible, context-sensitive framework.

Ultimately, credibility emerges as a negotiated outcome shaped by institutional norms, officer discretion, and broader social dynamics. By illuminating the multifaceted nature of credibility assessments and their interaction with legal mandates, organizational culture, and discretionary space, this study contributes to a deeper understanding of how justice is constructed and sometimes constrained within the criminal justice system. The implications are twofold, first, expanding research beyond domestic violence to include non-domestic battery cases, which remain underexplored. Second, recognizing the importance of cases that do not result in police reports, as these omissions create blind spots in crime data and policy development. Future research should examine how credibility interacts with discretion and structural constraints, aiming to reduce bias and ensure equitable treatment of victims across all case types.

References

Ask, K. (2010). A survey of police officers' and prosecutors' beliefs about crime victim behaviors. *Journal of Interpersonal Violence, 25*(6), 1132–1149. https://doi.org/10.1177/0886260509340535

Bostaph, L. G., King, L. L., & Brady, P. Q. (2021). How victim credibility and cooperation influence investigative decision-making: Examining DOJ's gender bias principles for investigating domestic and sexual violence. *Policing: An International Journal, 44*(4), 612–627. https://doi.org/10.1108/PIJPSM-02-2021-0018

Christie, N. (1986). The Ideal Victim. In E. Fattah (Ed.), *From crime policy to victim policy* (pp. 17–30). Palgrave Macmillan. https://doi.org/10.1007/978-1-349-08305-3_2

El Sayed, S. A., DeShay, R. A., Davis, J. B., Knox, K. N., & Kerley, K. R. (2022). A blue step forward: An exploratory study of law enforcement perceptions of intimate partner violence in the Southern United States. *Journal of Interpersonal Violence, 37*(9–10), 6514–6534. https://doi.org/10.1177/0886260520966675

Hess, K. M., & Wrobleski, H. M. (1996). *For the record: Report writing in law enforcement.* Innovative Systems.

Long, L. J. (2021). The Ideal Victim: A critical race theory (CRT) approach. *International Review of Victimology, 27*(3), 344–362. https://doi.org/10.1177/0269758021993339

Redwine, K. B (2003, October 26). The importance of the police report. Criminal Justice Institute School of Law Enforcement Supervision, Session XXII. https://www.cji.edu/wp-content/uploads/2019/04/importance_of_police_reports.pdf

Strobl, R. (2004). Constructing the victim: Theoretical reflections and empirical examples. *International Review of Victimology, 11*(2–3), 295–311. https://doi.org/10.1177/026975800401100206

Törnqvist, N. (2022). Drizzling sympathy: Ideal Victims and flows of sympathy in Swedish courts. *International Review of Victimology, 28*(3), 263–285. https://doi.org/10.1177/02697580211035586

Waaland, P., & Keeley, S. (1985). Police decision making in wife abuse: The impact of legal and extralegal factors. *Law and Human Behavior, 9*(4), 355–366. https://doi.org/10.1007/BF01044476

Wilson, M., & O'Brien, E. (2016). Constructing the Ideal Victim in the United States of America's annual trafficking in persons reports. *Crime, Law and Social Change, 65*(1–2), 29–45. https://doi.org/10.1007/s10611-015-9600-8

Methodology Appendix

Several sources of data were collected using different instruments, which I will describe in this appendix. Specifically, I will outline the types of data used, the instruments employed to collect them, the data collection process and procedures, data management practices, and the sample of officers interviewed. Because of the wide range of data gathered for this study, I have organized the description into two categories. The first category, organizational and context data, includes information related to GPD protocols and organizational context. The second category, battery case data, focuses on data collected from individual battery cases.

I chose to include this detailed description of how I conducted the study and the analytic phase because I believe transparency about the process is essential. Not only does this provide clarity for the reader, but I also hope it serves as a resource for other researchers, especially students, who are interested in conducting similar research. My goal is for this appendix to assist others in planning their studies by sharing both the successes and challenges I encountered. I hope that my experiences, including the obstacles I faced and the strategies I used to overcome

M. N. Eliasson, *Who Gets Believed?*, Palgrave's Critical Policing Studies,
https://doi.org/10.1007/978-3-032-22253-4

them, can help others in their efforts to seek knowledge and expand understanding across various fields. The study was approved by the University of Florida IRB.

Organizational Context

In this section, I will describe the data collected to provide insight into the practices, daily activities, and organizational context in which officers operate. Understanding this context was a key aspect of the study because it offered an opportunity to gain in-depth knowledge about GPD as an organization and informed the latter part of the research, where battery case data was collected.

In addition to interviewing officers about their procedures and practices, I conducted ride-alongs to better understand GPD operations. For example, I learned about the various shifts and geographical areas to which officers are assigned, which helped estimate when and where battery cases were most likely to occur. This section will outline the different types of data included in this category, along with the methods used to collect them.

Organizational Context Observations

I conducted several participatory observations of the organizational context during my fieldwork. Participatory observation allows the researcher to interact with participants for an extended period to learn about everyday activities, norms, values, interactions, and other important aspects that influence participants (Esterberg, 2002). For this study, participatory observation involved spending time with officers during ride-alongs, which refers to civilians accompanying police officers in their patrol cars during shifts. These observations were a critical tool that enabled me to immerse myself in officers' daily activities, gather data about GPD as an organization, learn more about individual officers, and observe interpersonal interactions between officers and civilians. Additionally, ride-alongs were essential for building rapport with officers, which facilitated access to battery case observations and interviews with the officers.

For the observations of the organizational context, I used two types of instruments, in addition to field notes, which I will describe more below. To learn more about GPD as an organization, I used and *Introductory Ride-Along Instrument* to outline the day-to-day activities officers conducted during their shifts, their interactions with other officers and civilians, their report-writing habits, and general investigation procedures. I used this instrument to record officers' behaviors, decisions, and to note questions about specific situations as they occurred during the ride-along. For example, if an officer's report was denied by a supervisor, I asked about the process for resubmitting the report, who made the decision to deny or approve reports, and when those decisions typically occur. Additionally, I made specific notes about the calls we attended, especially battery calls. I documented how many battery cases occurred during each shift, whether they were domestic or non-domestic, and the time they occurred, which helped me prepare instruments and schedule ride-alongs for collecting battery case data.

The *Introductory Ride-Along Instrument* focused on collecting information about practices and identifying questions or topics for further exploration while gathering battery data. It also helped establish a general understanding of the steps involved in officers' investigative procedures. The notes I recorded in this instrument combined jotting, where observations and questions were captured in keywords and short phrases (Emerson et al., 2011), with more detailed notes about battery case occurrences. After becoming familiar with GPD as an organization and transitioning to battery data collection, I used a *Ride-Along Instrument* to record observations of officers' general conduct during ride-alongs, the calls we attended, and the times they occurred. I also noted which officer I rode with, the time and shift, and the assigned zone. These notes were taken during the ride-along while I was in the patrol car.

In addition to the *Ride-Along Instrument*, I wrote field notes after each ride-along. Typically, I wrote one field note per ride-along, which ranged from one to three pages, depending on how many calls we attended that day. Depending on how busy the shift was, I either began writing field notes in the car when there were no calls or wrote them after the ride-along. Unlike the *Ride-Along Instrument*, which focused on structured observations and questions, the field notes contained thick descriptions of situations, behaviors, and interactions observed in context (Geertz, 2008). Hence the main difference between the field notes and the *Ride-Along Instrument* was that the field notes provided more in-depth descriptions of the calls we attended, including interactions officers had with victims of all types of crime, interactions with other officers, and descriptions of my personal interactions with officers, such as conversations in the patrol car.

Organizational Context Interviews

To learn more about GPD, I conducted semi-structured introductory interviews to gain insight into the organizational structure, departmental practices and procedures (such as report writing), and how officers make decisions on scene. The purpose of these interviews was to understand factors that influence officers' day-to-day tasks and the organizational context in which individual behavior occurs. More specifically, I aimed to identify aspects beyond officer-victim interactions that could shape officers' perceptions of victims, on-scene decisions, and police reports. The interviews provided valuable information about organizational structure, hierarchies, and case characteristics that were essential for understanding officers' perceptions and behaviors. They also revealed what organizational policies and procedures define expectations for managing battery incidents. I later contrasted these organizational expectations with actual observations of officers responding to battery cases.

Semi-structured interviews were chosen because they allowed discussion of specific topics while giving officers the flexibility to introduce additional subjects (Esterberg, 2002). Before entering the field, I developed an *Introductory Ride-Along Interview Guide* that outlined topics of interest. For example, I asked questions about staffing, shifts, zones, what a typical workday looks like, the arrest process, report writing procedures, and decision-making processes. The questions were primarily open-ended, enabling officers to expand their responses beyond narrow parameters often associated with closed-ended questions. This format encouraged officers to share broader perspectives and related topics they considered relevant (Denscombe, 2009). For instance, during one interview about zones and shifts, a GPD police captain explained how jurisdictions operate and described collaboration between GPD and other agencies.

The interviews were conducted either at the GPD police station or in patrol cars during introductory ride-alongs. The goal was to collect data that supplemented ride-along observations, ultimately combining both sources to develop a comprehensive understanding of GPD as an organization and its procedures and practices. This combined approach allowed me to compare organizational expectations with actual officer behavior in the field.

Organizational Documents

This study also utilized official GPD documents, most of which were obtained from the GPD website or provided by staff members. For example, information about staff demographics was obtained via email from a GPD staff member upon request. Additionally, I retrieved public documents from GPD's website, including the *General Investigation Procedures* and the *General Order Rules of Conduct*, which outlined GPD's rules and policies for officers' general conduct and report-writing practices. The *Domestic Violence and Dating Violence Investigations* document detailed GPD's policies for conducting investigations and writing reports for sexual and domestic victimizations. I also collected a zone map from GPD's website, which illustrated the different zones and sectors within Gainesville, FL.

These documents were used to provide background information on GPD's organizational structure, staff demographics, and the policies and rules governing officers' tasks and conduct. They informed which aspects of battery cases should be explored and were incorporated into the analysis to contrast organizational guidelines with observational and interview data. For example, the *General Investigation Procedures*, *General Order Rules of Conduct*, and *Domestic Violence and Dating Violence Investigations* documents provided insight into the guidelines GPD established for officers when conducting battery investigations. These guidelines were then compared with actual observations and interview responses from specific battery cases.

Battery Case Data

Since the primary focus of this study was to understand how police officers perceive victim credibility in non-domestic and domestic battery cases, data collection centered around battery cases. Because of this specific interest, I used a purposeful sampling strategy when selecting cases (Suri, 2011). To answer the research questions, I needed to collect information about credibility indicators displayed by victims during encounters with police, how officers discussed victim credibility after the encounter, and how it was represented in corresponding police reports. To capture this information, I relied on multiple data sources, including CAD records, police reports, interviews, and observations.

For each battery case, I conducted one observation of the interaction between victims and officers, at least one interview with the primary officer who wrote the report and interacted with the victim, a CAD record, and one police report (if generated). It is important to note that there was some variation in the amount of data collected for each case. For example, reports were not always generated, and the length of interviews or field notes varied depending on the duration of victim interactions. Despite these variations, the data collected for each case consistently included the elements listed above.

Based on what I learned about GPD as an organization and officers' day-to-day activities, I refined my instruments and note-taking methods for collecting battery case data. For example, I added items to the *Battery Case Instrument* to capture whether officers took photos of victims' injuries, asked about student or mental health status of victims or suspects, and whether a sworn complaint was written by the victim. I also refined the *Battery Case Interview Instrument* to ensure that questions about suspects were only asked if the officer had interacted with the suspect.

Computer-Aided Dispatch System

When an officer is dispatched to a call, they are briefed by the dispatcher over the radio with information about the incident, which is also typed into electronic call notes referred to by officers as "CAD." This information is typically based on details provided by the 911 caller and may include a description of the incident, the parties involved, the location, and any prior calls or history at that location. The call notes are updated as new information comes in, so officers often read the notes while driving to the scene, in addition to listening to dispatch. However, because the information is primarily based on the caller's report, it can be very limited. The information shared in the CAD was recorded on the *Battery Case Instrument.* I noted the exact time the call came in and the time we exited the car at the scene to determine when officers stopped receiving updates from dispatch. These notes helped me understand what information officers had before arriving and what details were shared about the incident and the victim. However, in addition to these notes, I also collected a digital copy of the CAD to ensure I did not miss any information in my notes I did during the call. After leaving the scene, I wrote down the incident number separately from my field notes and once the ride-along was complete, I emailed the Alachua County Audio Records Unit to request the CAD for the specific incident number. Within two to three days, the CAD was emailed to me free of charge under Florida's Sunshine Law on public records. Each battery case, therefore, had one CAD log for analysis.

The *CAD Instrument* was used to analyze the digital copy of the CAD and gather information about how the victim and suspect were described, what was known about the incident, whether children or witnesses were present, the relationship between the parties, and whether weapons, alcohol, or drugs were involved. It also captured any prior history of violence. These sections were coded using terms such as "yes," "no," or "unknown," along with short descriptive sentences. Additional space was provided for more detailed explanations when necessary. Sections of the CAD were highlighted and assigned codes written next to the relevant words or sentences on the CAD Instrument to ensure that descriptions could be directly linked to specific pieces of information in the CAD. Both my notes and the digital copy of the CAD were collected to capture as much information as possible, including cases where officers used earpieces and I could not hear their conversations with dispatch.

Battery Case Observation

I also utilized the *Battery Case Instrument* to collect data specifically related to each battery case. First, I recorded information received over the radio, details visible in the CAD, and information provided by officers about the incident. Second, I observed the victim's demeanor, officers' statements and demeanor, the environment where the interaction occurred, the number of officers on the scene, whether arrests were made, whether the victim had visible injuries, whether photos were taken of injuries, the identity of the 911 caller, the presence of witnesses, and the general procedures officers followed at the scene.

To evaluate common criteria of victim credibility, I drew on characteristics developed by Christie (1986) and Strobl (2004), as well as factors explored by other empirical scholars examining officers' perceptions of domestic and non-domestic batteries (Ask, 2010; Buzawa & Austin, 1993; Felson & Lantz, 2016; Finn & Stalans, 1997; Jasinski, 2003). However, due to the inductive nature of the study, I also documented additional aspects of interactions as they occurred to capture potential behavioral elements not mentioned in previous scholarship or by Christie and Strobl.

In addition to the *Battery Case Instrument*, I wrote field notes for each battery case. The main difference between the field notes and the *Battery Case Instrument* was that field notes were written after the ride-along, in a setting where I could focus entirely on writing. In contrast, notes in the *Battery Case Instrument* were usually taken during an incident or immediately afterward in the patrol car, requiring me to balance note-taking with observation and situational awareness for safety. Consequently, field notes tended to be longer and more detailed than the *Battery Case Instrument*. Before writing field notes, I reviewed the instrument to ensure all relevant aspects were included.

Like the *Battery Case Instrument*, all field notes were handwritten, but they were recorded on blank paper without predetermined prompts. On average, battery case notes were two to three handwritten pages and physical copies were scanned and filed with each Battery Case, labeled by ride-along number or case ID. The purpose of these additional field notes was not to duplicate information from the *Battery Case Instrument* but to provide more detailed descriptions of observed incidents and include thick descriptions (Geertz, 2008) of the context in which events occurred. For example, in the *Battery Case Instrument*, I might use descriptive words such as "crying" or "smiling," whereas in my field notes, I would write: "The victim displayed a wide range of emotions. They first appeared sad, they were crying and wiping tears from their face but later seemed calm while describing what happened with a steady voice and relaxed body language." Thus, the field notes served as an extension of the *Battery Case Instrument*, offering richer context and interpretive detail about emotions and behaviors.

Battery Case Interviews

The main goal of the interviews was to understand how officers, in their own words, described the incident, the victim, and their interaction with the victim. Specifically, I wanted to examine the language officers used when describing victims and incidents, and the factors they identified as essential to their positive assessment of victim credibility. By asking questions about the incident and the victim, I gathered information on a variety of factors that officers considered influential, which could then be analyzed alongside other data sources, such as police reports and my observations. The officer's perception of victim credibility from the interview was compared with my observations of that officer's interaction with the victim and the corresponding police report, if one was filed.

For each battery case I observed, I conducted a battery case interview using the *Battery Case Interview Instrument*. In these interviews, I asked officers to describe the incident and the victim, whether they found the victim credible and trustworthy, and what they based their perceptions on. For each battery case, at least one interview was conducted with the primary officer, defined as the officer who wrote the report (if one was generated) and interacted with the victim. In two cases, the primary officers declined to be interviewed, so I interviewed another officer who had interacted with the victim.

The primary condition for interviewing an officer was that they had interacted with the victim at the scene. Interaction was defined as a verbal exchange between the officer and the victim. This was to ensure that I could observe the interaction and then interview the officer about it. Despite multiple officers often being present, in some cases, only one officer was interviewed because that officer was the only one who interacted with the victim.

Although the interviews were semi-structured, all questions listed in the interview guide, except for two, were asked of all officers who met the interaction criteria. The two questions not asked in some interviews were "How would you describe the alleged defendant?" and "How would you describe the alleged defendant's demeanor during your encounter?" These questions were omitted if the officer had not interacted with the suspect. All other questions were asked of every officer, and at the end of each interview, officers were invited to provide additional comments by responding to "Is there anything else you would like to add?" This allowed officers to expand on their answers or raise topics they considered relevant.

Police Reports

Another type of data collected for each case was police reports. It is important to understand what is written and what is omitted in police reports because these reports are read by multiple criminal justice professionals and become a key resource for understanding what occurred at the scene (Miller & Pomerenke, 1989). The way information is presented in police reports can potentially influence decisions made at various stages of case processing and potentially affect case outcomes.

Existing literature on police reports often examines discrepancies between victim accounts in surveys and police reports (Averdijk & Elffers, 2012), general trends in characteristics or facts reported by officers (Acosta et al., 2013; Cazenave & Zahn, 1992; Tjaden & Thoennes, 2000), and the accuracy of reports (Beehr et al., 2004; Kassin et al.,

2017). While these studies provide valuable insights, few focus specifically on police practices and reporting during the initial stage of case processing. More importantly, current scholarship rarely explores in depth what information officers include or omit in relation to victims and how this relates to broader trends in reporting victim credibility. This study addresses that gap.

The goal of including police reports in this study was to understand how victims and their credibility are described by officers. By comparing observations and interviews with the content of police reports, I sought to identify potential discrepancies between how officers depict credibility in reports versus their statements during interviews and their behavior at the scene. Police reports typically include descriptions of individuals encountered at the scene, such as victims and alleged defendants, along with brief descriptions of the location and incident (Hess & Wrobleski, 1996; Redwine, 2003).

To examine how officers depict victims and victimization in their reports, I developed a *Police Report Instrument*. This instrument ensured that specific aspects were examined in each report and provided prompts related to how victims, suspects, the environment, and the incident were described. The instrument included both short descriptive words and longer sentences to capture report content. In addition to using the instrument, I read each report multiple times and highlighted relevant passages, which were then coded. Additionally the construction of the instrument was informed by the Ideal Victim characteristics developed by Christie (1986) and Strobl (2004), as well as factors identified by scholars studying officers' views of victim credibility in domestic and non-domestic battery cases (Ask, 2010; Buzawa & Austin, 1993; Felson & Lantz, 2016; Finn & Stalans, 1997; Jasinski, 2003; Landström et al., 2019).

The aim was to collect a police report for every case, however, not all cases generated a report. For cases where a report was available, it was obtained through an email request to the GPD public records division. Reports were retrieved by GPD records staff, who reviewed and redacted identifying information before providing them.

Data Collection and Procedures

Due to the extensive range of information sought and the different types of data that needed to be collected, I developed strategies for accessing and managing the data once collected. Having an organized approach to data collection and procedures allowed me to immerse myself in the field and gather a substantial amount of data within a limited timeframe, which was essential for answering the research questions posed. In the following section, I will provide an in-depth description of how I accessed the field, what a typical ride-along looked like, the data collection procedures and processes, and the strategies used for data management.

Getting Access to the Field

Police departments can be challenging spaces for researchers to access (Manning, 2015). Due to heightened scrutiny of police conduct in academia and the media, officers and administrators may be reluctant to allow outside researchers into their organization because they cannot control the information that will be generated about officers and the department. Another study highlights the tight-knit community of police officers, using terms such as the "thin blue line" to describe the loyalty and camaraderie that often exist among officers within the same agency and across policing organizations (Doreian & Conti, 2017). As a result, researchers may be viewed as outsiders with motives perceived as misaligned with officers' beliefs or attitudes about occupational conduct. Because of these challenges, building relationships and rapport with GPD officers was essential. These relationships were critical not only for obtaining substantive information about GPD's practices and procedures but also for identifying gatekeepers who could facilitate contact with additional officers and grant greater access to collect data for this study.

In December 2021, I made initial contact with GPD to express my interest in conducting ride-alongs and interviews with patrol officers. A GPD representative provided information about available shifts and sent liability waivers for me to sign. In late January 2022, GPD informed me that the ride-along program had been suspended due to the COVID-19 pandemic. After several email exchanges with GPD staff, I received approval at the end of February to conduct ride-alongs and interviews. This approval, however, only covered a limited number of ride-alongs. To conduct extended data collection over several months, I needed separate approval from an Assistant Chief since according to what I was told, civilians are typically allowed only one ride-along per year per GPD policy.

In March 2022, I began collecting data about GPD as an organization through interviews and ride-alongs. During this time, I maintained frequent communication with a staff member, referred to here as "L," who acted as a liaison between me and GPD. L facilitated communication with a Captain and an Assistant Chief, managed scheduling for ride-alongs, and handled liability waiver submissions. Two weeks into this process, I emphasized the importance of conducting multiple ride-alongs and interviewing officers about battery cases. I was asked to write a letter to the acting Police Chief explaining my research, its benefits for GPD, and why I chose GPD for this study. After submitting the letter, I received a call from the Assistant Chief, who asked about my motivations. He noted that multiple ride-alongs were typically reserved for recruits or trainees and described the process as an "administrative nightmare." I reiterated the importance of extended ride-alongs as the primary means of observing officers and battery cases. Shortly thereafter, L informed me that my request was approved under certain conditions. I had to sign a liability waiver before each ride-along, maintain contact with L for scheduling, and obtain pre-approval for each ride-along. Additionally, ride-alongs had to be distributed across all three shifts, day, evening, and midnight, and across different days of the week. I could not choose the officer I rode with, and GPD reserved the right to cancel ride-alongs if necessary. While these conditions posed challenges, approval from the Assistant Chief was crucial for the success of this study.

As the ride-alongs progressed, I built relationships with officers across shifts. When meeting officers for the first time, I explained that my research focused on victim interactions, mentioned prior ride-along experience in Washington, D.C., and shared that my father had been a police officer in Sweden. This information, combined with the extended time I spent in the field I think helped officers accept my presence. Several officers expressed surprise at the number of ride-alongs I completed and remarked that I was "one of them" because of my family background. A few weeks into collecting battery case data, officers began introducing me to others by saying, "she is good," which served as informal approval for my presence in their work environment. Ultimately, administrative approval and officers' acceptance were the two most important factors in gaining access to the field.

A "Typical" Ride-Along

The ride-alongs were split across three different shifts, however, the structure of the ride-alongs followed the same general format. During all ride-alongs, I wore civilian clothing without displaying any school affiliation, as requested by GPD. I typically wore black pants with either a long-sleeved or short-sleeved plain shirt. I always carried a black portfolio containing all instruments, pens, blank sheets of paper for field notes, and the audio recorder.

Each ride-along began with me arriving at the station approximately 15 minutes before the scheduled start time, which coincided with the officers' briefing (or roll call). I attended briefings fewer than five times during my fieldwork, so I often waited in the lobby while the briefing occurred. Although the briefing was an important part of the shift, I chose not to ask why I was not included, as I did not want to risk compromising my access to the field.

Officers picked me up either after their briefing or after being notified that they had a rider. Neither the officer nor I knew in advance who I would ride with. The decision was made by the Lieutenant or Sergeants on duty. Based on the few briefings I attended and conversations with patrol officers, it appeared that officers were selected based on four factors: volunteering to have a rider, having the highest badge number (indicating least seniority), being randomly chosen by the Lieutenant or Sergeants, or as punishment. The forms I signed for each ride-along did not specify detailed guidelines or practices beyond following the officer's instructions and wearing appropriate attire. There seemed to be no written standard procedure for officers. The experience described below reflects my personal observations and represents an overall summary of a typical ride-along.

The shift usually began with officers clearing the front seat for me, removing portable printers and paper organizers. I then explained my research and asked if they would agree to participate through a verbal informed consent, which all officers did. I also asked about safety protocols, such as their personal rules for exiting the car during calls and what to do if they were attacked or injured. Instructions were generally consistent: I could exit the car unless told otherwise, seek cover if the officer was hurt, and press the alarm button on the radio or laptop if possible. Some officers gave me a key to the car for shelter, and others explained how to access weapons stored in the vehicle.

During ride-alongs, officers gave me access to their software system, allowing me to view the call screen for current and pending calls and read CAD notes. I primarily used this access to monitor battery cases about to be dispatched.

When a call came in, the officer either was dispatched or self-dispatched. They always informed me of the type of call and either shared what they knew or told me to read the call notes. On occasions when we "ran code," meaning driving with lights and sirens, the officer always notified me beforehand. Upon arrival at the scene, I exited the car unless instructed otherwise. I stood a few feet behind the officer to overhear conversations with victims or suspects while maintaining safety. On several occasions, I was left alone with a victim at the scene or in the car while the officer pursued a suspect, but I was never left alone with a known suspect. If victims or suspects asked who I was, I explained that I was a researcher at UF studying police interactions with victims. If they asked questions or made statements, I clarified that I was not a police officer and directed them to speak with the officer.

Throughout the shift, we responded to calls in the officer's assigned zone and occasionally assisted in other zones at the sergeant's direction or the officer's initiative. When transporting a suspect to jail, the suspect sat in the back of the car in a secure compartment separated by bars and plexiglass. At the jail, I either walked through the lobby to join the officer in intake or waited in the car. During shifts, we made stops for meals, bathroom breaks, or returned to the station for supplies or to meet victims reporting crimes. I usually stayed for the entire shift, and the officer drove me home afterward. On a few occasions, I left early due to slow shifts with few calls or because the officer planned to work out at the station toward the end of the shift.

Data Management

I developed a system to manage the data as it was collected to ensure that it was organized and prepared for the analytical stage. In this section, I describe the system I used to manage, log, and file the different pieces of data. After each ride-along, I filed the physical copies of the instruments and observation notes. The ride-along instruments and field notes were stored in a secure folder organized by date and electronically logged in a spreadsheet. The spreadsheet recorded the following information: Anonymous officer ID, document ID, date, and time of the ride-along. To maintain anonymity, I kept a separate spreadsheet listing the anonymous officer ID alongside the officer's last name and rank.

If a battery occurred during the shift, I filed the ride-along instruments and field notes, along with physical copies of the battery case instrument and battery case interview after the shift. I then transferred the recorded interview to my password-protected laptop and transcribed it. Both the audio recording and transcription were filed in a folder labeled with the anonymous case number on a hard drive.

Next, I requested the CAD for the specific case using the incident number provided by the officers at the scene. This case number was stored separately from the battery case instrument, battery case interview, and battery case field notes to ensure that victims, suspects, and officers could not be identified. To manage the data for each case, I logged information about battery cases in a spreadsheet where I noted:

- anonymous case ID
- instrument and fieldnote IDs
- if the battery was non-domestic or domestic, gender and race of victim and suspect
- how many officers were interviewed

- anonymous officer ID
- if interviews had been transcribed
- if an arrest was made
- if a police report was generated
- if I had requested the CAD and police report and received them

These procedures were implemented to manage the large amount of data collected for each case and to ensure that anonymity was not compromised. This document was created solely for recordkeeping purposes and not for analytical purposes. In Table A.1 I provide an overview of the data.

Table A.1 Organizational context data overview

Source of data	Data	Information sought
Observations	Introductory ride-along instrument Introductory ride-along Fieldnotes Ride-along instrument Ride-along Fieldnotes	– Report writing process – Operational factors; jurisdiction, zones, shifts
Interviews	Introductory interview instrument Audio recording introductory interview Transcribed audio introductory interview	– Investigation habits – Report writing habits – Interactions with other officers – Interactions with victims, suspects and witnesses – Staffing – Terminology – Battery occurrence
Documents	Staff demographics Organizational chart Gainesville zone map General investigation procedures General order rules of conduct Domestic violence and dating violence investigations Code descriptions Statistics provided by GPD	– Organizational structure – Rules and protocols; conduct, investigations, report writing – Terminology

Data ID Codes

All the data, including instruments, field notes, interview recordings and transcripts, CADs, and police reports, were de-identified by removing dates, times, officers' names and ranks, and the names of victims, suspects, and witnesses, as well as incident numbers. These were replaced with anonymous ID codes. The de-identification process and creation of officer ID codes were implemented to increase protection of the identity of officers, victims, suspects, and witnesses. Additionally, each piece of data, including instruments, field notes, interview recordings and transcripts, CADs, and police reports, was assigned a separate ID code, and each battery case was given its own unique ID code.

Beyond protecting the identity of officers, this coding system provided a structured method for logging and identifying different pieces of data. The assigned codes were also used to locate information during analysis. For example, when coding field notes or interview transcripts, codes were attached to the data ID, which indicated the case number and page number, making it easier to trace specific information within the dataset.

Analytic Approach

In this study, I used inductive qualitative data triangulation to analyze the collected data. One of the key aspects of using an inductive approach is that the data determine which codes, categories, and themes or patterns are discussed in the findings (Denscombe, 2009). Although the findings in this study are expected to reflect organizational-, case-, and individual-level aspects that inform officers' perceptions in relation to policing, organizational, and victimological scholarship, this study did not aim to test a specific theory.

The goal of this analysis was to contextualize the factors that shape officers' perceptions regarding policing, organizational, and victimological scholarship, with a particular focus on the Ideal Victims concept developed by Christie (1986) and Strobl (2004). The primary interest was to examine what officers volunteered about victims and how often this topic was raised, which generated specific interest. The inductive approach made this possible because it centers on the voices and actions of officers (Esterberg, 2002), which was essential to uncover to answer the research questions.

Data Triangulation

I used qualitative data triangulation obtained through multiple qualitative methodologies informed by ethnographic methodological frameworks to understand police officers' perceptions of battery victims' credibility. More specifically, I relied on multiple sources of data collected through different qualitative methods to examine organizational-, case-, and individual-level factors that can influence officers' perceptions of victim credibility (Esterberg, 2002). The purpose of using data triangulation was to interpret the meaning of information found in various data sources and situate it within the broader context in which police carry out their daily tasks. The advantage of triangulating qualitative data is that it allows the researcher to verify whether findings are consistent across sources and to understand the context in which a phenomenon exists (Denscombe, 2009). To answer the research questions, I analyzed several types of data that needed to be compared and discussed in relation to each other, which is possible through triangulation.

Data triangulation is often used in qualitative projects where the goal is to achieve a holistic and contextual understanding of one or more phenomena (Leech & Onwuegbuzie, 2007). In this study, triangulation was essential because it enabled me to explore perceptions of credibility and how these were discussed by officers after the encounter and in corresponding police reports. Specifically, triangulation allowed me to identify which aspects of victim credibility were displayed or not displayed during interactions between officers and victims at the scene. This information was then contrasted with interviews with the primary officer, where they described their perceptions of the victim's credibility. By doing this, I could determine whether aspects of credibility observed during the encounter were mentioned in the interviews, or whether certain aspects were omitted. Additionally, I compared observations and interviews with corresponding police reports. For example, I examined whether aspects of credibility noted during observation or interview appeared in the police report, or whether they were mentioned in all three sources. Triangulation also allowed me to integrate organizational and contextual data with case-specific data to better understand which organizational factors influenced officers' work. For instance, I examined reporting practices and procedures to identify differences in how officers handled domestic battery reports compared to non-domestic battery reports.

Overall, data triangulation provided an opportunity to incorporate diverse data sources to examine credibility during case formation and assess variations in how officers discuss and depict victim credibility. Using multiple sources offered insight into the dynamic factors shaping officers' perceptions of credibility, which would not have been possible with a single source of data.

Coding

According to Coffey and Atkinson, qualitative coding has three core elements: "(a) noticing relevant phenomena, (b) collecting examples of those phenomena, and (c) analyzing those phenomena in order to find commonalities, differences, patterns, and structures" (1996, p. 29). Codes are typically short phrases or single words attached to a passage or sentence that carry symbolic meaning. Coding is therefore an interpretive act performed by the researcher when reviewing and analyzing data. Depending on the research questions, the type of data, and the study's objectives, different coding strategies may be selected (Saldaña, 2013).

Since I explored perceptions and the factors that inform them using several types of data, I employed multiple coding strategies to capture the various aspects under examination. For example, one coding strategy was used to understand how victims are described, while another was applied to examine officers' actions and behaviors during the case process. The advantage of using multiple coding strategies is that it enables a comprehensive exploration of diverse data and dimensions (Saldaña, 2013). In this section, I will outline the coding strategies applied in this study and explain the coding process.

Initial Coding

For the organizational and context data, I used initial coding, also referred to as open coding, following recommended general guidelines (Saldaña, 2013). Initial coding provides an opportunity to reflect on the content and nuances of the data while coding a broad range of material. It served as a way for me to become familiar with the data and establish the coding habits and procedures that I would apply throughout the study. Initial coding was specifically chosen for the organizational and context data because of the small sample size and its flexibility to code diverse elements such as officers' statements during interviews and shifts, as well as their behaviors and interactions with other officers or civilians.

Another purpose of analyzing organizational and context data was to learn more about GPD as an organization and the officers' daily tasks, which provided information that helped set up the battery case data collection and analysis. The findings from this stage were intended to contextualize the battery case data. By using initial coding for organizational and context data, I was able to create broad codes related to a wide range of topics. These codes did not generate precise themes but reflected loose categories such as officers' behaviors, case processes, organizational structure, decision-making, and operational aspects of patrol units.

When coding the organizational and context data, I combined line-by-line coding with coding of longer passages. A key part of this process was adding codes with question marks or parentheses to indicate uncertainty, which I then followed up on during subsequent data collection (Saldaña, 2013). For example, if I was unsure about the meaning of a statement or an observed behavior, I coded it with a word and a question mark, noted it, and asked about it during my next field visit. This approach allowed me to reflect on questions and address them in later observations.

Descriptive Coding

According to Saldana, descriptive coding "summarizes in a word or short phrase—most often a noun—the basic topic of a passage of qualitative data" (2013, p. 386). Tesch (1990) emphasizes that descriptive codes are not abbreviations of the content but rather identifiers of the topic. This means that "the topic is what is talked or written about. The content is the substance of the message" (1990, p. 119). The overarching goal of descriptive coding is to provide insight into what was seen and heard rather than capture the dynamic nuances of social interactions between individuals and groups (Wolcott, 1994).

In this study, descriptive coding was one of the strategies applied to the battery data. Although many scholars use descriptive coding as a default approach, this study specifically employed it because of its adaptability to various types of data within the same research. Additionally, since descriptive coding is noun-based (Saldaña, 2013), it aligns with the aim of understanding descriptions of victims and incidents shared by the police. Descriptive coding was, in this study, used to analyze how victims and victimization were discussed in CADs, by officers during interviews, in observations, and in police reports. More specifically, it was applied to label characteristics that officers described as influencing their perceptions of battery victims' credibility.

Process Coding

Since descriptive coding does not provide insight into participants' meanings and perspectives, additional coding strategies were employed to achieve the aim of understanding the factors that inform perceptions of victims' credibility. For some of the battery data, I used process coding in addition to descriptive coding, specifically to capture officers' actions.

Process coding focuses on actions in the data. Unlike descriptive coding, which is noun-based, process coding is verb-based (Saldaña, 2013). Actions are often situated within processes and can be described as "processes also imply actions intertwined with the dynamics of time, such as those things that emerge, change, occur in sequences, or become strategically implemented through time" (Hennink et al., 2011, p. 253). According to Saldana (2013), process coding is particularly useful for examining routines and rituals in human life, which occur in interactions and can be linked to psychological concepts such as identity and memory. Because this study explores officers' interactions with victims and their actions during the case process, situated within routine daily activities, process coding was an effective tool for analyzing these actions and interactions and situating them within the broader processes and contexts officers operate in. Process coding can reveal the routine nature of certain actions or disruptions and changes in routine. In this study, it was used to determine whether there were variations in how officers interacted with some victims compared to others.

Simultaneous Coding

Qualitative data often have non-distinct boundaries, meaning that the data collected sometimes require multiple coding strategies to fully address the research questions. Since this study examines officers' perceptions of victim credibility and the contexts in which these perceptions occur, a wide range of data was collected through observations, interviews, and reports. Some of these data, particularly those obtained through observations, combined actions, interactions, and conversations. To capture these complexities, both descriptive coding and process coding were applied to the observational data. This approach is known as simultaneous coding, which involves incorporating two or more coding strategies (Saldaña, 2013). In this case, descriptive and process coding were used together.

Simultaneous coding was conducted by reviewing the data and assigning either a descriptive code or a process code to some passages, and in certain cases, applying both codes to parts of the same passage (Saldaña, 2013). For example, when analyzing notes from observations of interactions between victims and officers, codes were assigned to describe the content of statements made by victims or officers. At the same time, codes were applied to capture actions performed by either party before, during, or immediately after the interaction. These codes were distinguished by their structure: Noun-based for descriptive codes and verb-based for process codes. To differentiate them clearly, each code was preceded by a letter "D" for descriptive and "P" for Process, such as "D truth" and "P Crying."

Pattern Coding

Different strategies of coding can be applied in different cycles, which will be discussed in more depth in the next section. After coding data once, it is common for researchers to return to the data to recode it or to look for patterns and trends in the existing codes. After using descriptive and process coding, I applied pattern coding. Pattern coding is explained as "grouping those summaries into a smaller number of categories, themes, or concepts" (Saldaña, 2013, p. 316). The codes created through pattern coding are explanatory codes that identify themes or explanations by organizing material from the first round or cycle of codes into meaningful units of analysis.

Pattern coding is a useful strategy because it enables the researcher to create themes and helps lay the groundwork for cross-case analysis, which is valuable in this study since it explores trends across a wide range of domestic and non-domestic battery cases (Miles et al., 2014). Pattern coding provides a more holistic approach to coding, making multiple types of data and large numbers of codes manageable. It also situates data and codes within larger processes, allowing the researcher to identify patterns across extensive sets of codes (Saldaña, 2013).

Coding Process

The organizational and context data were coded using initial coding (Saldaña, 2013), which was conducted consecutively as data collection occurred. Coding during data collection allowed me to become familiar with the data and coding procedures while making notes about questions or observations that required further exploration during subsequent observations or interviews. These data were coded in one cycle since the goal was not to identify overarching themes in officers' statements or behaviors but rather to learn more about their procedures and daily tasks. This phase of data collection was exploratory in nature.

The coding of the battery data was completed in a two-step process that encompassed two cycles labeled "cycle 1" and "cycle 2." According to Saldana, the benefit of coding in two cycles is that it allows the researcher to first focus on the substantive content of the data and then, during the second cycle, synthesize and conceptualize larger patterns. This approach also provides a structured process for categorizing codes developed through different strategies across various types of data.

In cycle 1, the goal was to summarize segments of data labeled with codes. During this cycle, I used descriptive coding to code CAD, interviews, and police reports to examine how victims and incidents were described. Additionally, I used simultaneous coding, combining descriptive coding and process coding, to analyze observational data and capture officers' actions at the scene, interactions with victims, and exchanges during these interactions.

For cycle 2, I used pattern coding to review the codes created in cycle 1 and develop categories based on those codes. The primary goal of cycle 2 was to identify patterns by grouping the summarized segments and codes generated through descriptive and process coding.

Analytical Procedure

In this section, I will describe the steps taken to analyze the data after it was coded. First, I will explain the procedures for the organizational and context data. Second, I will outline the process for the battery case data. Third, I will describe how the data were ultimately triangulated to answer the research questions posed.

Organizational Context Data

The organizational and context data were coded simultaneously as they were collected. Once the data had been transcribed and the notes completed after each interview and ride-along, I coded the data using initial coding and logged the codes in the codebook. I also wrote down any questions that arose during coding and explored these questions in subsequent ride-alongs or interviews.

The codes developed from reviewing interview transcripts, introductory ride-along instruments, field notes, and documents were categorized. Although the data were coded separately, they were analyzed using triangulation to determine whether codes and categories appeared across the three types of data. Most codes appeared in more than one type of data but reflected different aspects of the same concept. For example, the code "report writing" appeared in rules and policies for general investigations, in interviews when officers described the process, and in observational notes when I observed officers writing reports. Thus, the same code reflected different nuances: How officers are instructed to write reports, how they describe the process, and the procedures they follow when writing reports.

Battery Case Data

Each battery case was coded individually and by data source. I examined how incidents and victims were described using codes generated through descriptive coding and pattern coding in observational data, interviews, and police reports to understand how credibility was discussed and depicted by officers. I also reviewed process codes to capture victim and officer interactions, as well as general behavior observed during the case process, such as whether officers wrote a report or made an arrest. This analysis provided insight into officers' conduct in each case and helped identify factors influencing investigative practices in domestic and non-domestic cases.

During this stage, I focused on understanding which aspects of victim credibility were observed at the scene, how they were depicted and discussed in interviews, and whether they appeared in corresponding police reports. Specifically, I identified which aspects were mentioned or omitted and how they were discussed to determine similarities or differences across case formation. If multiple officers were interviewed for a case, I examined whether their perceptions varied.

After analyzing credibility in individual cases, I grouped cases by type: domestic or non-domestic. This distinction was important because these case types differ in scholarly attention and in factors such as the nature of relationships between parties, which relate to the Ideal Victim concept (Christie, 1986) and relevant legislation. Within each group, cases were further categorized based on whether a report was generated. Thus, cases were labeled as domestic or non-domestic and as having a report or not. I then analyzed similarities and differences in how credibility was discussed in cases that produced reports versus those that did not, within each group. Finally, I compared domestic and non-domestic cases to identify variations in credibility discussions across these categories. In the attached Table A.2, I provide an example of a visualization of the overview of the credibility factors.

As a final step, I contextualized the credibility aspects discussed and depicted by officers using the Ideal Victim characteristics developed by Christie (1986) and Strobl (2004), along with previous empirical findings on officers' perceptions of credibility in domestic and non-domestic victimizations. The aim was not to test the Ideal Victim concept but to use it as a framework for interpreting findings. Specifically, I examined whether the aspects mentioned by officers aligned with Christie's idea of factors shaping perceptions of victims, victimization, and victim–suspect dynamics. I also explored whether differences emerged in credibility discussions between domestic and non-domestic cases, given Christie's suggestion that domestic violence victims, particularly women, face greater challenges in being perceived as Ideal Victims.

Methodological Limitations

As with all research methodologies and all data, there are limitations to the strategies and data used in this study. In this section, I will discuss three major methodological limitations and how they were addressed. Specifically, I will examine officers altering their statements or behavior due to my presence, the limited input I had on when I could do

Table A.2 Interview credibility factors

Case	Cooperation/ Motivation	Info/ Story	Evidence	Witness	Injury/ Mark	Relationship	History	Suspect admission	Demeanor
Non-domestic batteries									
Non-report yielding cases									
5		–		+					+
6	–	=							
7		+		+					
8	+	+		+					+
15	–	–		–	=				–
26		+,+			–				
27	+	+							
34		+	+	–	–, +				–
Report yielding cases									
10	+		–		–				
12	+	+	+	+					
14	+			–	–				+
21	–	–							–
23	+	+	+						=
28	=				+				=
Domestic batteries									
Non-report yielding cases									
1				+					
13	+								+
16			+						
22		–		+	–				
32		+	+		+				
Report yielding cases									
2	+	+				+			
3	–/+	–		+		=			

Case	Cooperation/ Motivation	Info/ Story	Evidence	Witness	Injury/ Mark	Relationship	History	Suspect admission	Demeanor
4	+	+, +	+, +			=	+		+
9	–	–	–		–				–
11		+, +			+			+, +	
17		+							
18		+	+						
19				+					
20		+					+	+	
24	–							–	
25				+					+
29		+				=			+
30	+	+					+	+	+, +
31		+					+		
33		+	+, –						

(+) = Positive Impact, (-) = Negative Impact, (=) = Neutral, First symbol = Primary Officer, Second symbol = Second Officer, Third symbol = Third Officer ride-alongs, and the consistency of the quantity of data collected in each battery case.

The data in this study relied on observations, interviews, and texts, which allow for capturing a wide range of nuances in how police officers perceive victim credibility. However, there is always a possibility that officers alter their behavior or perceptions because they want to provide socially acceptable answers or simply refuse to participate in the study. For example, consistent with other qualitative and ethnographic scholarship that uses interviews to collect data, there is always a risk of the interview effect. The interview effect refers to interviewees responding in a specific way because they seek approval from the interviewer or believe the interviewer expects certain answers, which leads them to alter their responses to fit those expectations (Denscombe, 2009). To minimize this, I maintained a neutral facial expression and avoided language or mannerisms that could suggest approval or disapproval during interviews. Despite these efforts, it is important to acknowledge that officers may still have been influenced by the interview effect and, in some cases, provided answers they perceived as socially acceptable or aligned with what they thought I wanted to hear. Therefore, while interviews were an essential part of this study, the responses are analyzed with an awareness of the potential influence of the interview effect.

Police officers are under extensive public scrutiny, which may lead them to alter their behavior or statements to avoid presenting negative behavior or comments in front of me, or they may choose not to participate in interviews. This limitation cannot be disregarded, as it could impact the findings of this study. Fortunately, only 2 officers out of the 38 approached declined to be interviewed, so participation was not a major issue. To minimize the risk of officers adjusting their behavior, I took two steps. First, I spent extended time with the officers during ride-alongs, staying for entire shifts to build trust and make it harder for them to maintain altered behavior for 10 hours or more. I rode with many officers multiple times and encountered the same officers on several calls, which allowed me to observe them over longer periods. Second, I used data triangulation to answer research questions, collecting different types of data that reflected officers' perceptions of victim credibility. This approach enabled me to contextualize patterns found in one type of data with insights from others. Although officers could still alter their behavior or statements, having multiple data sources provided a broader perspective on their views of victim credibility.

Another important limitation was that I could not freely choose when to do ride-alongs, which zone I would be in, or which officer I would ride with. Although I provided GPD with a schedule of days and shifts I was available, and this was often followed by scheduling staff, my rides were ultimately controlled by GPD. Practically, this meant that even though some zones had more battery cases than others, I could not request to ride in a specific zone. GPD instructed me to spread my rides across all shifts and days of the week, which prevented me from selecting times when batteries were more likely to occur, such as weekends and evenings. To address this, I ensured that I had at least one weekend shift and one evening shift each week, alternating every other week. Another limitation was that although a battery might occur during a shift in a neighboring zone, I was assigned to one specific officer for safety reasons. If the officer I was riding with was handling a call and a battery occurred elsewhere, I could not leave to observe the battery call. While this affected my ability to collect cases, it was a necessary condition for conducting the study. To meet my target number of cases, I extended my time in the field and increased the number of weekly ride-alongs.

A third methodological challenge was the consistency of the quantity of data collected for each battery case. Although equal amounts of data for each case are desirable from a research standpoint, achieving this in practice is difficult. For example, I aimed to collect police reports for the battery cases I observed, but not all battery cases result in police reports. Consequently, although one research question focused on how officers describe victims in police reports, I had fewer reports than cases, limiting the sample size for examining perceptions of victim credibility across different stages of a case. This is a significant methodological limitation, but it also contributes to the study's findings by highlighting the implications of officers' discretionary power and variations in reporting practices across battery cases. Another example of limited data occurred in cases involving language barriers between victims or suspects and officers. Although translators were often available, in some incidents they were not present at the scene, requiring officers to communicate to the best of their ability, which affected the amount of information I could record. These limitations could impact the findings of this book, but they are also important because they underscore the dynamic nature of police work and the reality of limited information in some cases. Despite these challenges, I believe the findings succeed in their purpose of highlighting the many factors that inform officers' perceptions.

References

Acosta, D. F., Gomes, V. L. D. O., & Barlem, E. L. D. (2013). Profile of police reports related to violence against women. *Acta Paulista de Enfermagem, 26*(6), 547–553. https://doi.org/10.1590/S0103-21002013000600007

Alderden, M. A., & Ullman, S. E. (2012). Creating a more complete and current picture: Examining police and prosecutor decision-making when processing sexual assault cases. *Violence Against Women, 18*, 525–551. https://doi.org/10.1177/1077801212453867

Alexius, K. (2020). The exposed child in a qualitative study of cases at the Swedish schools inspectorate. An ideal or not-so-ideal victim? *Pedagogy, Culture & Society, 28*(3), 367–382. https://doi.org/10.1080/14681366.2019.1649296

Anderson, E. (2000). *Code of the street: Decency, violence, and the moral life of the inner city*. WW Norton & Company.

Aspholm, R. (2020). *Views from the streets: The transformation of gangs and violence on Chicago's south side*. Columbia University Press.

Averdijk, M., & Elffers, H. (2012). The discrepancy between survey-based victim accounts and police reports revisited. *International Review of Victimology, 18*(2), 91–107. https://doi.org/10.1177/0269758011432955

Ambrozewicz, P., Hammond, C., & Fido, D. (2024). Ending the stigma of male domestic violence and abuse victims: A mixed-methods study. *Journal of*

M. N. Eliasson, *Who Gets Believed?*, Palgrave's Critical Policing Studies,
https://doi.org/10.1007/978-3-032-22253-4

Criminal Justice, 93, 102222. https://doi.org/10.1016/j.jcrimjus.2024.102222

Ask, K. (2010). A survey of police officers' and prosecutors' beliefs about crime victim behaviors. *Journal of Interpersonal Violence, 25*(6), 1132–1149. https://doi.org/10.1177/0886260509340535

Ba, B. A., Knox, D., Mummolo, J., & Rivera, R. (2021). The role of officer race and gender in police-civilian interactions in Chicago. *Science, 371*, 696–702. https://doi.org/10.1126/science.abd8694

Bachman, R. (1994). Victim's perceptions of initial police responses to robbery and aggravated assault: Does race matter? *Journal of Quantitative Criminology, 12*, 363–390. https://doi.org/10.1007/BF02354424

Balenovich, J., Grossi, E., & Hughes, T. (2008). Toward a balanced approach: Defining police roles in responding to domestic violence. *American Journal of Criminal Justice, 33*, 19–31. https://doi.org/10.1007/s12103-007-9028-5

Barling, J. (1996). The prediction, experience, and consequences of workplace violence. In G. R. VandenBos & E. Q. Bulatao (Eds.), *Violence on the job: Identifying risks and developing solutions* (pp. 29–49). American Psychological Association. https://doi.org/10.1037/10215-001

Basic, G. (2015). Constructing "ideal victim" stories of Bosnian war survivors. *Social Inclusion, 3*(4), 25–37. https://doi.org/10.17645/si.v3i4.249

Baskin, D. (2018). *Casualties of community disorder: Women's careers in violent crime*. Routledge.

Benson, M. L., Fox, G. L., DeMaris, A., & Van Wyk, J. (2003). Neighborhood disadvantage, individual economic distress and violence against women in intimate relationships. *Journal of Quantitative Criminology, 19*(3), 207–235. https://doi.org/10.1023/A:1024930208331

Bittner, E. (1970). *The functions of the police in modern society*. Aronson.

Blaustein, J. (2015). *Speaking truths to power: Policy ethnography and police reform in Bosnia and Herzegovina*. Oxford University Press.

Black, A., Lumsden, K., & Hadlington, L. (2019). 'Why Don't you block them?' Police officers' constructions of the ideal victim when responding to reports of interpersonal cybercrime. In K. Lumsden & E. Harmer (Eds.), *Online othering* (pp. 355–378). Palgrave Studies in Cybercrime and Cybersecurity). Springer International Publishing. https://doi.org/10.1007/978-3-030-12633-9_15

Bollingmo, G. C., Wessel, E. O., Eilertsen, D. E., & Magnussen, S. (2007). Credibility of the emotional witness: A study of ratings by police investigators. *Psychology, Crime & Law, 14*, 29–40. https://doi.org/10.1007/s10979-006-9024-1

Bostaph, L. G., King, L. L., & Brady, P. Q. (2021). How victim credibility and cooperation influence investigative decision-making: Examining DOJ's gender bias principles for investigating domestic and sexual violence. *Policing: An International Journal, 44*(4), 612–627. https://doi.org/10.1108/PIJPSM-02-2021-0018

Braga, A. A., Brunson, R. K., & Drakulich, K. M. (2019). Race, place, and effective policing. *Annual Review of Sociology, 45*, 535–555. https://doi.org/10.1146/annurev-soc-073018-022541

Brown, J. (2007). From cult of masculinity to smart macho: Gender perspectives on police occupational culture. *Sociology of Crime, Law and Deviance, 8*(1), 205–226. https://doi.org/10.1016/S1521-6136(07)08008-6

Beehr, T. A., Ivanitskaya, L., Glaser, K., Erofeev, D., & Canali, K. (2004). Working in a violent environment: The accuracy of police officers' reports about shooting incidents. *Journal of Occupational and Organizational Psychology, 77*(2), 217–235. https://doi.org/10.1348/096317904774202153

Belknap, J. (1995). Law enforcement officers' attitudes about the appropriate responses to woman battering. *International Review of Victimology, 4*(1), 47–62. https://doi.org/10.1177/026975809500400104

Bowker, L. H. (1982). Police services to battered women: Bad or not so bad? *Criminal Justice and Behavior, 9*(4), 476–494. https://doi.org/10.1177/0093854882009004005

Bostaph, L. G., King, L. L., & Brady, P. Q. (2021). How victim credibility and cooperation influence investigative decision-making: examining DOJ's gender bias principles for investigating domestic and sexual violence. *Policing: An International Journal, 44*(4), 612–627. https://doi.org/10.1108/PIJPSM-02-2021-0018

Burcar, V. (2013). Doing masculinity in narratives about reporting violent crime: Young male victims talk about contacting and encountering the police. *Journal of Youth Studies, 16*(2), 172–190. https://doi.org/10.1080/13676261.2012.704992

Buzawa, E. S., & Austin, T. (1993). Determining police response to domestic violence victims: The role of victim preference. *American Behavioral Scientist, 36*(5), 610–623. https://doi.org/10.1177/0002764293036005006

Buzawa, E. S., Buzawa, C. G., & Stark, E. D. (2015). *Responding to domestic violence: The integration of criminal justice and human services*. Sage Publications.

Cain, M. (1973). Society and the policeman's role. *Routledge*. https://doi.org/10.4324/9781315688541

Cazenave, N. A., & Zahn, M. A. (1992). Women, murder, and male domination: Police reports of domestic violence in Chicago and Philadelphia. In E. C. Viano (Ed.), *Intimate violence: Interdisciplinary perspectives* (pp. 83–97). Hemisphere Publishing Corporation.

Christie, N. (1986). The ideal victim. In E. Fattah (Ed.), *From crime policy to victim policy* (pp. 17–30). Palgrave Macmillan. https://doi.org/10.1007/978-1-349-08305-3_2

Campbell, B. A., Menaker, T. A., & King, W. R. (2015). The determination of victim credibility by adult and juvenile sexual assault investigators. *Journal of Criminal Justice, 43*(1), 29–39. https://doi.org/10.1016/j.jcrimjus.2014.12.001

Contreras, R. (2013). *The stickup kids: Race, drugs, violence, and the American dream*. University of California Press.

Coulter, M. L., Kuehnle, K., Byers, R., & Alfonso, M. (1999). Police-reporting behavior and victim-police interactions as described by women in a domestic violence shelter. *Journal of Interpersonal Violence, 14*(12), 1290–1298. https://doi.org/10.1177/088626099014012004

Cordner, G. (2017). Police culture: Individual and organizational differences in police officer perspectives. *Policing: An International Journal, 40*(1), 11–25. https://doi.org/10.1108/PIJPSM-07-2016-0116

Crank, J. P. (2014). *Understanding police culture*. Routledge. https://doi.org/10.4324/9781315721255

Cunha, O., Carvalho, F., de Castro Rodrigues, A., Cruz, A. R., & Gonçalves, R. A. (2022). Attitudes of police recruits towards offenders: The impact of the police training on attitudinal change. *Journal of Police and Criminal Psychology, 37*(1), 162–172. https://doi.org/10.1007/s11896-021-09484-5

Clark, V. E. (2021). Victim-blaming discourse underpinning police responses to domestic violence: A critical social work perspective. *Social Work & Policy Studies: Social Justice, Practice and Theory, 4*(1), 1–15. https://openjournals.library.sydney.edu.au/SWPS/article/view/14959

Cross, C. (2018). Denying victim status to online fraud victims: The challenges of being a "non-Ideal Victim". In M. Duggan (Ed.), *Revisiting the ideal victim concept* (pp. 243–262). Policy Press. https://doi.org/10.1332/policypress/9781447338765.003.0015

Data USA. (2023). *Gainesville, Florida about*. https://datausa.io/profile/geo/gainesville-fl/

DeJong, C., Burgess-Proctor, A., & Elis, L. (2008). Police officer perceptions of intimate partner violence: An analysis of observational data. *Violence and Victims, 23*(6), 683–696. https://doi.org/10.1891/0886-6708.23.6.683

Denscombe, M. (2009). *Ground rules for social research: Guidelines for good practice*. Open University Press.

Demirkol, I. C., & Nalla, M. K. (2020). Police culture: An empirical appraisal of the phenomenon. *Criminology & Criminal Justice, 20*(3), 319–338. https://doi.org/10.1177/1748895818823832

DeAngelo, G., Toger, M., & Weisburd, S. (2023). Police response time and injury outcomes. *The Economic Journal, 133*(654), 2147–2177. https://doi.org/10.1093/ej/uead035

Dorfman, D. N. (1999). Proving the lie: Litigating police credibility. *American Journal of Criminal Law, 26*(3), 455–504. http://digitalcommons.pace.edu/lawfaculty/533/

Doreian, P., & Conti, N. (2017). Creating the thin blue line: Social network evolution within a police academy. *Social Networks, 50*, 83–97. https://doi.org/10.1016/j.socnet.2017.03.011

Duggan, M. (2018). *Revisiting the ideal victim': Developments in critical victimology*. Policy Press. https://doi.org/10.1332/policypress/9781447338765.001.0001

Dukes, K. N., & Gaither, S. E. (2017). Black racial stereotypes and victim blaming: Implications for media coverage and criminal proceedings in cases of police violence against racial and ethnic minorities. *Journal of Social Issues, 73*(4), 789–807. https://doi.org/10.1111/josi.12248

Eitle, D. (2005). The influence of mandatory arrest policies, police organizational characteristics, and situational variables on the probability of arrest in domestic violence cases. *Crime & Delinquency, 51*(4), 573–597. https://doi.org/10.1177/0011128705277784

El Sayed, S. A., DeShay, R. A., Davis, J. B., Knox, K. N., & Kerley, K. R. (2022). A blue step forward: An exploratory study of law enforcement perceptions of intimate partner violence in the southern United States. *Journal of Interpersonal Violence, 37*(9–10), 6514–6534. https://doi.org/10.1177/0886260520966675

Eliasson, M. N. (2022). A qualitative examination of Swedish police officers' perceptions of victim culpability. *Victims & Offenders, 19*(2), 160–178. https://doi.org/10.1080/15564886.2022.2091069

Emerson, R. M., Fretz, R. I., & Shaw, L. L. (2011). *Writing ethnographic fieldnotes*. University of Chicago Press.

Engel, R. S., Sobol, J. J., & Worden, R. E. (2000). Further exploration of the demeanor hypothesis: The interaction effects of suspects' characteristics and demeanor on police behavior. *Justice Quarterly, 17*(2), 235–258. https://doi.org/10.1080/07418820000096311

Epstein, D., & Goodman, L. A. (2018). Discounting women: Doubting domestic violence survivors' credibility and dismissing their experiences. *University Pennsylvania Law Review, 167*, 399.

Ellison, L. (2002). Prosecuting domestic violence without victim participation. *The Modern Law Review, 65*(6), 834–858. https://doi.org/10.1111/1468-2230.00412

Epstein, D., & Goodman, L. A. (2019). Discounting women: Doubting domestic violence survivors' credibility and dismissing their experiences. *University of Pennsylvania Law Review, 167*(2), 399–462. https://scholarship.law.georgetown.edu/facpub/2037

Esterberg, K. G. (2002). *Qualitative methods in social research*. McGraw-Hill.

Faragher, J. M. (2016). *Eternity street: Violence and justice in frontier Los Angeles*. WW Norton & Company.

Farrell, A., Owens, C., & McDevitt, J. (2014). New laws but few cases: Understanding the challenges to the investigation and prosecution of human trafficking cases. *Crime, Law and Social Change, 61*, 139–168. https://doi.org/10.1007/s10611-013-9442-1

Fassin, D. (2013). *The moral world of law enforcement* (p. 49). Institute of Advanced Studies.

Fassin, D. (Ed.). (2017). *Writing the world of policing: The difference ethnography makes*. University of Chicago Press.

Federal Bureau of Investigation. (2019). *Full-time law enforcement employees by population group, percent male and female*. https://ucr.fbi.gov/crime-in-the-u.s/2019/crime-in-the-u.s.-2019/topic-pages/tables/table-74

Felson, R. B., Messner, S. F., & Hoskin, A. (1999). The victim-offender relationship and calling the police in assaults. *Criminology, 37*(4), 931–948. https://doi.org/10.1111/j.1745-9125.1999.tb00510.x

Felson, R. B., & Lantz, B. (2016). When are victims unlikely to cooperate with the police? *Aggressive Behavior, 42*(1), 97–108. https://doi.org/10.1002/ab.21626

Finn, M. A., & Stalans, L. J. (1997). The influence of gender and mental state on police decisions in domestic assault cases. *Criminal Justice and Behavior, 24*(2), 157–176. https://doi.org/10.1177/0093854897024002002

Fleming, J. C., & Franklin, C. A. (2021). Predicting police endorsement of myths surrounding intimate partner violence. *Journal of Family Violence, 36*(4), 407–416. https://doi.org/10.1007/s10896-020-00178-w

Florida Senate. (2025a). *Fla. stat. Chapter 784.03*. Florida Senate. https://www.leg.state.fl.us/statutes/index.cfm?App_mode=Display_Statute&Search_String=&URL=0700-0799/0784/Sections/0784.03.html

Florida Senate. (2025b). *Fla. stat. Chapter 741.28*. Florida Senate https://www.leg.state.fl.us/statutes/index.cfm?mode=View%20Statutes&SubMenu=1&App_mode=Display_Statute&Search_String=741.28&URL=0700-0799/0741/Sections/0741.28.html

Fohring, S. (2018). Revisiting the non-ideal victim. In M. Duggan (Ed.), *Revisiting the 'ideal victim': Developments in critical victimology* (pp. 195–210). https://doi.org/10.1332/policypress/9781447338765.003.0012

Franklin, C. A., Goodson, A., & Garza, A. D. (2019). Intimate partner violence among sexual minorities: Predicting police officer arrest decisions. *Criminal Justice and Behavior, 46*(8), 1181–1199. https://doi.org/10.1177/0093854819834722

Frohmann, L. (1991). Discrediting victims' allegations of sexual assault: Prosecutorial accounts of case rejections. *Social Problems, 38*, 213–226. https://doi.org/10.2307/800530

Frohmann, L. (1997). Convictability and discordant locales: Reproducing race, class, and gender ideologies in prosecutorial decision-making. *Law and Society Review, 31*, 531–555. https://doi.org/10.2307/3054045

Figley, C. R. (2013). *Trauma and its wake*. Routledge.

Fisher, S. Z. (1993). Just the facts, ma'am: Lying and the omission of exculpatory evidence in police reports. *New England Law Review, 28*(1), 1–62. https://scholarship.law.bu.edu/faculty_scholarship/906

Florida Senate. (2023). Fla. Stat. Chapter 741.29. Florida Senate. https://www.flsenate.gov/laws/statutes/2023/741.29

Florida Senate. (2025). Fla. Stat. Chapter 901.15. Florida Senate. https://www.leg.state.fl.us/Statutes/index.cfm?App_mode=Display_Statute&URL=0900-0999/0901/Sections/0901.15.html

Geertz, C. (2008). Thick description: Toward an interpretive theory of culture. In *The cultural geography reader* (pp. 41–51). Routledge.

García, E., García, F., & Lila, M. (2011). Police attitudes toward policing partner violence against women: Do they correspond to different psychosocial profiles? *Journal of Interpersonal Violence, 26*(1), 189–207. https://doi.org/10.1177/0886260510362892

Gainesville Police Department. (2022, December). *Staffing records*. Retrieved from Gainesville Police Department.

Garner, R. (2005). Police attitudes: The impact of experience after training. *Applied Psychology in Criminal Justice, 1*(1), 56–70.

Gainesville Police Department. (2023a). General Order 26.1 Rules Of Conduct. https://public.powerdms.com/GPD/tree/documents/265

Gainesville Police Department. (2023b). General Order 40.6 General Investigation Procedures for Domestic and Dating Violence. https://public.powerdms.com/GPD/tree/documents/313

Gainesville Police Department. (2023c). General Order 42.2 General Investigation Procedures. https://public.powerdms.com/GPD/tree/documents/325

Glomseth, R., Gottschalk, P., & Solli-Saether, H. (2007). Occupational culture as determinant of knowledge sharing and performance in police investigations. *International Journal of the Sociology of Law, 35*(2), 96–107. https://doi.org/10.1016/j.ijsl.2007.03.003

Goodson, A. J. (2020). *Heterosexual and same-sex intimate partner violence: Police attributions of victim culpability*. Doctoral dissertation, Sam Huston State University. https://hdl.handle.net/20.500.11875/2758

Harrison, L. A., & Esqueda, C. W. (2000). Effects of race and victim drinking on domestic violence attributions. *Sex Roles, 42*, 1043–1057. https://doi.org/10.1023/A:1007040701889

Hennink, M., Hutter, I., & Bailey, A. (2011). Qualitative research methods. *SAGE Publications*.

Hessick, C. B. (2007). Violence between lovers, strangers, and friends. *Washington University Law Review, 85*(2), 343–407. https://openscholarship.wustl.edu/law_lawreview/vol85/iss2/3

Hickman, L. J., & Simpson, S. S. (2003). Fair treatment or preferred outcome? The impact of police behavior on victim reports of domestic violence incidents. *Law & Society Review, 37*(3), 607–634. https://doi.org/10.1111/1540-5893.3703005

Hirschel, D., Buzawa, E., Pattavina, A., & Faggiani, D. (2007). Domestic violence and mandatory arrest laws: To what extent do they influence police arrest decisions. *Journal of Criminal Law and Criminology, 98*(1), 255–298. https://www.jstor.org/stable/40042852

Horwitz, S. H., Mitchell, D., LaRussa-Trott, M., Santiago, L., Pearson, J., Skiff, D. M., & Cerulli, C. (2011). An inside view of police officers' experience with domestic violence. *Journal of Family Violence, 26*(8), 617–625. https://doi.org/10.1007/s10896-011-9396-y

Huisman, K., Martinez, J., & Wilson, C. (2005). Training police officers on domestic violence and racism: Challenges and strategies. *Violence Against Women, 11*(6), 792–821. https://doi.org/10.1177/1077801205276110

Hirschel, J. D., Hutchison, I. W., Dean, C. W., & Mills, A. M. (1992). Review essay on the law enforcement response to spouse abuse: Past, present, and future. *Justice Quarterly, 9*(2), 247–283. https://doi.org/10.1080/07418829200091361

Holdaway, S. (1983). *Inside the British police: A force at work*. Basil Blackwell.

Holloway, C. P., & Wiener, R. L. (2018). Abuse history and culpability judgments: Implications for battered spouse syndrome. *Psychology, Public Policy, and Law, 24*(3), 279–291. https://doi.org/10.1037/law0000167

Hess, K. M., & Wrobleski, H. M. (1996). *For the record: Report writing in law enforcement*. Innovative Systems.

Inzunza, M. (2022). The significance of victim ideality in interactions between crime victims and police officers. *International Journal of Law, Crime and Justice, 68*, 1–12. https://doi.org/10.1016/j.ijlcj.2021.100522

Ingram, J. R., Terrill, W., & Paoline, E. A., III. (2018). Police culture and officer behavior: Application of a multilevel framework. *Criminology, 56*(4), 780–811. https://doi.org/10.1111/1745-9125.12192

Jasinski, J. L. (2003). Police involvement in incidents of physical assault: Analysis of the redesigned National Crime Victimization Survey. *Journal of Family Violence, 18*, 143–150. https://doi.org/10.1023/A:1023512420703

Jägervi, L. (2014). Who wants to be an ideal victim? A narrative analysis of crime victims' self-presentation. *Journal of Scandinavian Studies in Criminology and Crime Prevention, 15*(1), 73–88. https://doi.org/10.1080/14043858.2014.893479

James, L., James, S., & Vila, B. (2018). The impact of work shift and fatigue on police officer response in simulated interactions with citizens. *Journal of Experimental Criminology, 14*, 111–120. https://doi.org/10.1007/s11292-017-9294-2

Johnson, B., Golub, A., & Dunlap, E. (2000). The rise and decline of hard drugs, drug markets, and violence in inner-city New York. In A. Blumstein & J. Wallman (Eds.), *The crime drop in America* (pp. 164–206). Cambridge University Press.

Kang, J. H., & Lynch, J. P. (2014). Calling the police in instances of family violence: Effects of victim–offender relationship and life stages. *Crime & Delinquency, 60*(1), 34–59. https://doi.org/10.1177/0011128709359655

Kassin, S. M., Kukucka, J., Lawson, V. Z., & DeCarlo, J. (2017). Police reports of mock suspect interrogations: A test of accuracy and perception. *Law and Human Behavior, 41*(3), 230–243. https://doi.org/10.1037/lhb0000225

Kraska, P. B. (1996). Enjoying militarism: Political/personal dilemmas in studying US police paramilitary units. *Justice Quarterly, 13*(3), 405–429. https://doi.org/10.1080/07418829600093031

Kwak, H., Dierenfeldt, R., & McNeeley, S. (2019). The code of the street and cooperation with the police: Do codes of violence, procedural injustice, and police ineffectiveness discourage reporting violent victimization to the police? *Journal of Criminal Justice, 60*, 25–34. https://doi.org/10.1016/j.jcrimjus.2018.11.001

LaFree, G. D. (1981). Official reactions to social problems: Police decisions in sexual assault cases. *Social Problems, 28*, 582–594. https://doi.org/10.2307/800232

Landström, S., Ask, K., & Sommar, C. (2015). The emotional male victim: Effects of presentation mode on judged credibility. *Scandinavian Journal of Psychology, 56*(1), 99–104. https://doi.org/10.1111/sjop.12176

Lee, J., Zhang, Y., & Hoover, L. T. (2013). Police response to domestic violence: Multilevel factors of arrest decision. *Policing: an International Journal of Police Strategies & Management, 36*(1), 157–174. https://doi.org/10.1108/13639511311302524

Leech, N. L., & Onwuegbuzie, A. J. (2007). An array of qualitative data analysis tools: A call for data analysis triangulation. *School Psychology Quarterly, 22*(4), 557–584. https://doi.org/10.1037/1045-3830.22.4.557

Leatherby, L., & Oppel, R. A. (2020). Which police departments are as diverse as their communities. *New York Times*, 23.

LeCount, R. J. (2017). More black than blue? Comparing the racial attitudes of police to citizens. *Sociological Forum, 32*(1), 1051–1072. https://doi.org/10.1111/socf.12367

Lewis, J. A., Hamilton, J. C., & Elmore, J. D. (2019). Describing the ideal victim: A linguistic analysis of victim descriptions. *Current Psychology*, (9), 1. https://doi.org/10.1007/s12144-019-00347-1

Lipsky, S., Caetano, R., & Roy-Byrne, P. (2009). Racial and ethnic disparities in police-reported intimate partner violence and risk of hospitalization among women. *Women's Health Issues, 19*(2), 109–118. https://doi.org/10.1016/j.whi.2008.09.005

Loader, I., & Mulcahy, A. (2003). *Policing and the condition of England: Memory, politics and culture*. Oxford University Press.

Long, L. J. (2021). The ideal victim: A critical race theory (CRT) approach. *International Review of Victimology, 27*(3), 344–362. https://doi.org/10.1177/0269758021993339

Loftus, B. (2009). *Police culture in a changing world.* Oxford Academic. https://doi.org/10.1093/acprof:oso/9780199560905.001.0001

Lum, C. (2011). The influence of places on police decision pathways: From call for service to arrest. *Justice Quarterly, 28*(4), 631–665. https://doi.org/10.1080/07418825.2010.526130

Maguire, M. (2012). Criminal investigation and crime control. In *Handbook of policing* (pp. 430–464). Willan.

Manning, P. K. (2015). Researching policing using qualitative methods. In *The Routledge handbook of qualitative criminology* (pp. 265–282). Routledge.

Mancini, C., & Pickett, J. T. (2017). Reaping what they sow? Victim-offender overlap perceptions and victim blaming attitudes. *Victims & Offenders, 12*(3), 434–466. https://doi.org/10.1080/15564886.2015.1093051

Martin, S. E. (1994). "Outsider within" the station house: The impact of race and gender on black women police. *Social Problems, 41*(3), 383–400. https://doi.org/10.2307/3096969

McLaughlin, E. M. (2006). *The new policing.* Sage.

Merriam-Webster. (2025a). *Credibility.* In Merriam-Webster.com dictionary. Retrieved October 15, 2025, from https://www.merriam-webster.com/dictionary/credibility

Merriam-Webster. (2025b). *Legitimacy.* In Merriam-Webster.com dictionary. Retrieved October 15, 2025, from https://www.merriam-webster.com/dictionary/legitimacy?src=search-dict-box

Miller, M., & Pomerenke, P. (1989). Police reports must be reader based. *Law and Order, 37*(9), 66–69. https://www.ojp.gov/pdffiles1/Digitization/120641NCJRS.pdf

Miles, M. B., Huberman, A. M., & Saldaña, J. (2014). *Qualitative data analysis: A methods sourcebook.* SAGE Publications.

Myhill, A., & Bradford, B. (2013). Overcoming cop culture? Organizational justice and police officers' attitudes toward the public. *Policing: an International Journal of Police Strategies & Management, 36*(2), 338–356. https://doi.org/10.1108/13639511311329732

Myhill, A., & Johnson, K. (2016). Police use of discretion in response to domestic violence. *Criminology & Criminal Justice, 16*(1), 3–20. https://doi.org/10.1177/1748895815590202

Neuman, J. H., & Baron, R. A. (1998). Workplace violence and workplace aggression: Evidence concerning specific forms, potential causes, and preferred targets. *Journal of Management, 24*(3), 391–419. https://doi.org/10.1016/S0149-2063(99)80066-X

O'Neal, E. N. (2019). "Victim is not credible": The influence of rape culture on police perceptions of sexual assault complainants. *Justice Quarterly, 36*(1), 127–160. https://doi.org/10.1080/07418825.2017.1406977

O'Neal, E. N., & Hayes, B. E. (2020). "A rape is a rape, regardless of what the victim was doing at the time": Detective views on how "problematic" victims affect sexual assault case processing. *Criminal Justice Review, 45*(1), 26–44. https://doi.org/10.1177/0734016819842639

Overstreet, N. M., & Quinn, D. M. (2016). The intimate partner violence stigmatization model and barriers to help seeking. In *Social psychological perspectives on Stigma* (pp. 109–122). Routledge.

Pahl, J. (2016). *Private violence and public policy: The needs of battered women and the response of the public services*. Routledge. https://doi.org/10.4324/9781315562100

Patterson, G. T. (2004). Evaluating the effects of child abuse training on the attitudes, knowledge, and skills of police recruits. *Research on Social Work Practice, 14*(4), 273–280. https://doi.org/10.1177/1049731503262390

Pearlman, D. N., Zierler, S., Gjelsvik, A., & Verhoek-Oftedahl, W. (2003). Neighbor-hood environment, racial position, and risk of police-reported domestic violence: A contextual analysis. *Public Health Reports, 118*(1), 44–58. https://doi.org/10.1093/phr/118.1.44

Petherick, W. A., & Turvey, B. (2009). *Forensic victimology: Examining violent crime victims in investigative and legal contexts*. Elsevier.

Phillips, A., & de Roos, M. S. (2022). Gender stereotypes and perceptions of stranger violence: Attributions of blame and motivation. *International Journal of Offender Therapy and Comparative Criminology, 69*(1), 43–61. https://doi.org/10.1177/0306624X221124849

Pich, J., & Roche, M. (2020). Violence on the job: The experiences of nurses and midwives with violence from patients and their friends and relatives. *Healthcare, 8*(4), 1–12. https://doi.org/10.3390/healthcare8040522

Piquero, N. L., Piquero, A. R., Craig, J. M., & Clipper, S. J. (2013). Assessing research on workplace violence, 2000–2012. *Aggression and Violent Behavior, 18*(3), 383–394. https://doi.org/10.1016/j.avb.2013.03.001

Phillips, A., & de Roos, M. S. (2022). Gender stereotypes and perceptions of stranger violence: Attributions of blame and motivation. *International Journal*

of Offender Therapy and Comparative Criminology, Online first. https://doi.org/10.1177/0306624X221124849
Phillips, A., & de Roos, M. S. (2025). Gender stereotypes and perceptions of stranger violence: Attributions of blame and motivation. *International Journal of Offender Therapy and Comparative Criminology, 69*(1), 43–61. https://doi.org/10.1177/0306624X221124849
Poteyeva, M., & Sun, I. Y. (2009). Gender differences in police officers' attitudes: Assessing current empirical evidence. *Journal of Criminal Justice, 37*(5), 512–522. https://doi.org/10.1016/j.jcrimjus.2009.07.011
Punch, M. (1979). *Policing the inner city: A study of Amsterdam's Warmoesstraat*. Springer.
Redwine, K. B (2003, October 26). The importance of the police report. Criminal Justice Institute School of Law Enforcement Supervision, Session XXII. https://www.cji.edu/wp-content/uploads/2019/04/importance_of_police_reports.pdf
Reiner, R. (2017). Is police culture cultural? *Policing: A Journal of Policy and Practice, 11*(3), 236–241. https://doi.org/10.1093/police/paw046
Ricciardelli, R. (2018). "Risk it out, risk it out": Occupational and organizational stresses in rural policing. *Police Quarterly, 21*(4), 415–439. https://doi.org/10.1177/1098611118772268
Ricciardelli, R., Spencer, D. C., & Dodge, A. (2020). "Society wants to see a true victim": Police interpretations of victims of sexual violence. *Feminist Criminology, 16*(2), 216–235. https://doi.org/10.1177/1557085120970270
Riedel, M. (2017). A perspective on stranger violence. In W. Laufer & F. Adler (Eds.), *The criminology of criminal law* (pp. 29–52). Routledge. https://doi.org/10.4324/9781315131535
Rios, V. M. (2017). *Human targets: Schools, police, and the criminalization of Latino youth*. University of Chicago Press. https://doi.org/10.7208/chicago/9780226091044.001.0001
Rollwagen, H., & Jacob, J. C. (2018). The victim–offender relationship and police charging decisions for juvenile delinquents: How does social distance moderate the impact of legal and extralegal factors? *Youth Violence and Juvenile Justice, 16*(4), 378–394. https://doi.org/10.1177/1541204017710315
Rubinstein, J. (1980). *City police*. Macmillan.
Russell, B. (2018). Police perceptions in intimate partner violence cases: The influence of gender and sexual orientation. *Journal of Crime and Justice, 41*(2), 193–205. https://doi.org/10.1080/0735648X.2017.1282378

Russell, B., & Sturgeon, J. A. (2019). Police evaluations of intimate partner violence in heterosexual and same-sex relationships: Do experience and training play a role? *Journal of Police and Criminal Psychology, 34*(1), 34–44. https://doi.org/10.1007/s11896-018-9279-8

Ryan, C., Silvio, D., Borden, T., & Ross, N. M. (2022). A review of pro-arrest, pro-charge, and pro-prosecution policies as a response to domestic violence. *Journal of Social Work, 22*(1), 211–238. https://doi.org/10.1177/1468017320979956

Saldaña, J. (2013). *The coding manual for qualitative researchers*. Sage Publications. http://digital.casalini.it/9781529755992

Saunders, D. G., & Size, P. B. (1986). Attitudes about woman abuse among police officers, victims, and victim advocates. *Journal of Interpersonal Violence, 1*(1), 25–42. https://doi.org/10.1177/088626086001001003

Sherman, L. W., Schmidt, J. D., & Rogan, D. P. (1992). *Policing domestic violence*. The Free Press.

Sherman, L. W. (2020). Targeting American policing: Rogue cops or rogue cultures? *Cambridge Journal of Evidence Based Policing, 4*, 77–88. https://doi.org/10.1007/s41887-020-00046-z

Sherman, L. W., & Berk, R. A. (1984). The specific deterrent effects of arrest for domestic assault. *American Sociological Review, 49*(2), 261–272. https://doi.org/10.2307/2095575

Schwöbel-Patel, C. (2018). The 'ideal' victim of international criminal law. *European Journal of International Law, 29*(3), 703–724. https://doi.org/10.1093/ejil/chy056

Skogan, W. G., & Hartnett, S. M. (1999). *Community policing, Chicago style*. Oxford University Press.

Skogan, W. G. (2006a). *Police and community in Chicago: A tale of three cities*. Oxford University Press. https://doi.org/10.1093/acprof:oso/9780195154580.001.0001

Skogan, W. (2006b). Asymmetry in the impact of encounters with police. *Policing and Society, 16*(2), 99–126. https://doi.org/10.1080/10439460600662098

Skolnick, J. H. (1966). *Justice without trial: Law enforcement in democratic society*. Wiley.

Sleath, E., & Bull, R. (2012). Comparing rape victim and perpetrator blaming in a police officer sample: Differences between police officers with and without special training. *Criminal Justice and Behavior, 39*(5), 646–665. https://doi.org/10.1177/0093854811434696

Sleath, E., & Bull, R. (2017). Police perceptions of rape victims and the impact on case decision making: A systematic review. *Aggression and Violent Behavior, 34*, 102–112. https://doi.org/10.1016/j.avb.2017.02.003

Sokoloff, N. J., & Dupont, I. (2005). Domestic violence at the intersections of race, class, and gender: Challenges and contributions to understanding violence against marginalized women in diverse communities. *Violence Against Women, 11*(1), 38–64. https://doi.org/10.1177/1077801204271476

Stewart, A., & Maddren, K. (1997). Police officers' judgements of blame in family violence: The impact of gender and alcohol. *Sex Roles, 37*, 921–933. https://doi.org/10.1007/BF02936347

Stewart, E. A., & Simons, R. L. (2010). Race, code of the street, and violent delinquency: A multilevel investigation of neighborhood street culture and individual norms of violence. *Criminology, 48*(2), 569–605. https://doi.org/10.1111/j.1745-9125.2010.00196.x

Stogner, J., Miller, B. L., & McLean, K. (2020). Police stress, mental health, and resiliency during the COVID-19 pandemic. *American Journal of Criminal Justice, 45*(4), 718–730. https://doi.org/10.1007/s12103-020-09548-y

Storey, J. E., & Strand, S. (2017). The influence of victim vulnerability and gender on police officers' assessment of intimate partner violence risk. *Journal of Family Violence, 32*(1), 125–134. https://doi.org/10.1007/s10896-016-9905-0

Strom, K. J., Warner, T. D., Tichavsky, L., & Zahn, M. A. (2014). Policing juveniles: Domestic violence arrest policies, gender, and police response to child–parent violence. *Crime & Delinquency, 60*(3), 427–450. https://doi.org/10.1177/0011128710376293

Strobl, R. (2004). Constructing the victim: Theoretical reflections and empirical examples. *International Review of Victimology, 11*(2–3), 295–311. https://doi.org/10.1177/026975800401100206

Serrano-Montilla, C., Lozano, L. M., Alonso-Ferres, M., Valor-Segura, I., & Padilla, J. L. (2023). Understanding the components and determinants of police attitudes toward intervention in intimate partner violence against women: A systematic review. *Trauma, Violence, & Abuse, 24*(1), 245–260. https://doi.org/10.1177/15248380211029398

Sun, I. Y., & Payne, B. K. (2004). Racial differences in resolving conflicts: A comparison between black and white police officers. *Crime & Delinquency, 50*(4), 516–541. https://doi.org/10.1177/0011128703259298

Sun, I. Y. (2006). Police response to victims of domestic and non-domestic violence. *Journal of Health and Human Services Administration, 29*(2), 145–172. http://www.jstor.org/stable/25790685

Tapp, S. N., & Coen, E. J. (2025). *Criminal victimization, 2024*. Bureau of Justice Statistics. https://bjs.ojp.gov/document/cv24.pdf

Tatum, K. M., & Pence, R. (2015). Factors that affect the arrest decision in domestic violence cases. *Policing: An International Journal of Police Strategies & Management, 38*(1), 56–70. https://doi.org/10.1108/PIJPSM-07-2014-0075

Taylor, T. J., Holleran, D., & Topalli, V. (2009). Racial bias in case processing: Does victim race affect police clearance of violent crime incidents?. *Justice Quarterly, 26*(3), 562–591. https://doi.org/10.1080/07418820802266462

Tesch, R. (1990). *Qualitative research: Analysis types and software tools*. Falmer Press.

Tjaden, P., & Thoennes, N. (2000). The role of stalking in domestic violence crime reports generated by the Colorado Springs Police Department. *Violence and Victims, 15*(4), 427–441. https://doi.org/10.1891/0886-6708.15.4.427

Törnqvist, N. (2022). Drizzling sympathy: Ideal victims and flows of sympathy in Swedish courts. *International Review of Victimology, 28*(3), 263–285. https://doi.org/10.1177/02697580211035586

van Doorn, J., & Koster, N. N. (2019). Emotional victims and the impact on credibility: A systematic review. *Aggression and Violent Behavior, 47*, 74–89. https://doi.org/10.1016/j.avb.2019.03.007

Van Maanen, J. (1973). Working the street; a developmental view of police behavior. In H. Jacobs (Ed.), *Volume III of the annals of criminal justice* (pp. 1–92). Sage Publishing.

Van Maanen, J. (1975). Police socialization: A longitudinal examination of job attitudes in an urban police department. *Administrative Science Quarterly, 20*(2), 207–228. https://doi.org/10.2307/2391695

Van Maanen, J. (2011). *Tales of the field: On writing ethnography*. University of Chicago Press.

Van Wijk, J. (2013). Who is the 'little old lady 'of international crimes? Nils Christie's concept of the ideal victim reinterpreted. *International Review of Victimology, 19*(2), 159–179. https://doi.org/10.1177/0143034312472770

Vigil, J. D. (2003). Urban violence and street gangs. *Annual Review of Anthropology, 32*(1), 225–242. https://doi.org/10.1146/annurev.anthro.32.061002.093426

Waaland, P., & Keeley, S. (1985). Police decision making in wife abuse: The impact of legal and extralegal factors. *Law and Human Behavior, 9*(4), 355–366. https://doi.org/10.1007/BF01044476

Waasdorp, T. E., Bagdi, A., & Bradshaw, C. P. (2009). Peer victimization among urban, predominantly African American youth: Coping with relational aggression between friends. *Journal of School Violence, 9*(1), 98–116. https://doi.org/10.1080/15388220903341372

Watson, A. C., Corrigan, P. W., & Ottati, V. (2004). Police officers' attitudes toward and decisions about persons with mental illness. *Psychiatric Services, 55*(1), 49–53. https://doi.org/10.1176/appi.ps.55.1.49

Westley, W. A. (1970). *Violence and the police: A sociological study of law, custom, and morality*. MIT Press.

Westmarland, L. (2005). Police ethics and integrity: Breaking the blue code of silence. *Policing and Society, 15*(2), 145–165. https://doi.org/10.1080/10439460500071721

Wilson, J. M. (2012). Articulating the dynamic police staffing challenge: An examination of supply and demand. *Policing: An International Journal of Police Strategies & Management, 35*(2), 327–355. https://doi.org/10.1108/13639511211230084

Wilson, M., & O'Brien, E. (2016). Constructing the ideal victim in The United States of America's annual trafficking in persons reports. *Crime, Law and Social Change, 65*(1–2), 29–45. https://doi.org/10.1007/s10611-015-9600-8

Wolcott, H. F. (1994). *Transforming qualitative data: Description, analysis, and interpretation*. Sage.

Wolfe, S. E., & Piquero, A. R. (2011). Organizational justice and police misconduct. *Criminal Justice and Behavior, 38*(4), 332–353. https://doi.org/10.1177/0093854810397739

Xie, M., Pogarsky, G., Lynch, J. P., & McDowall, D. (2006). Prior police contact and subsequent victim reporting: Results from the NCVS. *Justice Quarterly, 23*(4), 481–501. https://doi.org/10.1080/07418820600985339

Younglove, J. A., Kerr, M. G., & Vitello, C. J. (2002). Law enforcement officers' perceptions of same sex domestic violence: Reason for cautious optimism. *Journal of Interpersonal Violence, 17*(7), 760–772. https://doi.org/10.1177/088626050201700704

Yu, H., & Monas, N. (2020). Recreating the scene: An investigation of police report writing. *Journal of Technical Writing and Communication, 50*(1), 35–55. https://doi.org/10.1177/0047281618812441

Index

M. N. Eliasson, *Who Gets Believed?*, Palgrave's Critical Policing Studies, https://doi.org/10.1007/978-3-032-22253-4

FSC
www.fsc.org
MIX
Papier | Fördert
gute Waldnutzung
FSC® C083411

Zeitfracht Medien GmbH
Ferdinand-Jühlke-Straße 7
99095 Erfurt, Deutschland
produktsicherheit@kolibri360.de